About Test Prep Connection:

Welcome to RBP Books' Connection series. You have select
for your child or your students. Rainbow Bridge Publishing (RBP) has been the leader in summer educational materials for the past ten years. Now with their Connection series, RBP has expanded to year-round educational support materials for children at home and at school.

Their newest release, *Test Prep Connection,* provides students with focused practice in taking reading, language arts, mathematics, science, and social studies tests. *Test Prep Connection* is designed to help reinforce and develop standardized test-taking skills and skills based on NCTM (National Council of Teachers of Mathematics) and NCTE (National Council of Teachers of English) standards for third-grade students.

Anyone who understands children and the nature of learning would agree that a standardized test cannot fully measure a child's understanding, a teacher's effectiveness, or a school's performance. A standardized test is merely a measure of a child's or a group of children's performance on a given day and under certain circumstances. However, since schools and school systems are being held accountable for student performance, some means of providing objective information is essential. Thus, standardized tests have become a popular tool for measuring achievement.

The purpose of this book is to help students improve performance on standardized tests. The authors have carefully targeted topics known to give students the most difficulty—for instance, drawing inferences, estimation, and problem solving. In addition, since many other test prep books do not address science or social studies, the authors of this series have included test prep exercises in these areas as well in grades 3–5.

The content of *Test Prep Connection Grade 3* is grade-specific and based on recent editions of the following standardized achievement tests:

✔ California Achievement Tests (CAT)

✔ Comprehensive Tests of Basic Skills (CTBS)

✔ Iowa Tests of Basic Skills (ITBS)

✔ Metropolitan Achievement Tests (MAT)

✔ Standard Achievement Tests (SAT)

As you use *Test Prep Connection Grade 3*, you will find a table of contents that will guide you through the skills covered and an answer key that allows you to follow your child's progress. A sample answer sheet is also included, which you can copy and use to familiarize your child with the format of standardized achievement tests and provide practice in filling in answers.

Dear Parents and Educators,

Thank you for choosing this Rainbow Bridge Publishing educational product for your children and students. We take great pride in being involved with your educational experience. Some people say that math will always be math, and reading will always be reading, but we do not share that opinion. Reading, math, spelling, writing, geography, science, history, and other academic subjects will always be some of life's most fulfilling adventures and should be taught with passion both at home and in the classroom. Because of this, we at Rainbow Bridge Publishing try to capture and encourage this passion in every product we create.

It is our mission to provide materials that not only explain, but also amaze; not only review, but also encourage; not only guide, but also lead. Every product contains clear, concise instructions; appropriate sample work; and engaging, grade-appropriate content created by classroom teachers and writers that is based on national standards to support your best educational efforts. We hope you enjoy our company's products as you embark on your adventure. Thank you for bringing us along.

Sincerely,

George Starks
Associate Publisher
Rainbow Bridge Publishing

Test Prep Connection™ • Grade 3

Written by Connie York, M.Ed., and Leland Graham, Ph.D.

For information, call or write: Rainbow Bridge Publishing, Inc. • PO Box 571470 • Salt Lake City, Utah 84157-1470 • Tel: (801) 268-8887

Publisher
Scott G. Van Leeuwen

Associate Publisher
George Starks

Series Creator
Michele Van Leeuwen

Illustrations
Amanda Sorensen

Visual Design and Layout
Andy Carlson, Robyn Funk, Zachary Johnson, Amanda Sorensen

Editorial Director
Paul Rawlins

Copy Editors and Proofreaders
Kim Carlson, Melody Feist, Jeanna Mason

Please visit our website at
www.summerbridgeactivities.com
for supplements, additions, and corrections to this book.

First Edition 2004

For orders call 1-800-598-1441
Discounts available for quantity orders.

ISBN: 1-932210-86-5

PRINTED IN THE UNITED STATES OF AMERICA
10 9 8 7 6 5 4 3 2 1

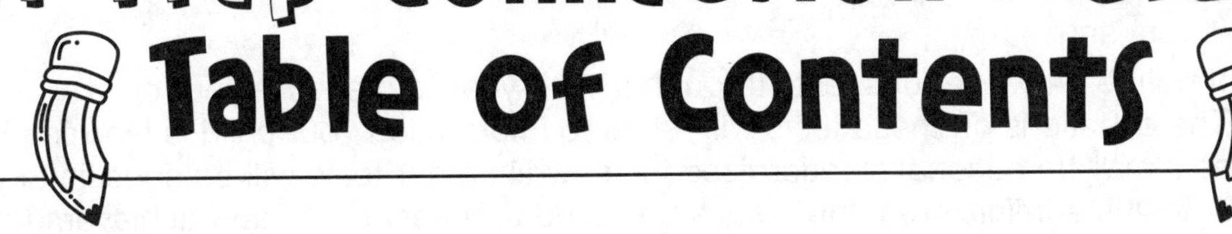

Test Prep Connection—Grade 3

Table of Contents

To Parents

Dear Parent:

Your school will be giving various tests throughout the year to measure your child's performance. The questions on these tests will relate to information your child is learning in school. Some of the tests may be national standardized tests, while other tests will be specific to your state. Whatever test is administered, the results are used to measure student achievement.

Often, even though children know the subject matter, they may not do well on the tests. Test anxiety is frequently created by a fear of the unknown: What questions will be asked? What happens if my score is low? In addition, the test environment for a standardized test can be quite different from the normal test-taking routine, since children are given a limited length of time to complete each section of the test.

The purpose of *Test Prep Connection Grade 3* is to help you as a parent work with your child in order to decrease his/her test anxiety. The book contains practice test exercises that will familiarize your child with test directions, format, and simulated content. A sample answer sheet is included to give your child practice in filling in answers on a separate sheet.

As a parent, you can help your child perform on the test as well as he/she is able. Here are some suggestions:

- ✏ Look over the practice exercises that your child has completed, and review troublesome content.
- ✏ Practice using a timer with your child to start and end an exercise.
- ✏ Emphasize the following test-taking tips with your child:
    - Read all the directions carefully.
    - Look over the whole test section before you begin.
    - Read all the answer choices before you choose one.
    - Do not spend too much time on any one question.
    - Use all the time you are given. Look back over your answers.
    - Stay calm and focus on the test.
- ✏ Be sure your child gets a good night's sleep the night before the test.
- ✏ On the morning of the test, allow plenty of time for a good breakfast.

By spending time with your child practicing these sample exercises, you will show your child that you are interested in how he/she performs on the standardized achievement tests. Good luck!

Sincerely,

Connie York, M.Ed., and Leland Graham, Ph.D.
Authors of *Test Prep Connection Grade 3*

Test-Taking Tips

- It is important to do your best on standardized tests because the test results are used to compare your performance with other students in your school and to compare your school with other schools.

- Studying for standardized tests may seem difficult, but the things you learn in school will help you do well on these tests. One of the best ways to prepare for standardized tests is to work hard all year and learn as much as you can.

- Be sure to have a good eraser and an extra, sharpened #2 pencil.

- Always read all of the directions carefully before you begin. Listen to the instructions that your teacher gives you.

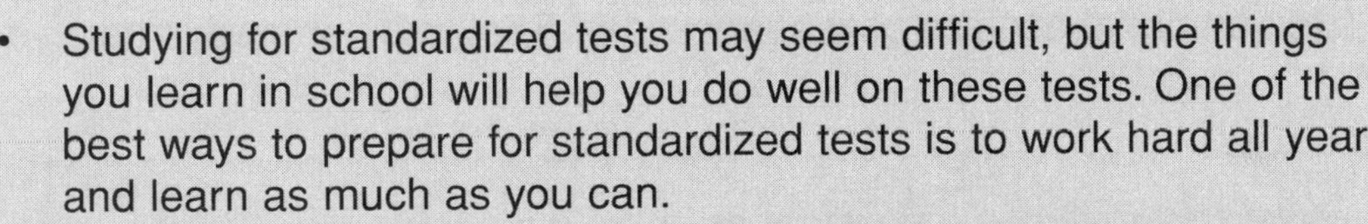

- Pay attention to the STOP and GO ON signs at the bottom of each page.

- Read each item carefully. Then read all the answer choices even though you may think you know the answer.

- If you do not find the answer that you think is correct, review the answer choices. If you are sure that the correct answer is not given, fill in the bubble for "Not given."

- If you do not know the correct answer, eliminate the answers you know are wrong. Then, choose the best answer from the choices that remain.

- Use scratch paper to work your answers if your teacher tells you it is permitted.

- **Be sure to mark your answers correctly.**

  - ✏ Fill in the answer space completely. ○ ● ○ **Correct**
  - ✏ Mark only one answer. ● ● ○ **Wrong**
  - ✏ Make your mark dark and solid. ○ ○ ⊘ **Wrong**

Test-Taking Tips

Sometimes it is necessary to guess on a standardized test. Some questions may ask about content that has not been included in your textbook. Other questions may be difficult, or you may not remember the answer. On many standardized tests, if you do not answer a question it will be scored as a wrong answer. When that is the case, it is important to answer each question.

If you have to guess, here are some suggestions for making the best guess you possibly can on a multiple choice test. (Remember, these are only suggestions. They will not always help you choose the correct answer.)

1. Select an answer that matches the grammar in the question. For example, in the question below, answer B is wrong because the grammar is incorrect.
   Question:
   Third graders who want to score high on achievement tests ________
   Ⓐ should never do their homework.
   Ⓑ has not gotten a good night's sleep.
   Ⓒ should always do their homework.
   Ⓓ pay close attention to the teacher's directions.

2. Select answers that contain words such as *many, often, some, usually,* and *frequently.*

3. Do not select answers that contain words such as *all, always, every, never,* and *none.*

4. If there are answers that say about the same thing, do not select either answer.

5. If there are answers that are opposite from each other, select one of these answers.

6. Select the answer "All of the above" or "Not given."

7. Select the longest answer.

8. Select an answer toward the middle.

Name Date

Synonyms

Directions: Read each item. Choose the word that means the same or about the same as the underlined word.

Examples:

A. We saw a large herd of cows in the field.

- ● group
- Ⓑ line
- Ⓒ sign
- Ⓓ pile

B. I could not hear the music because of the din in the room.

- Ⓕ crowd
- Ⓖ people
- ● noise
- Ⓙ laughter

Remember that a synonym is a word that means the same or about the same as another word.

Practice

1. Discard those newspapers when you have finished reading them.

- Ⓐ Keep
- Ⓑ Throw away
- Ⓒ Hide
- Ⓓ Shred

2. Hurricane Isabel was a fierce storm.

- Ⓕ meek
- Ⓖ easy
- Ⓗ strong
- Ⓙ weak

3. The trip to the beach is a seven-hour journey.

- Ⓐ trip
- Ⓑ wait
- Ⓒ walk
- Ⓓ vehicle

4. The mountain peak was covered in snow.

- Ⓕ side
- Ⓖ tree
- Ⓗ trail
- Ⓙ top

5. We used a spade to dig the hole for the new tree.

- Ⓐ shovel
- Ⓑ hammer
- Ⓒ spoon
- Ⓓ cup

6. An octopus has eight long tentacles.

- Ⓕ eyes
- Ⓖ arms
- Ⓗ spots
- Ⓙ shoes

STOP

Name Date

Antonyms

Directions: Read each item. Choose the word that means the opposite of the underlined word.

Examples:

A. The wealthy man made a large donation to our school.

Ⓐ handsome Ⓑ generous
● poor Ⓓ excited

B. The theater required an adult to be with all children.

Ⓕ mother Ⓖ friend
Ⓗ father ● child

Remember that an antonym is a word that means the opposite of the underlined word.

Practice

1. Jerry is a newcomer in our friendly neighborhood.

Ⓐ stranger
Ⓑ old-timer
Ⓒ neighbor
Ⓓ workman

2. The boy made an intelligent decision.

Ⓕ foolish
Ⓖ smart
Ⓗ easy
Ⓙ useless

3. Julie was cautious when the strange dog approached her.

Ⓐ frightened
Ⓑ careless
Ⓒ silly
Ⓓ friendly

4. My grandmother is very old and frail.

Ⓕ pretty
Ⓖ strong
Ⓗ fat
Ⓙ smart

5. The puppy followed a zigzag path from his bed to his bowl.

Ⓐ straight
Ⓑ crooked
Ⓒ slow
Ⓓ quick

6. I had a loaded hot dog at the baseball game last night.

Ⓕ delicious
Ⓖ footlong
Ⓗ plain
Ⓙ beef

STOP

Name _______________ Date _______________

Homophones

Directions: Read each item. The answer choices sound the same but mean different things. Choose the answer that makes sense in the sentence.

Examples:

A. _____ will be a picnic for all third grade students.

- ● There
- Ⓑ Their
- Ⓒ They're
- Ⓓ Not given

B. Our class will usually spend one or _____ hours at the picnic.

- Ⓕ to
- Ⓖ too
- ● two
- Ⓙ Not given

Remember that homophones are words that sound the same but mean different things.

Practice

1. Susan was _____ frightened that she could not move.

- Ⓐ so
- Ⓑ sew
- Ⓒ sow
- Ⓓ Not given

2. Pull on the _____ to make the horse stop.

- Ⓕ reign
- Ⓖ rein
- Ⓗ rain
- Ⓙ Not given

3. I have a new _____ of tennis shoes.

- Ⓐ pair
- Ⓑ pare
- Ⓒ pear
- Ⓓ Not given

4. Mrs. McCoy asked me to _____ the question on the board.

- Ⓕ right
- Ⓖ write
- Ⓗ rite
- Ⓙ Not given

5. The golfer called _____ when he hit the ball.

- Ⓐ for
- Ⓑ four
- Ⓒ fore
- Ⓓ Not given

6. Is that _____ dog barking in the yard?

- Ⓕ there
- Ⓖ they're
- Ⓗ their
- Ⓙ Not given

STOP

Name Date

Words in Context

Directions: There are two sentences in each of these items. Read both sentences. Choose the word that fits in both sentences.

Examples:

A. The river had a swift _____.
Have you read the _____ paper?

● current
Ⓑ bank
Ⓒ daily
Ⓓ tissue

B. I had the ball in my _____.
He could not _____ the handle.

Ⓕ pocket
● grasp
Ⓗ glove
Ⓙ touch

Remember, only one word fits in both sentences.

Practice

1. I just read a good _____.
What a _____ idea that is!

Ⓐ book
Ⓑ great
Ⓒ story
Ⓓ novel

2. I have finished the _____.
Please _____ your paper.

Ⓕ outline
Ⓖ draw
Ⓗ story
Ⓙ color

3. _____ me when you are ready.
The traffic _____ is green.

Ⓐ call
Ⓑ signal
Ⓒ light
Ⓓ see

4. A hungry tiger _____ its prey.
The corn _____ were brown.

Ⓕ hunts
Ⓖ cobs
Ⓗ stalks
Ⓙ walks

5. The tree _____ over the house.
The radio _____ were very tall.

Ⓐ towers
Ⓑ stations
Ⓒ branches
Ⓓ songs

6. Will you _____ to help us?
My uncle is a _____ fireman.

Ⓕ tall
Ⓖ volunteer
Ⓗ ask
Ⓙ brave

STOP

Name Date

Words in Context

Directions: Sometimes two words that are spelled the same can be said in different ways. Choose the word that fits in both sentences.

Examples:

A. The _____ blew very hard.
I will _____ the clock.

Ⓐ set
Ⓑ breeze
Ⓒ read
● wind

B. The large _____ lay in the mud.
_____ the seeds in the garden.

Ⓕ pig
Ⓖ weed
● sow
Ⓙ water

Remember, only one word fits in both sentences.

Practice

1. The _____ is hot and dry.
Don't go away and _____ me.

Ⓐ leave
Ⓑ weather
Ⓒ desert
Ⓓ street

2. The brown horse is in the _____.
The _____ in my pencil broke.

Ⓕ lead
Ⓖ eraser
Ⓗ race
Ⓙ pen

3. The performer took a _____.
She wore a _____ in her hair.

Ⓐ seat
Ⓑ song
Ⓒ clip
Ⓓ bow

4. He caught a large _____ in the lake.
He sings _____ in the choir.

Ⓕ songs
Ⓖ fish
Ⓗ bass
Ⓙ loudly

5. A _____ rolled down her cheek.
There is a _____ in his shirt.

Ⓐ tear
Ⓑ rip
Ⓒ button
Ⓓ sad

6. I love to _____ Harry Potter books.
I have _____ all five of the books.

Ⓕ bought
Ⓖ hear
Ⓗ read
Ⓙ buy

STOP

Name Date

Sample Vocabulary Test

Directions: Read the phrase with the underlined word. Find the word below that means the same or almost the same as the underlined word.

Examples:

A. accept the invitation
Ⓐ reject ● welcome Ⓑ decline Ⓓ discard

B. reply to the invitation
Ⓕ ask Ⓗ plead Ⓖ demand ● answer

1. terrified little child
Ⓐ sad
Ⓑ hungry
Ⓒ scared
Ⓓ happy

2. inspect the hospital
Ⓕ examine
Ⓖ repair
Ⓗ watch
Ⓙ make

3. the main idea
Ⓐ unusual
Ⓑ important
Ⓒ minor
Ⓓ other

4. punctured the football
Ⓕ put air into
Ⓖ put a hole in
Ⓗ tossed
Ⓙ hit hard

5. thoroughly prepared for the test
Ⓐ completely
Ⓑ sometimes
Ⓒ rarely
Ⓓ almost

6. the spacious house
Ⓕ roomy
Ⓖ attractive
Ⓗ cramped
Ⓙ restricted

7. have a brief recess
Ⓐ extended
Ⓑ wild
Ⓒ quiet
Ⓓ short

8. stare at the television
Ⓕ gaze
Ⓖ reach
Ⓗ sit
Ⓙ listen

Name Date

Directions: For numbers 9–13, find the word that means the opposite of the underlined word.

9. demolish the building
   - Ⓐ paint
   - Ⓑ photograph
   - Ⓒ build
   - Ⓓ climb

10. the opposite meaning
   - Ⓕ same
   - Ⓖ first
   - Ⓗ right
   - Ⓙ good

11. put the car in drive
   - Ⓐ garage
   - Ⓑ road
   - Ⓒ reverse
   - Ⓓ street

12. a marine mammal
   - Ⓕ furry
   - Ⓖ land
   - Ⓗ soft
   - Ⓙ fierce

13. a major mistake
   - Ⓐ big
   - Ⓑ serious
   - Ⓒ slight
   - Ⓓ important

Directions: For numbers 14–18, find the word that fits in both sentences.

14. We saw boats off the _____.
    _____ your bike down the hill.
   - Ⓕ ride
   - Ⓖ beach
   - Ⓗ ocean
   - Ⓙ coast

15. A large _____ was in the pasture.
    _____ the car carefully.
   - Ⓐ drive
   - Ⓑ steer
   - Ⓒ bull
   - Ⓓ cow

16. The boat had a _____ of three.
    I helped _____ the boat.
   - Ⓕ steer
   - Ⓖ sail
   - Ⓗ crew
   - Ⓙ paint

17. Chipper stole third _____.
    Carl shot from the _____ line.
   - Ⓐ base
   - Ⓑ foul
   - Ⓒ front
   - Ⓓ side

18. I _____ to that idea.
    Place the _____ in the bag.
   - Ⓕ agree
   - Ⓖ thing
   - Ⓗ listen
   - Ⓙ object

STOP

Name Date

Following Directions

Directions: Read each item carefully. Then choose the correct answer.

Example: The teacher read the test directions to the students. She said, "Fill in the circle for the correct answer. Be sure to fill the circle completely. Make your mark heavy and dark."

A. If the correct answer is "C," which one shows the correctly marked answer?

Ⓐ 

Ⓒ 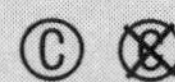

Ⓓ 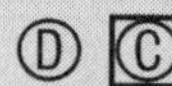

Be sure to follow the directions exactly.

1. The physical education teacher told the students to follow these directions: Start at X and take 3 steps; then turn right and take 3 steps; turn right again and take 3 steps; turn right once more and take 3 steps.

Which figure shows the path the students should have followed?

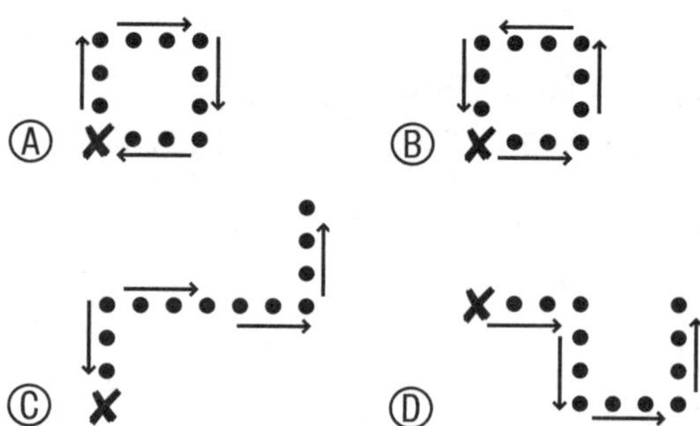

2. Read these directions: Draw a square. Put the letter "O" inside the square. Draw a straight line diagonally through the square with the letter "B" at one end and the number "6" at the other end.

If you follow the directions, which of the following could not be the correct answer?

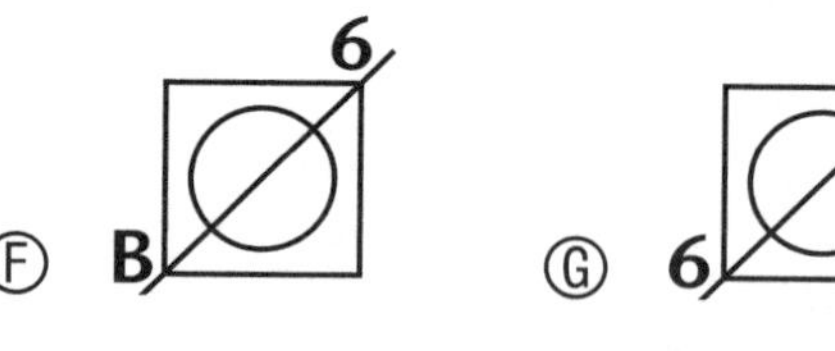

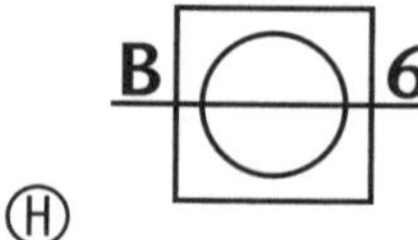

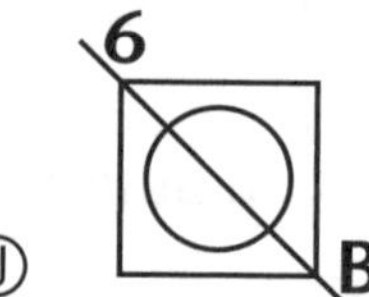

3. Mark the correct set of directions for making a turkey and cheese sandwich.

Ⓐ Spread mayonnaise between a slice of turkey and a slice of cheese.
Ⓑ Put mayonnaise, turkey, and cheese between two slices of bread.
Ⓒ Put mayonnaise and bread between the turkey and cheese.
Ⓓ Put turkey and cheese between bread and put mustard on the top.

Name Date

4. The teacher said to the students, "Put your name at the top left of your paper, the date at the top right, and number 1–5 using Roman numerals.

If Lisa followed the directions carefully, which one shows her paper?

Ⓕ 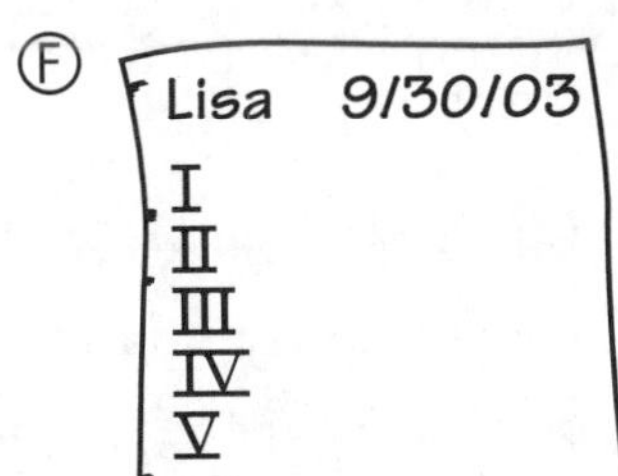

Ⓖ 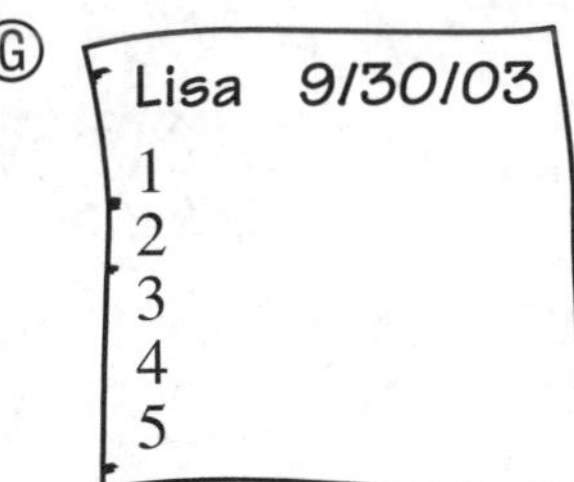

Ⓗ 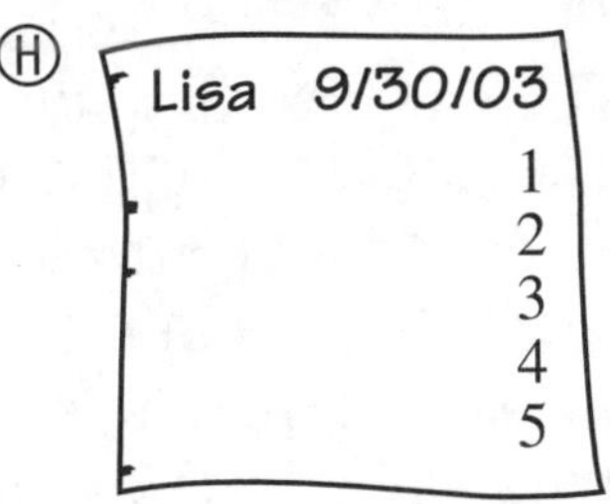

Ⓙ 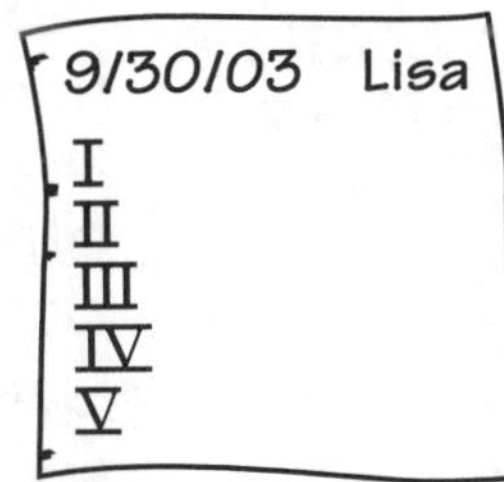

5. The librarian told her assistant to separate the fiction books from the nonfiction books and place each group in alphabetical order.

Choose the one that shows the books arranged correctly.

Ⓐ 

Ⓑ 

Ⓒ 

Ⓓ 

6. Follow these directions to draw a face: Draw a circle with two circles for eyes, a small triangle for a nose, and a line curved upward for a smile. Put an ear on each side and some short straight lines on the top for hair. Add a bow tie under the chin.

Mark the one that shows the face drawn correctly.

STOP

Name Date

Main Idea

Directions: Read each paragraph carefully. Decide what the paragraph is mainly about. Mark the best answer.

Example: Hawaii is located in the Pacific Ocean. It consists of a chain of eight main islands. The largest island is named Hawaii. The capital of Hawaii is Honolulu, which is on the island of Oahu. Hawaii was the last state added to the United States. Beautiful flowers and trees grow in Hawaii, along with pineapples.

A. What is the main idea of this paragraph?

Ⓐ The capital of Hawaii is Oahu.
Ⓑ Pineapples grow in Hawaii.
Ⓒ Hawaii was the last U.S. state.
● Hawaii is a state in the Pacific Ocean.

Be sure to choose the main idea of the paragraph.

1. "I have a dream" is a phrase from a very famous speech given by Dr. Martin Luther King, Jr. Dr. King was a minister and a leader in the Civil Rights Movement. He believed in treating everyone fairly and encouraged people to try to change things in peaceful ways. He gave his famous speech in Washington, D.C., in 1963.

Ⓐ Dr. King gave a famous speech.
Ⓑ Dr. King was a minister.
Ⓒ Dr. King was peaceful man.
Ⓓ He gave his speech in 1963.

2. "The Tortoise and the Hare" is a well-known story that teaches a lesson about not giving up. The tortoise and the hare were in a race. The hare, who was much faster than the tortoise, was so sure he would win the race that he stopped to take a nap. The tortoise, who knew he would have to work very hard to win, just kept plodding along without stopping. Soon he passed the sleeping hare and won the race.

Ⓕ The hare won the race.
Ⓖ The hare lost the race.
Ⓗ Don't give up if you want to win.
Ⓙ The hare took a nap.

Name Date

3. Walt Disney was a famous American filmmaker. Many of his movies are animated cartoons, but the Disney Studios have also made nature films, films with live actors, and television programs. Some of his most famous movies are *Snow White and the Seven Dwarfs*, *Cinderella*, and *Sleeping Beauty*. Donald Duck and Mickey Mouse are two of his most famous characters. Disneyland in California and Walt Disney World in Florida are two large amusement parks that are based on Disney characters and ideas.

Ⓐ Donald Duck and Mickey Mouse are two famous Disney characters.
Ⓑ Walt Disney was a famous American filmmaker.
Ⓒ Walt Disney World is in Florida.
Ⓓ *Cinderella* is a popular Disney movie.

4. An atlas is a book of maps. In mythology, Atlas was a Titan who was famous because he was so strong. When the Titans were defeated by Zeus, Atlas was condemned to hold the earth and sky on his shoulders forever. A picture of Atlas holding the earth is often used on the front of a book of maps.

Ⓕ Atlas holds the earth and the sky.
Ⓖ There's a reason an atlas sometimes has a picture of Atlas.
Ⓗ Atlas holds the sky on his shoulders.
Ⓙ Zeus defeated the Titans.

5. The Statue of Liberty is a giant statue that represents freedom. It stands on an island in the New York Harbor. The statue is of a woman raising a torch in her right hand and holding a tablet in her left hand. France gave the statue to the United States. It was brought across the ocean in sections and put back together on the island where "Lady Liberty" now stands. The Statue of Liberty was the first landmark that many immigrants saw as they neared their new home in the U.S.

Ⓐ The Statue of Liberty is also called "Lady Liberty."
Ⓑ She is holding a torch and a tablet.
Ⓒ The Statue of Liberty is on an island in New York Harbor.
Ⓓ The Statue of Liberty has an interesting story.

Name Date

Recognizing Details

Directions: Read the paragraph carefully. Find the best answer to each question that follows the paragraph.

Example:

Australia's flag has a deep blue background and white stars. The British Union Jack, which is red, white, and blue, is in the corner. The largest star stands for the Commonwealth of Australia.

A. What color is the background of Australia's flag?

Ⓐ light blue
Ⓑ dark green
Ⓒ deep purple
● deep blue

First, read the paragraphs carefully for details, and then read the questions. Refer to the paragraph to answer the questions.

Australia is the only country that is also a continent. Australia is the sixth largest country in the world and the smallest continent. Australia is often referred to as being "down under" because it lies entirely in the southern hemisphere.

Most of the population in Australia lives in cities. Australia's two largest cities, Sydney and Melbourne, are the most populated areas. Sydney is Australia's oldest and largest city. It is located on a beautiful, huge, deep harbor called Port Jackson. In 2000, Sydney was the host for the Summer Olympics. Melbourne, a dignified and elegant city, hosted the 1956 Olympics. Canberra became Australia's capital city in 1926. Adelaide, a lovely, quiet city, is the capital of South Australia. Perth, host for the America's Cup sailing races for four years, is the capital of Western Australia, and Brisbane is the capital of Queensland.

The kangaroo is the most famous of Australia's native animals. The kangaroo is a member of the marsupial family. Marsupials carry their young in a pouch. The kangaroo can hop at speeds of up to 40 miles per hour (64 kph). Australia has many other unique animals not found anywhere else in the world, like dingoes, duck-billed platypuses, wombats, and koalas. The dingo is a mammal believed to have evolved from the wolf and wild dog. Early natives used dingoes to hunt. The duck-billed platypus is the world's only egg-laying mammal. Wombats and koalas are marsupials like kangaroos.

GO ON

Name Date

1. Besides Melbourne, what other Australian city has hosted the Summer Olympics?

Ⓐ Canberra
Ⓑ Sydney
Ⓒ Adelaide
Ⓓ Perth

2. Australia is often referred to as being _____ _____ because it lies entirely in the southern hemisphere.

Ⓕ huge, deep
Ⓖ oldest, largest
Ⓗ down under
Ⓙ lovely, quiet

3. What is Australia's largest and oldest city?

Ⓐ Adelaide
Ⓑ Canberra
Ⓒ Melbourne
Ⓓ Sydney

4. What Australian mammal is believed to have descended from the wolf and the wild dog?

Ⓕ koala
Ⓖ platypus
Ⓗ kangaroo
Ⓙ dingo

5. Australia is the only country that is also a _____.

Ⓐ continent
Ⓑ hemisphere
Ⓒ capital
Ⓓ harbor

6. Australia's most famous animal is the _____.

Ⓕ dingo
Ⓖ wombat
Ⓗ kangaroo
Ⓙ koala

7. What Australian city has been the host for the America's Cup sailing races?

Ⓐ Brisbane
Ⓑ Perth
Ⓒ Adelaide
Ⓓ Sydney

8. What is the world's only egg-laying mammal?

Ⓕ kangaroo
Ⓖ platypus
Ⓗ dingo
Ⓙ koala

STOP

Name

Date

Drawing Inferences

Directions: Read each paragraph or story. Choose the best answer to each question.

Example: Joe played on his school baseball team. During the first game of the season, he struck out every time he came to bat. He started going to the batting cages three times a week to practice. By the end of the season, he had one of the highest batting averages of any player.

A. Why did Joe become a better batter by the end of the season?

● He practiced.
Ⓑ He wanted to.
Ⓒ He just had a bad game.
Ⓓ His coach gave him tips.

Read each paragraph carefully for clues that suggest the correct answer.

1. When you have been running or playing hard, your body cools itself by sweating. A dog, however, does not sweat. Panting is the way the dog's body cools itself after exercise or play. Laura and her dog, Coco, had just come inside, and Coco was panting hard.

What had Laura and Coco probably been doing outside?

Ⓐ sitting under a tree
Ⓑ taking a nap
Ⓒ playing ball
Ⓓ riding in the car

2. Judy wore a jacket to school this morning, but she came home without it. She told her mother she had forgotten it.

What can you guess about the weather?

Ⓕ It is raining.
Ⓖ It got colder during the day.
Ⓗ It got warmer during the day.
Ⓙ Not given

Name Date

3. George was working on a long report for school. He was typing it on his computer. He had finished typing five pages when his mother called him to dinner. A thunderstorm came up while they were eating, and the lights went out for a few minutes. Later, when George's mom went to check on him, he was typing page two of his report. When she asked him why he was retyping page two, George said,

Ⓐ "I didn't like the way it looked."
Ⓑ "I forgot to save it, and it got erased during the storm."
Ⓒ "It was no good."
Ⓓ "I like to type."

4. In *The Sorcerer's Apprentice*, Mickey Mouse works for the sorcerer, sweeping and mopping and doing other chores. One day, without permission, he borrows the sorcerer's magic hat and uses magical commands to make the brooms bring buckets of water to clean the floor. Mickey then falls asleep, but he wakes up when the room becomes flooded. He tries telling the brooms to stop bringing water, but they do not stop.

Why don't the brooms stop when Mickey tells them to?

Ⓕ They don't want to.
Ⓖ They like floods.
Ⓗ They are stubborn.
Ⓙ Mickey doesn't use the magic word.

5. Sylvia had been invited to spend the night with some friends. Her mother told her to feed the dog, clean her room, and unload the dishwasher as soon as she got home from school on Friday, or she could not go. On Monday, Marla asked Sylvia why she did not come to the sleepover party. Marla answered,

Ⓐ "I did not finish my chores."
Ⓑ "I broke my leg."
Ⓒ "I was not invited."
Ⓓ "I was out of town."

6. For Joe's science project, he decided to plant grass seed in several different types of dirt to see which grew the best. He planted his seeds, watered them, and put them under a light in the basement. He checked on them daily and watered them regularly for the first two weeks. All the pots of grass were growing. Then he did not check on them for ten days. When he went to see how they were growing, all his pots of grass were brown and dead.

The seeds probably died because

Ⓕ Joe forgot to turn the light off.
Ⓖ someone sprayed them with weed killer.
Ⓗ Joe forgot to water them.
Ⓙ none of the dirt was good.

Name Date

Drawing Conclusions

Directions: Read each paragraph or story. Choose the best answer.

Example: Everyone in the York family was busy unpacking boxes. Jay and Will were excited when they found their boxes of videos because the den in this house had room for a large-screen television. The boys also each had their own bedroom. When they went to bed that night, they were tired but happy.

A. What were the Yorks most likely doing?

Ⓐ getting ready to watch movies
Ⓑ packing for a vacation
● moving into a new house
Ⓓ cleaning out the den

Use the information in the paragraphs to draw the best conclusion.

1. Mrs. Conyers' third grade class was planning a surprise birthday party for her. Several mothers were getting cake, ice cream, balloons, and party favors. They had gotten permission from the principal to have the party after lunch. The children had taken up a collection to buy Mrs. Conyers a special present. When she opened the present, she was thrilled. It was something she had always wanted for her classroom.

Why did the children want to give their teacher a birthday party?

Ⓐ She was old.
Ⓑ The students liked her.
Ⓒ The students didn't want a test.
Ⓓ Their mothers suggested it.

2. Mr. Crane's class was going on a field trip. He asked his students to bring a notebook and a pencil. They also needed to bring a sack lunch. Mr. Crane told them to wear comfortable clothes and shoes because they would be outside for most of the day.

Where were the students going?

Ⓕ to the symphony
Ⓖ to the planetarium
Ⓗ to the zoo
Ⓙ to the puppet museum

Name Date

3. Chile lies south of the equator, and so its seasons are opposite of those in the Northern Hemisphere. Summer lasts from late December to late March, and winter lasts from late June to late September. Parts of Chile's northern desert may not have rain for years, but the region is not especially hot. The Central Valley has a mild climate, with dry summers and rainy winters. Santiago receives about 14 inches (36 cm) of rain annually, while in Puerto Montt, it rains about 325 days per year. The total rainfall there can be up to 200 inches (500 cm).

In one part of Chile, it rains

Ⓐ every day.
Ⓑ every other day.
Ⓒ almost every day.
Ⓓ only 14 days annually.

4. Basketball was invented in the United States in 1891. By the mid-1900s, it had become the world's most popular indoor sport. Today, millions crowd into gyms and arenas to watch their favorite teams. Millions more watch games on TV. In the U.S., thousands of elementary schools, high schools, and colleges sponsor amateur teams for both male and female players. Some of the best male players in the world compete as professionals in the National Basketball Association (NBA). Both young people and adults enjoy playing on neighborhood playgrounds, in backyards, in alleys, and on driveways.

Basketball is a popular form of

Ⓕ recreation.
Ⓖ confusion.
Ⓗ commotion.
Ⓙ distraction.

5. The rhinoceros is a huge animal with short, stocky legs, thick skin, and little hair. Some rhinos have one or two slightly curved horns that project from their nose. The horns grow throughout the life of the rhinoceros. They are made of something similar to a combination of hair and fingernails. Some people believe that powdered rhinoceros horns have special healing powers. Poachers, people who illegally hunt animals, have killed thousands of rhinoceroses.

So many rhinoceroses have been killed that they might become

Ⓐ poached.
Ⓑ hunted.
Ⓒ horned.
Ⓓ extinct.

Name Date

Fiction

Directions: Read each story or paragraph carefully. Then mark the best answer for each question about the story.

Example: Melanie was so excited that she could barely sit still in school. Today her new puppy was coming home! Melanie had picked her out from nine puppies in the litter. They were all so cute that Melanie had to make a hard decision. She chose this one because of its four white feet, and she was going to call her puppy Belle.

A. What would be the best title for this paragraph?

Ⓐ Making a Decision
● Melanie's New Puppy
Ⓒ A Hard Day at School
Ⓓ Belle's Feet

Be sure to read the paragraph and each question carefully. Look back at the paragraph if you need help.

Shannon had a wonderful dollhouse that her grandfather had built for her. It had two bedrooms, a playroom, den, living room, dining room, kitchen, two bathrooms, and a basement. It even had a laundry room. He had painted it gray with blue shutters to match Shannon's own house. He had wallpapered it with her favorite colors, blue and white. Shannon's whole family was enjoying furnishing the dollhouse. They had bought some of the furniture, and they were making lamps, rugs, vases, and other accessories from beads, toothpaste tops, and other things they found around their house. They had bought several books that told them how to make all kinds of miniatures for the dollhouse. Shannon's favorite room was the storage room in the basement because they had filled it with miniature toys. It was almost like a museum.

1. How many rooms were in the dollhouse?

Ⓐ 7
Ⓑ 10
Ⓒ 11
Ⓓ 14

2. Where did Shannon get her dollhouse?

Ⓕ at the toy store
Ⓖ at a garage sale
Ⓗ from a catalog
Ⓙ from her grandfather

GO ON

Name Date

When Bill was six years old, he convinced his dad to take him fishing for the first time. They did not have a tent, so they rigged up the back of their old station wagon as a camper. They put an old mattress in it, and Bill's mother made curtains to hang at the windows. They gathered up some old pots and a grill to cook on, and they stowed all their fishing gear in the back. Soon they were off. They drove for about two hours and arrived at their campsite in time to fix dinner and go to bed. Early the next morning, they got their fishing rods and went to the river to fish. By lunchtime they had caught several nice trout, but it began to rain, so they dashed back to their "camper." They tossed their fishing poles in and climbed in and slammed the door. "Snap" went Bill's fishing rod. Bill was disappointed, but he had souvenirs to take home anyway, so the rain and a broken rod didn't spoil his first fishing trip.

3. What is the best title for this story?
- Ⓐ Bill's First Fishing Trip
- Ⓑ A Broken Fishing Rod
- Ⓒ A Rained-Out Trip
- Ⓓ Great Souvenirs

4. What happened to Bill's fishing pole?
- Ⓕ He dropped it in the river.
- Ⓖ He lost it in the rainstorm.
- Ⓗ A large fish took it away.
- Ⓙ He closed the car door on it.

5. What were Bill's souvenirs?
- Ⓐ the fish he had caught
- Ⓑ a stuffed fish he bought
- Ⓒ his wet clothes
- Ⓓ his broken fishing rod

6. Where did Bill and his dad fish?
- Ⓕ in a lake
- Ⓖ in the ocean
- Ⓗ in a river
- Ⓙ at a fish hatchery

7. In this story, <u>convinced</u> means
- Ⓐ forced.
- Ⓑ talked him into.
- Ⓒ begged.
- Ⓓ pitched a fit.

8. Why was Bill disappointed?
- Ⓕ He didn't catch any fish.
- Ⓖ Their camper was too small.
- Ⓗ His fishing rod broke.
- Ⓙ His dad fussed at him.

9. How did Bill feel about his first fishing trip?
- Ⓐ angry
- Ⓑ disappointed
- Ⓒ happy
- Ⓓ wet

10. How long did Bill and his dad fish before it began to rain?
- Ⓕ two hours
- Ⓖ about half a day
- Ⓗ until morning
- Ⓙ until bedtime

Name Date

Nonfiction

Directions: Read each paragraph carefully. Then choose the best answer.

Example: P. T. Barnum, an American entertainer in the 1800s, is best known for his circus, "The Greatest Show on Earth." Some people who went to his circus became angry because the "freaks" he advertised were not really alive. They were made from parts of stuffed animals put together. After he died, his circus became part of the Ringling Brothers and Barnum & Bailey Circus.

A. Who was P. T. Barnum?

- Ⓐ the man who invented "freaks"
- Ⓑ a circus performer
- ● the man who started Barnum & Bailey Circus
- Ⓓ one of the Ringling Brothers

Be sure to read each question and the answers carefully. Look back in the paragraph if you need help.

The Beatles were a very popular singing group from England in the 1960s. Their names were John Lennon, Ringo Starr, Paul McCartney, and George Harrison. They were so popular that when they performed, many people in the audience would scream and become hysterical. This was known as "Beatlemania."

1. How many Beatles were there?

- Ⓐ 4
- Ⓑ 8
- Ⓒ 3
- Ⓓ 5

2. Hysterical behavior by the audience was called

- Ⓕ "McCartneyism."
- Ⓖ "Hysterical."
- Ⓗ "Beatlemania."
- Ⓙ "Popular."

A volcano is a cone-shaped mountain that forms when molten rock and other materials force their way from deep in the earth to the surface. This hot lava destroys everything in its path as it flows down the side of the mountain.

3. When a volcano erupts, what causes the damage?

- Ⓐ noise
- Ⓑ shaking
- Ⓒ smoke
- Ⓓ lava

GO ON

Name Date

The name *dinosaur* comes from the Greek word for "monstrous lizard." Dinosaurs were reptiles that were the main form of life on earth for millions of years. Dinosaurs are now extinct. Scientists are not certain why the dinosaurs all died, but one theory is that the earth became too cold for them to survive. Some dinosaurs, such as the tyrannosaurus rex, were meat eaters. Others, such as the brontosaurus, were plant eaters. The triceratops got its name from the three bony spines that came out of its head. Some dinosaurs were so gigantic that the ground shook when they walked, yet others were small enough to fly. Most dinosaurs had tiny brains.

4. What were the spines on the triceratops' head probably used for?
- Ⓕ decoration
- Ⓖ defense
- Ⓗ to help it run
- Ⓙ to keep it warm

5. The word <u>extinct</u> means
- Ⓐ monstrous lizard.
- Ⓑ meat eater.
- Ⓒ very large.
- Ⓓ no longer living.

6. If dinosaurs had tiny brains, you might think that
- Ⓕ they were not very smart.
- Ⓖ they had tiny heads, too.
- Ⓗ they were extinct.
- Ⓙ they did not need a brain.

7. The best title for this paragraph is
- Ⓐ What Dinosaurs Ate.
- Ⓑ Monstrous Lizard.
- Ⓒ The Difference in Dinosaurs.
- Ⓓ All about Dinosaurs.

8. To which group did dinosaurs belong?
- Ⓕ birds
- Ⓖ mammals
- Ⓗ reptiles
- Ⓙ fish

9. What may have caused dinosaurs to become extinct?
- Ⓐ They were not very smart.
- Ⓑ The earth cooled off.
- Ⓒ They killed each other.
- Ⓓ They were millions of years old.

STOP

Name Date

Sample Comprehension Test

Directions: Read each paragraph and the questions that follow. Choose the best answer to each question.

Example:

Sesame Street is a children's television program that began in the 1960s. The characters are live actors and puppets called Muppets. They use songs and short skits to teach young children the letters of the alphabet and numbers. They also teach things such as cooperation and kindness.

A. For whom would *Sesame Street* be most appropriate?

Ⓐ your grandmother
Ⓑ your teenage brother
● your 4-year-old cousin
Ⓓ you

Read each paragraph and each question carefully. Look back in the paragraph if you need help.

The United States has two neighboring countries in North America: Canada and Mexico. To the north is Canada, whose first settlers in 1604 were the French. Instead of states, Canada has provinces. Its capital is Ottawa, and its largest city is Toronto. Both French and English are spoken in Canada. Canada and the U.S. work together to buy and sell goods to other countries.

To the south of the United States is Mexico. Mexico is much smaller than either the U.S. or Canada. Native Americans, such as the Aztecs and Mayas, originally lived in Mexico. The Spanish came in the 1500s. Spanish is the main language of Mexico. Mexico has much fertile land, but it is hard to cultivate. Mexico is a poorer country than Canada and the U.S. Many Mexicans try to come to the United States to find jobs. Mexico City is the capital of Mexico and the largest city.

1. Traveling north to south, what is the correct order of these countries?

Ⓐ Mexico, U.S., Canada
Ⓑ U.S., Canada, Mexico
Ⓒ Mexico, Canada, U.S.
Ⓓ Canada, U.S., Mexico

2. Which language is not a major one in these countries?

Ⓕ English
Ⓖ Spanish
Ⓗ Portuguese
Ⓙ French

Name Date

3. What is the main idea of these paragraphs?
   Ⓐ The U.S. has two North American neighbors.
   Ⓑ Canada was settled by the French.
   Ⓒ The Spanish settled Mexico.
   Ⓓ Canadian Provinces

4. A province is similar to a
   Ⓕ capital.
   Ⓖ large city.
   Ⓗ country.
   Ⓙ state.

5. What are the capitals of Canada and Mexico?
   Ⓐ Toronto and Mexico City
   Ⓑ Ottawa and Mexico City
   Ⓒ Toronto and Ottawa
   Ⓓ Maya and Aztec

Directions: Carefully read the paragraph, and answer each question.

Everything is made up of matter. Matter exists in three states: solid, such as wood; liquid, like water; or gas, such as water vapor. Matter can change from one state to another when its temperature changes. When ice melts and becomes water, it changes from a solid to a liquid. Freezing water changes it from a liquid to a solid. Evaporation occurs when water changes from its liquid state to steam or water vapor. This can happen when water boils and turns to steam or when a puddle dries up. When dew forms, water changes its state from water vapor, a gas in the air, to a liquid on the grass. This is called condensation.

6. When a cup of cold liquid gets wet on the outside, it is an example of
   Ⓕ evaporation.
   Ⓖ condensation.
   Ⓗ melting.
   Ⓙ matter.

7. Which one could not evaporate?
   Ⓐ wood
   Ⓑ water
   Ⓒ lemonade
   Ⓓ coffee

Name Date

8. What are the three states of matter?
   Ⓕ liquid, dew, solid
   Ⓖ gas, water vapor, dew
   Ⓗ solid, liquid, evaporation
   Ⓙ solid, gas, liquid

9. Which changes are opposites?
   Ⓐ condensing, melting
   Ⓑ evaporating, freezing
   Ⓒ freezing, melting
   Ⓓ melting, evaporating

10. What has occurred when a wet bathing suit dries?
   Ⓕ condensation
   Ⓖ evaporation
   Ⓗ melting
   Ⓙ freezing

11. Which one would not change state by freezing?
   Ⓐ milk
   Ⓑ a soda
   Ⓒ a penny
   Ⓓ orange juice

12. What can cause matter to change its state?
   Ⓕ temperature change
   Ⓖ evaporation
   Ⓗ condensation
   Ⓙ steam

13. Which one could change its state by melting?
   Ⓐ an apple
   Ⓑ a Popsicle
   Ⓒ a pencil
   Ⓓ a pretzel

Directions: Read each paragraph and each question carefully. Then choose the best answer to each question.

John Chapman was an American pioneer who was born in Massachusetts in 1774. He is much better known by the name Johnny Appleseed. He was called Johnny Appleseed because he gave apple seeds and saplings to families who were moving west from Pennsylvania, and he traveled to Ohio sowing seeds as he went. He wandered through Ohio, Indiana, and Pennsylvania for over 40 years, tending to the apple orchards he had planted and helping settlers plant their own orchards. Everyone recognized him because of his ragged clothes and unusual behavior. Many pictures show him wearing a cooking pot turned upside down on his head for a hat. He died near Fort Wayne, Indiana, in 1845.

Name Date

14. Where was John Chapman born?
   Ⓕ Indiana
   Ⓖ Ohio
   Ⓗ Pennsylvania
   Ⓙ Massachusetts

15. What does sapling mean?
   Ⓐ seed
   Ⓑ small tree
   Ⓒ advice
   Ⓓ fertilizer

16. Which word does not describe Johnny Appleseed?
   Ⓕ selfish
   Ⓖ helpful
   Ⓗ wanderer
   Ⓙ farmer

17. The best title for this story is
   Ⓐ Wandering John.
   Ⓑ The Man with Odd Behavior.
   Ⓒ John Chapman, American Pioneer.
   Ⓓ Johnny Appleseed.

Directions: Read the paragraph, and choose the best answer to each question.

Polar bears are large white bears that live in arctic parts of North America. They usually live on drifting ice packs, but sometimes they travel for long distances inland. They are very strong swimmers; sometimes they swim 20 to 30 miles at a time. The polar bear's body is long and sleek, with a long neck and a small head. Their fur is very thick and yellowish white all over. The polar bear is the only bear that has fur on the soles of its feet. The fur helps them grip the ice. Polar bears can run 25 miles (40 km) per hour on ice. They are omnivorous, but their main food is marine animals such as seals and young walruses. In summer they eat plants that grow along the shore.

18. The word omnivorous means
   Ⓕ eats plants and meat.
   Ⓖ eats only plants.
   Ⓗ eats only animals.
   Ⓙ is on a diet.

19. Polar bears have fur on their feet
   Ⓐ to keep them warm.
   Ⓑ to help them move quietly.
   Ⓒ to help them grip the ice.
   Ⓓ to help them swim faster.

20. Which does not describe the polar bear's body?
   Ⓕ sleek
   Ⓖ furry
   Ⓗ yellowish white
   Ⓙ omnivorous

21. Polar bears travel by
   Ⓐ swimming and running.
   Ⓑ swimming only.
   Ⓒ running only.
   Ⓓ drifting.

Name Date

Capitalization

Language

Directions: For A and items 1–3, mark the letter under the word that should be capitalized. If the sentence is correct, mark the letter for "None." For B and items 4–5, mark the answer that shows the correct capitalization.

Examples:

A.
Jack London was born on market Street in San Francisco. None
Ⓐ ● Ⓒ Ⓓ

B. His name at birth was
Ⓕ John griffith Chaney.
Ⓖ John Griffith chaney.
● John Griffith Chaney.
Ⓙ john Griffith Chaney.

Sentences and proper nouns begin with capital letters.

1. he was the son of William Chaney, an astrologer and journalist.
Ⓐ Ⓑ Ⓒ Ⓓ

2. His father deserted jack's mother, Flora, before Jack was born.
Ⓕ Ⓖ Ⓗ Ⓙ

3. Later, Flora married John London, a civil War veteran. None
Ⓐ Ⓑ Ⓒ Ⓓ

4. Jack attended _____ only through the eighth grade.
Ⓕ Oakland preparatory School
Ⓖ oakland preparatory school
Ⓗ Oakland Preparatory School
Ⓙ Oakland Preparatory school

5. Jack London's most notable book, _____, is considered to be an all-time classic.
Ⓐ *The call of the Wild*
Ⓑ *The Call Of the Wild*
Ⓒ *The Call of the Wild*
Ⓓ *the Call of the wild*

Name Date

Capitalization

Directions: For items 6–12, mark the answer that shows the correct capitalization.

Example:

C. Ⓐ Coco loves to chase Cats.
Ⓑ My mother baked Brownies.
Ⓒ Which is your favorite TV Program?
● My family will go to New York for Christmas.

Practice

6. Ⓕ Can you name a Country in Africa?
Ⓖ What do people speak in spain?
Ⓗ My family lived in South africa for two years.
Ⓙ When I graduate, I would like to live in Amsterdam, Holland.

7. Ⓐ Mrs. Margaret starks is a great teacher.
Ⓑ Brandon elementary is only two blocks from my house.
Ⓒ My sister and I walk to school every day.
Ⓓ The third grade class is going to the Grant park Zoo.

8. Ⓕ Isabelle and Jane are twin sisters.
Ⓖ My mother met senator Rogers.
Ⓗ Have you seen mrs. Moore?
Ⓙ The grand prize was presented to uncle Jessie.

9. Ⓐ My brother jerry will be nine years old tomorrow.
Ⓑ We visited the Grand Canyon.
Ⓒ Who is your favorite Author?
Ⓓ Mrs. ross is a great third grade teacher.

10. Ⓕ It was so hot last july.
Ⓖ Tanya wrote a letter to renee.
Ⓗ Is Erica singing in the chorus?
Ⓙ The Andes mountains are in Chile.

11. Ⓐ The smallest state is Rhode Island.
Ⓑ This year Christmas is on thursday.
Ⓒ Bring a quart of carnation milk.
Ⓓ She bought Apples, bananas, and pears.

12. Ⓕ My father donated blood to the American red cross.
Ⓖ His sister Tina arrived from Brazil today.
Ⓗ Dr. harrison gave my father a physical.
Ⓙ Principal york greeted the students.

Name Date

Punctuation

Language

Directions: For A and items 1–4, mark the letter that shows the punctuation mark that should be at the end of the sentence. If the sentence is correct, mark the letter for "None." For B and items 5–6, mark the answer that shows the part of the sentence where the punctuation is incorrect.

Examples:

A. What time did you finish your homework

Ⓐ . Ⓑ ,

● ? Ⓓ None

B. Ⓕ Michael and I will be Ⓖ going to practice after

● school Will you meet Ⓙ us after practice?

Always look for missing punctuation at the end of the sentence. Next, look for any missing punctuation inside the sentence. If the punctuation is correct, mark the space "None."

1. Thursday night was so stormy that we could not watch television

Ⓐ . Ⓑ ? Ⓒ ! Ⓓ None

2. Look out The dog will get out of the fence!

Ⓕ . Ⓖ ? Ⓗ ! Ⓙ None

3. Can you call Diane to help you finish the project

Ⓐ . Ⓑ ? Ⓒ ! Ⓓ None

4. The two workers finished their job early today

Ⓕ . Ⓖ ? Ⓗ ! Ⓙ None

5. Ⓐ Please bring crayons, paper,
Ⓑ glue, and scissors to the art
Ⓒ class on Saturday morning.
Ⓓ No mistakes

6. The principal ______ announced the writing contest winners.

Ⓕ hasnt' Ⓖ hasn't Ⓗ hasnt Ⓙ has'nt

Name Date

Directions: For items 7–14, mark the answer for the correct punctuation of the underlined part.

7. Which one is Jacks coat?

Ⓐ Jacks.
Ⓑ Jack's
Ⓒ Jacks;
Ⓓ Jack"s

8. Mother said, "Come in from the cold and warm yourself

Ⓕ ."
Ⓖ ?"
Ⓗ .
Ⓙ !'

9. A pair of skates, a softball bat and a glove were left out in the rain.

Ⓐ ;
Ⓑ :
Ⓒ ,
Ⓓ "

10. Tiger Woods, a famous golfer, has won every major golf tournament

Ⓕ .
Ⓖ ?
Ⓗ ,
Ⓙ "

11. By the way how far is it to the bowling alley?

Ⓐ ,
Ⓑ :
Ⓒ ;
Ⓓ Correct as is

12. Has your mother ever visited Chicago Illinois?

Ⓕ .
Ⓖ ,
Ⓗ ;
Ⓙ Correct as is

13. The stranded woman screamed, "Help

Ⓐ ."
Ⓑ ,"
Ⓒ ?"
Ⓓ !"

14. Jenicas cell phone was lost at the ball game.

Ⓕ Jenica.s
Ⓖ Jenica's
Ⓗ Jenicas"
Ⓙ Correct as is

STOP

Name Date

Capitalization and Punctuation

Language

Directions: Read this paragraph. The paragraph will have groups of underlined words. After reading the paragraph, answer items 1–4 about the capitalization and punctuation in the underlined parts.

Garth Brooks, who was born in Tulsa oklahoma (1) blasted onto the country music scene. He sings country but (2) he moves with the energy of a rock star during his concerts. His impact on music has been powerful. in fact Garth changed (3) the path of country music. At first he sold boots in a shoe store during the day and he sang (4) at local clubs at night. Finally, a talent scout discovered Garth in a talent show. In 1991, he recorded his third album Ropin' the wind and (5) the album sold four million copies before it was released. In 2000 Garth (6) took time off to spend with his three daughters. He wanted to say Daddy loves you in (7) person.

1. In sentence 1, Tulsa oklahoma is best written as

Ⓐ Tulsa, Oklahoma
Ⓑ Tulsa, Oklahoma,
Ⓒ Tulsa oklahoma
Ⓓ Tulsa Oklahoma,

2. In sentence 3, in fact Garth is best written as

Ⓕ in fact Garth
Ⓖ In fact Garth
Ⓗ In fact, Garth
Ⓙ in Fact, Garth

3. In sentence 5, album Ropin' the wind and is best written as

Ⓐ Album, 'Ropin' the wind' And
Ⓑ album, *Ropin' the Wind*, and
Ⓒ "album Ropin' the Wind" and
Ⓓ album, *"Ropin' The Wind*, And

4. In sentence 7, say Daddy loves you in is best written as

Ⓕ say, "Daddy loves you," in
Ⓖ say, Daddy loves you, in
Ⓗ say "Daddy loves you" in
Ⓙ say, "Daddy Loves You," in

GO ON

Name Date

Directions: Choose the answer that is written correctly and shows the correct capitalization and punctuation.

5.

Ⓐ i saw the movie twice last week.
Ⓑ Her sister is in rhode Island?
Ⓒ Watch out!
Ⓓ Can you watch my baby brother.

6.

Ⓕ Alaska is the largest state.
Ⓖ Chads birthday is tomorrow.
Ⓗ the pot of beans boiled over!
Ⓙ I want to go too.

7.

Ⓐ My dog sadie had puppies.
Ⓑ "What should we do for his birthday?" asked Tommy.
Ⓒ Please, hand me that book?
Ⓓ Ally wore her new Hat, today!

8.

Ⓕ Why dont we bake cookies?
Ⓖ My family visited alaska last summer.
Ⓗ My grandparents live in Toronto, Canada.
Ⓙ Dont go near that fire.

9.

Ⓐ Who forgot to empty the trash?
Ⓑ Isn't that mrs. Drake.
Ⓒ The president lives in the White house.
Ⓓ Mrs. Warren asked, Who wants to take this report to the office?

10.

Ⓕ We celebrate thanksgiving in November
Ⓖ What time does your plane leave friday?
Ⓗ we need to wear a jacket to the Ball Game tonight.
Ⓙ My mother's friend has such beautiful hair.

11.

Ⓐ Joseph painted a picture in Art class today;
Ⓑ bob Thomas ran only one mile in the Race.
Ⓒ Our neighborhood swimming pool always opens in june.
Ⓓ *Curious George* is one of my favorite books.

12.

Ⓕ October 8 2003
Ⓖ October 8, 2003
Ⓗ october 8, 2003
Ⓙ october 8 2003

13.

Ⓐ David and John want to play Basketball on saturday.
Ⓑ The desserts were not ready when Mrs. Bush promised.
Ⓒ my grandfather now lives in Reno Nevada!
Ⓓ How many Hamburgers did Joey eat at the Birthday Party?

Name Date

Spelling

Directions: For A and items 1–6, find the word that fits in the sentence and is spelled correctly. For B–C and items 7–9, find the word that is spelled incorrectly. If there are no mistakes, mark "No mistakes."

Examples:

A. Brownies are my _____ dessert.
- Ⓐ favorit
- Ⓑ favorrite
- ● favorite
- Ⓓ favorete

B.
- Ⓕ vegetable
- ● stomick
- Ⓗ opposite
- Ⓙ worker
- Ⓚ No mistakes

C.
- Ⓐ enemy
- Ⓑ captain
- Ⓒ language
- Ⓓ business
- ● No mistakes

Try not to look at the words too long. They will all look misspelled.

Practice

1. Mark your _____ for the next event.
- Ⓐ calunder
- Ⓑ calender
- Ⓒ calendar
- Ⓓ calundar

2. My mother is _____ with those streets.
- Ⓕ familiar
- Ⓖ familyer
- Ⓗ familyar
- Ⓙ familier

3. The ships took _____ courses to America.
- Ⓐ seperit
- Ⓑ separite
- Ⓒ separete
- Ⓓ separate

4. My brother left his _____ on the bus.
- Ⓕ luggiage
- Ⓖ luggage
- Ⓗ lugage
- Ⓙ lujage

5. _____ turn is it to take out the garbage?
- Ⓐ Whoose
- Ⓑ Whose
- Ⓒ Who's
- Ⓓ Whoos

6. Please park your car in the _____.
- Ⓕ garege
- Ⓖ gargee
- Ⓗ garegge
- Ⓙ garage

7.
- Ⓐ practice
- Ⓑ playground
- Ⓒ stairway
- Ⓓ grasshoper
- Ⓔ No mistakes

8.
- Ⓕ leader
- Ⓖ diffrence
- Ⓗ guard
- Ⓙ Thursday
- Ⓚ No mistakes

9.
- Ⓐ ninetey
- Ⓑ elephant
- Ⓒ potatoes
- Ⓓ mountain
- Ⓔ No mistakes

GO ON

Name Date

Spelling

Directions: For items 10–22, find the word that is spelled incorrectly. Mark "No mistakes" if there are no errors.

10.
- Ⓕ guitar
- Ⓖ basketball
- Ⓗ directions
- Ⓙ surface
- Ⓚ No mistakes

11.
- Ⓐ yesterday
- Ⓑ messiage
- Ⓒ neighbor
- Ⓓ useful
- Ⓔ No mistakes

12.
- Ⓕ fraight
- Ⓖ manage
- Ⓗ copy
- Ⓙ address
- Ⓚ No mistakes

13.
- Ⓐ ballon
- Ⓑ teacher
- Ⓒ Tuesday
- Ⓓ swimming
- Ⓔ No mistakes

14.
- Ⓕ trouble
- Ⓖ birthday
- Ⓗ describ
- Ⓙ certain
- Ⓚ No mistakes

15.
- Ⓐ thirsty
- Ⓑ takeing
- Ⓒ backpack
- Ⓓ children
- Ⓔ No mistakes

16.
- Ⓕ thoughtless
- Ⓖ dissagree
- Ⓗ wouldn't
- Ⓙ taught
- Ⓚ No mistakes

17.
- Ⓐ pitcher
- Ⓑ wrinkle
- Ⓒ Halloween
- Ⓓ written
- Ⓔ No mistakes

18.
- Ⓕ squeeze
- Ⓖ declare
- Ⓗ midnight
- Ⓙ tomorow
- Ⓚ No mistakes

19. Please don't lean against that table in the hallway. No mistakes
Ⓐ Ⓑ Ⓒ Ⓓ

20. There are twenty childern in the third grade class. No mistakes
Ⓕ Ⓖ Ⓗ Ⓙ

21. My sister is sleepy becauz she had trouble falling asleep. No mistakes
Ⓐ Ⓑ Ⓒ Ⓓ

22. Our family loves to eat around the dinning room table. No mistakes
Ⓕ Ⓖ Ⓗ Ⓙ

GO ON

Name Date

Spelling

Directions: For items 23–31, find the word that is spelled incorrectly. Mark "No mistakes" if there are no errors.

23. Thomas had purchased two tickets to the musicial concert. No mistakes
Ⓐ Ⓑ Ⓒ Ⓓ

24. To stay healthy, a person should exercise and eat corectly. No mistakes
Ⓕ Ⓖ Ⓗ Ⓙ

25. An artist is one who is talented and skilled in any of the fine arts. No mistakes
Ⓐ Ⓑ Ⓒ Ⓓ

26. Why is raising bunny rabbitts a great hobby? No mistakes
Ⓕ Ⓖ Ⓗ Ⓙ

27. I allways have so much fun when our classmates work with clay. No mistakes
Ⓐ Ⓑ Ⓒ Ⓓ

28. Michele wants to write a scarey ghost story for class. No mistakes
Ⓕ Ⓖ Ⓗ Ⓙ

29. Everybody in my class wears a backpack to school. No mistakes
Ⓐ Ⓑ Ⓒ Ⓓ

30. Jennifer carefully cut the sanwich in two and gave her a half. No mistakes
Ⓕ Ⓖ Ⓗ Ⓙ

31. Learning how to use computers has been so helpfull. No mistakes
Ⓐ Ⓑ Ⓒ Ⓓ

GO ON

Name ______ Date ______

Spelling

Directions: For items 32–38, read each sentence. Then choose the word that fits in the sentence and is spelled correctly.

Example: **D.** Don't watch television _____ doing your homework.

● while
Ⓖ wile
Ⓗ wheil
Ⓙ whil

32. Susie could not _____ the teacher when he gave the directions.

Ⓕ here
Ⓖ heer
Ⓗ hear
Ⓙ her

33. The boys lost _____ baseball when it went over the fence.

Ⓐ they're
Ⓑ their
Ⓒ there
Ⓓ thier

34. Jack will be _____ years old on his birthday.

Ⓕ ait
Ⓖ ate
Ⓗ eight
Ⓙ hait

35. The doll broke _____ arm when it fell off the shelf.

Ⓐ it's
Ⓑ its
Ⓒ its'
Ⓓ itss'

36. What did you name _____ new guinea pig?

Ⓕ youre
Ⓖ you're
Ⓗ your
Ⓙ yore

37. The new library books _____ ready to be checked out.

Ⓐ were
Ⓑ where
Ⓒ wear
Ⓓ we're

38. Will you please help me _____ my science report that is due tomorrow?

Ⓕ write
Ⓖ rite
Ⓗ right
Ⓙ reight

STOP

Name Date

Sample Language Mechanics Test

Language

Directions: Read the following paragraph with the numbered lines. Then mark the answer below that shows incorrect spelling, capitalization, or punctuation in each line.

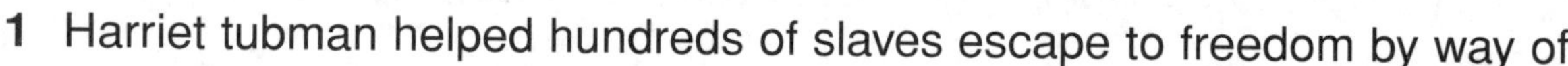

1 Harriet tubman helped hundreds of slaves escape to freedom by way of

2 the Underground Railroad. She was an excaped slave herself, and during

3 the Civil War she served as a nurse and a spy for the Union Army, The

4 Underground Railroad wasn't really a railroad. it was a series of houses

5 and safe places that slave's could use to escape to freedom in the North.

6 They would travel from one "station" to the next at night?

1.

Ⓐ tubman
Ⓑ Harriet
Ⓒ hundreds
Ⓓ freedom

2.

Ⓕ Underground
Ⓖ Railroad
Ⓗ excaped
Ⓙ during

3.

Ⓐ Civil
Ⓑ War
Ⓒ served
Ⓓ Army,

4.

Ⓕ wasn't
Ⓖ really
Ⓗ railroad
Ⓙ it

5.

Ⓐ places
Ⓑ slave's
Ⓒ freedom
Ⓓ North.

6.

Ⓕ travel
Ⓖ "station"
Ⓗ next
Ⓙ night?

GO ON

Name Date

Sample Language Mechanics Test

Directions: Choose the sentence that has no mistakes in spelling, punctuation, or capitalization.

7.

Ⓐ Halloween is on Friday, October 31, this year.
Ⓑ Halloween is on Friday October 31, this year.
Ⓒ Halloween is on friday, October 31 this year.
Ⓓ Halloween is on Friday, October 31 this year

8.

Ⓕ My dog Kobe likes to play in the Sprinkler during the summer.
Ⓖ My dog Kobe, likes to play in the sprinkler during the summer.
Ⓗ My dog Kobe likes to play in the sprinkler during the summer.
Ⓙ My dog Kobe likes to play in the sprinkler during the Summer.

9.

Ⓐ Joshua goes to school mows lawns and works at Conyers Sports Arena.
Ⓑ Joshua goes to school, mows lawns, and works at conyers sports arena.
Ⓒ Joshua goes to School, mows lawns, and works at Conyers Sports Arena.
Ⓓ Joshua goes to school, mows lawns, and works at Conyers Sports Arena.

10.

Ⓕ Sherry bought chocolate, jaw breakers, and chewing gum at the store.
Ⓖ sherry bought chocolate, jaw breakers, and chewing gum at the store.
Ⓗ Sherry bought chocolate, jaw breakers, and chewing gum at the store
Ⓙ Sherry bought chocolate jaw breakers and chewing gum at the store.

11.

Ⓐ Where is Santiago locatted on the map of South America?
Ⓑ Where is Santiago located on the map of South America?
Ⓒ Where is santiago located on the map of South America.
Ⓓ Where is Santiago located on the map of south america?

Name Date

Sample Language Mechanics Test

Directions: For items 12–25, find the word that is spelled incorrectly. Mark "No mistakes" if there are no errors.

12.
- Ⓕ hairy
- Ⓖ gentley
- Ⓗ knowing
- Ⓙ frown
- Ⓚ No mistakes

13.
- Ⓐ general
- Ⓑ bubble
- Ⓒ aren't
- Ⓓ certian
- Ⓔ No mistakes

14.
- Ⓕ hobbies
- Ⓖ pennies
- Ⓗ butterflies
- Ⓙ ponies
- Ⓚ No mistakes

15.
- Ⓐ giraffe
- Ⓑ aligator
- Ⓒ raccoon
- Ⓓ lizard
- Ⓔ No mistakes

16.
- Ⓕ quiet
- Ⓖ picture
- Ⓗ capitial
- Ⓙ dairy
- Ⓚ No mistakes

17.
- Ⓐ gnaw
- Ⓑ wrinkle
- Ⓒ crumb
- Ⓓ knowlege
- Ⓔ No mistakes

18.
- Ⓕ twelfith
- Ⓖ eleventh
- Ⓗ fourth
- Ⓙ seventh
- Ⓚ No mistakes

19.
- Ⓐ moonlight
- Ⓑ sunset
- Ⓒ thunderstorm
- Ⓓ waterfall
- Ⓔ No mistakes

20.
- Ⓕ wonderful
- Ⓖ driest
- Ⓗ largest
- Ⓙ happeir
- Ⓚ No mistakes

21. Write the contraction for each word on your list. No mistakes
Ⓐ Ⓑ Ⓒ Ⓓ

22. The old judge ordered slients in the courtroom. No mistakes
Ⓕ Ⓖ Ⓗ Ⓙ

23. Christine listed the prices on the sheet in sequense. No mistakes
Ⓐ Ⓑ Ⓒ Ⓓ

24. The insturment used for moving the cursor is the mouse. No mistakes
Ⓕ Ⓖ Ⓗ Ⓙ

25. The computer part that looks like a telivision is the monitor. No mistakes
Ⓐ Ⓑ Ⓒ Ⓓ

STOP

Name Date

Nouns and Pronouns

Directions: For A and items 1–4, choose the answer that completes the sentence best. For B and items 5–8, choose the answer that could take the place of the underlined word or words.

Examples:

A. ___ loves to play Trivial Pursuit.

Ⓐ Them
Ⓑ We
● He
Ⓓ Him

B. I gave the books to <u>Mrs. Carter.</u>

Ⓕ him.
Ⓖ hers.
Ⓗ she.
● her.

If you have trouble, try reading the sentence quietly with each word in the blank.

Practice

1. ___ made a perfect score on the test.

Ⓐ He Ⓑ Him
Ⓒ Her Ⓓ Them

2. Mother gave ______ some cookies.

Ⓕ they Ⓖ we
Ⓗ she Ⓙ them

3. The teacher let ______ play outside longer today.

Ⓐ we Ⓑ us
Ⓒ they Ⓓ his

4. Please give the dog ______ bone.

Ⓕ him Ⓖ hers
Ⓗ its Ⓙ it's

5. <u>Mary</u> had a little lamb.

Ⓐ It Ⓑ She
Ⓒ He Ⓓ They

6. There is a hole in <u>Tom's</u> sock.

Ⓕ her Ⓖ their
Ⓗ his Ⓙ its

7. <u>Joe and David</u> have lost their money.

Ⓐ Their Ⓑ Them
Ⓒ He Ⓓ They

8. Please take <u>Coco</u> for a walk.

Ⓕ her Ⓖ she
Ⓗ them Ⓙ they

STOP

Name Date

Nouns and Pronouns

Directions: For A and items 1–4, choose the answer that completes the sentence best. For B and items 5–8, choose the answer that could take the place of the underlined word or words.

Examples:

A. Help _____ move this table.
- Ⓐ his
- Ⓑ we
- ● me
- Ⓓ it

B. George of the Jungle is funny.
- Ⓕ Him
- ● He
- Ⓗ His
- Ⓙ Her

If you have trouble, try reading the sentence with each word in the blank.

Practice

1. The twins fooled _____ teacher.
- Ⓐ us
- Ⓑ we
- Ⓒ their
- Ⓓ its

2. We found _____ lost puppy.
- Ⓕ our
- Ⓖ them
- Ⓗ I
- Ⓙ him

3. _____ cannot get the jar open.
- Ⓐ Him
- Ⓑ Her
- Ⓒ Them
- Ⓓ I

4. Did you borrow _____ jacket?
- Ⓕ my
- Ⓖ it
- Ⓗ me
- Ⓙ I

5. When did Sally get sick?
- Ⓐ her
- Ⓑ she
- Ⓒ it
- Ⓓ me

6. Where did you get the new computer?
- Ⓕ them
- Ⓖ their
- Ⓗ it
- Ⓙ her

7. Jill is invited to the party.
- Ⓐ Her
- Ⓑ She
- Ⓒ Hers
- Ⓓ They

8. Send the note to Uncle Bob.
- Ⓕ her.
- Ⓖ he.
- Ⓗ his.
- Ⓙ him.

STOP

Name Date

Verbs

Directions: For A and items 1–4, choose the answer that completes the sentence best. For B and items 5–8, choose the sentence with the correct form of the verb.

Examples:

A. What made the bridge _____?

Ⓐ collapsed
● collapse
Ⓒ collapsing
Ⓓ collapses

B.

Ⓕ They have ate dinner.
Ⓖ They eat dinner an hour ago.
● They ate dinner at 6:00.
Ⓙ They eaten steak for dinner.

If you have trouble, try reading the sentence quietly to yourself.

Practice

1. The teacher said, "___ down!"

Ⓐ Settling Ⓑ Settled
Ⓒ Had settled Ⓓ Settle

2. Jamie has _____ to the store.

Ⓕ gone Ⓖ went
Ⓗ done gone Ⓙ go

3. Mary Lou _____ down the steps.

Ⓐ fallen Ⓑ fell
Ⓒ has fell Ⓓ fellen

4. Have you ever been ___?

Ⓕ ski Ⓖ skied
Ⓗ going ski Ⓙ skiing

5.

Ⓐ Connie type the report.
Ⓑ Jeff write the report.
Ⓒ The teacher read the report.
Ⓓ Mother help with the report.

6.

Ⓕ Matt walked the dog.
Ⓖ Jay feed the dog.
Ⓗ Taylor brushing the dog.
Ⓙ Wes had pet the dog.

7.

Ⓐ Can you helped me with this?
Ⓑ Are you finished the book?
Ⓒ May I borrow your pen?
Ⓓ Did she dropping the paper?

8.

Ⓕ Dig the hole was hard work.
Ⓖ It was easy to move the bush.
Ⓗ I liked to watered it.
Ⓙ Watch it grow is fun.

Name Date

Verbs

Directions: For A and items 1–4, choose the answer that completes the sentence best. For B and items 5–8, choose the sentence that does not use the correct form of the verb.

Examples:

A. Barry ___the game on television.

● watched
Ⓑ watching
Ⓒ watch
Ⓓ is watched

B.

Ⓕ Jane made her bed neatly.
Ⓖ She brushed her teeth.
● Mother fix her breakfast.
Ⓙ Jane got on the school bus.

If you have trouble, try reading the sentence quietly to yourself.

Practice

1. The dolphins ______ in the water.

Ⓐ jumping Ⓑ jumped
Ⓒ has jumped Ⓓ is jumping

2. Joan ______ the cake batter well.

Ⓕ stirred Ⓖ stirring
Ⓗ stir Ⓙ was stir

3. Mike helped ______ his room.

Ⓐ painting Ⓑ painted
Ⓒ paint Ⓓ paints

4. She will be ______ home soon.

Ⓕ come Ⓖ went
Ⓗ came Ⓙ coming

5.

Ⓐ The team played well.
Ⓑ They scored many points.
Ⓒ They made few errors.
Ⓓ The coach were proud.

6.

Ⓕ The chair felt very comfortable.
Ⓖ Goldilocks fallen asleep.
Ⓗ The bears woke her up.
Ⓙ Frightened, she ran away.

7.

Ⓐ The tacos tasting delicious.
Ⓑ They were messy to eat.
Ⓒ Jose spilled some on his shirt.
Ⓓ His mother said it was okay.

8.

Ⓕ The test questions were easy.
Ⓖ Sam knew he had did well.
Ⓗ The teacher graded the test.
Ⓙ Sam was very happy.

STOP

Name Date

Adjectives

Directions: For A and items 1–4, choose the best answer to complete each sentence. For B and items 5–8, choose the sentence with an adjective underlined.

Examples:

A. In autumn, the leaves on the trees turn _____ colors.
- ● pretty
- Ⓑ prettier
- Ⓒ prettiest
- Ⓓ more prettier

B.
- Ⓕ They <u>were</u> tired after the game.
- Ⓖ <u>He</u> is a very talented player.
- ● The fans were really <u>happy</u>.
- Ⓙ They <u>scored</u> a lot of points.

Remember that an adjective is a word that describes a noun.

Practice

1. Football players are _____ and fast.
- Ⓐ strong
- Ⓑ strongly
- Ⓒ stronger
- Ⓓ strongest

2. Yesterday was such a _____ day!
- Ⓕ rainier
- Ⓖ rainiest
- Ⓗ most rainiest
- Ⓙ rainy

3. Those brownies were _____.
- Ⓐ deliciouser
- Ⓑ delicious
- Ⓒ deliciously
- Ⓓ deliciousest

4. What a _____ dress that is.
- Ⓕ lovelier
- Ⓖ loveliest
- Ⓗ love
- Ⓙ lovely

5.
- Ⓐ The <u>painting</u> is quite colorful.
- Ⓑ It was done by a <u>famous</u> artist.
- Ⓒ His <u>name</u> was Pablo Picasso.
- Ⓓ He <u>was</u> a great painter.

6.
- Ⓕ I just read a <u>wonderful</u> book.
- Ⓖ It <u>was</u> a mystery.
- Ⓗ The <u>hero</u> was brave and smart.
- Ⓙ In the end, he solved the <u>case</u>.

7.
- Ⓐ Our <u>class</u> went on a field trip.
- Ⓑ We <u>visited</u> the space museum.
- Ⓒ <u>It</u> was really fun.
- Ⓓ My <u>favorite</u> part was seeing the old space suits.

8.
- Ⓕ Jamie <u>has</u> a new puppy.
- Ⓖ It is <u>soft</u> and black.
- Ⓗ It has huge <u>paws</u> and long ears.
- Ⓙ He <u>adopted</u> it from the pound.

STOP

Name Date

Adverbs

Directions: For A and items 1–4, choose the best answer to complete each sentence. For B and items 5–8, choose the sentence with an adverb underlined.

Examples:

A. The orchestra played ____.

- Ⓐ beautiful
- ● beautifully
- Ⓒ more beautiful
- Ⓓ most beautiful

B.

- Ⓕ The track meet was <u>exciting</u>.
- Ⓖ The runners were <u>speedy</u>.
- ● They finished the race <u>quickly</u>.
- Ⓙ The high <u>jump</u> was exciting.

Remember that an adverb is a word that describes a verb, an adjective, or another adverb. Adverbs often end in *ly.*

Practice

1. The race cars went really ____.

- Ⓐ fast
- Ⓑ fastly
- Ⓒ faster
- Ⓓ fastest

2. Pierre learned English ____.

- Ⓕ quicker
- Ⓖ quickest
- Ⓗ quickly
- Ⓙ quick

3. The dogs barked ____.

- Ⓐ loud
- Ⓑ louder
- Ⓒ most loud
- Ⓓ loudly

4. That is a _____ written paper.

- Ⓕ nice
- Ⓖ nicely
- Ⓗ nicest
- Ⓙ nicer

5.

- Ⓐ Maria's new house is <u>huge</u>.
- Ⓑ She <u>will</u> move in next week.
- Ⓒ The <u>sunniest</u> room is hers.
- Ⓓ She chose it <u>carefully</u>.

6.

- Ⓕ We <u>rented</u> a movie last night.
- Ⓖ It was so <u>funny</u>!
- Ⓗ The actors were <u>really</u> good.
- Ⓙ They played <u>their</u> parts well.

7.

- Ⓐ We <u>went</u> camping last week.
- Ⓑ During the <u>night</u> we heard a loud noise.
- Ⓒ It was a bear <u>raiding</u> the garbage can.
- Ⓓ The movie was <u>very</u> scary!

8.

- Ⓕ Maude is talking very <u>quietly</u>.
- Ⓖ She has a new <u>baby</u> brother.
- Ⓗ She is really excited <u>about</u> Will.
- Ⓙ She is looking forward to <u>baby-sitting</u> him.

Name Date

Sentences

Directions: For A and sentences 1–5, mark the sentence that is written correctly. For B and sentences 6–8, mark the one that is not a sentence.

Examples:

A.

- Ⓐ My favorite ice cream.
- Ⓑ Is chocolate ice cream.
- ● Chocolate is my favorite ice cream.
- Ⓓ Do not like vanilla.

B.

- Ⓕ I like to read mysteries.
- ● Not science fiction.
- Ⓗ I do not like fairy tales either.
- Ⓙ I just renewed my library card.

Remember that a sentence must have a noun and a verb.

Practice

1.

- Ⓐ Mandy did her homework.
- Ⓑ Always does it quickly.
- Ⓒ Never does a poor job.
- Ⓓ Turns it in on time.

2.

- Ⓕ Leaves all over the yard.
- Ⓖ Raked them into a pile.
- Ⓗ Jumped into the piles.
- Ⓙ We raked leaves all morning.

3.

- Ⓐ Had a pizza party.
- Ⓑ At Pizzaria Pronto.
- Ⓒ Dion had a birthday party.
- Ⓓ For his birthday.

4.

- Ⓕ Four bags of groceries.
- Ⓖ Suddenly the bag broke.
- Ⓗ Went to the grocery store.
- Ⓙ Broken jars everywhere.

5.

- Ⓐ Brad has new sneakers.
- Ⓑ Has new socks, too.
- Ⓒ Tried on many pairs.
- Ⓓ At three sports stores.

6.

- Ⓕ We played on the playground.
- Ⓖ There were swings and slides.
- Ⓗ Also a jungle gym.
- Ⓙ It was so much fun.

7.

- Ⓐ Jane had six new puppies.
- Ⓑ Four black and two tan.
- Ⓒ They were born Monday.
- Ⓓ Three were boys, and three were girls.

8.

- Ⓕ Dad bought a new car.
- Ⓖ His old one broke down.
- Ⓗ Tried out several kinds.
- Ⓙ He decided on a convertible.

Name Date

Sentences

Directions: Read each pair of underlined sentences. Then choose the answer that shows the best way to combine the sentences.

Example: **A.** Traffic was awful on the highway.
There was road construction.

● Traffic was awful on the highway because there was road construction.
Ⓑ There was road construction and the traffic was awful on the highway.
Ⓒ Awful traffic was on the highway with road construction.
Ⓓ Traffic was awful on the highway and there was road construction.

Read each answer, and decide which sentence sounds best.

Practice

1. Mark studied hard for the geography test.
Mark made the highest grade in the class.

Ⓐ Mark studied hard for the geography test and Mark made the highest grade in the class.
Ⓑ Mark hardly studied for the highest grade in the class on the geography test.
Ⓒ Mark studied hard for the geography test, so he made the highest grade in the class.
Ⓓ The highest grade in the class was made by Mark, and he studied hard for the geography test.

2. Claire is a very good soccer player.
She plays goalie for the Spurs.

Ⓕ Claire is a very good soccer player, she plays goalie for the Spurs.
Ⓖ Claire is a very good soccer player who plays goalie for the Spurs.
Ⓗ Claire plays goalie for the Spurs and Claire is a very good soccer player.
Ⓙ Claire is a very good goalie and she plays soccer for the Spurs.

Name _______________ Date _______________

Paragraphs

Directions: Carefully read the paragraph with the blank. Choose the answer that is the best topic sentence for the paragraph.

Example:

A. _______________ They stay in constant motion by beating their wings very fast—50 to 75 beats per second. These tiny birds use so much energy that they feed constantly. They feed on insects and nectar from flowers.

Ⓐ Hummingbirds are brightly colored birds.
● Hummingbirds are tiny and interesting birds.
Ⓒ Hummingbirds vary in size.
Ⓓ Hummingbirds are small birds related to swifts.

Remember, the topic sentence tells what the rest of the paragraph is about.

1. _______________ The sun and our solar system are part of the Milky Way. The whole galaxy rotates around the Milky Way's center. The Milky Way is shaped like a spiral. It has about a hundred billion stars.

Ⓐ The galaxy rotates around the center.
Ⓑ The Milky Way is a galaxy.
Ⓒ The Milky Way is shaped like a spiral.
Ⓓ The Milky Way has about a hundred billion stars.

2. _______________ Scientists think that enormous clouds of gas and dust started to condense to form stars. The rest of the gas and dust became a thin layer where other stars are still forming. There are young stars and old stars in the Milky Way.

Ⓕ The Milky Way has young and old stars.
Ⓖ Gas and dust condense to form stars.
Ⓗ Stars are still forming in the Milky Way.
Ⓙ The Milky Way is made of stars, gas, and dust.

Name Date

Paragraphs

Directions: For items 3 and 4, read each topic sentence. Then choose the answer that best finishes the paragraph.

Remember that all the sentences in a paragraph should be about the same topic.

Practice

3. Crossword puzzles are fun to work, and you can learn from them, too.
   - Ⓐ You can improve your spelling. Sometimes they are frustrating.
   - Ⓑ They help you learn new words and improve your spelling. Sometimes there is a riddle or poem hidden in the answers.
   - Ⓒ They help improve your vocabulary. Sometimes the answers are too hard.
   - Ⓓ They have words that are spelled down and across. The answers must fit together in the puzzle.

4. Rivers School has a fall festival every year that I always like to go to.
   - Ⓕ Last year it rained and all the booths had to be moved inside. The building was very crowded.
   - Ⓖ Madeleine caught a fish at the go fishing booth. She named it Spot.
   - Ⓗ There are many games and booths at the festival with fun activities, such as face painting, bowling, and ringtoss. There is a lot of good food, too.
   - Ⓙ My favorite is the dunking booth. I always get a hot dog and popcorn.

Directions: Read the paragraph. Choose the sentence that does not belong.

5. Columbus Day is celebrated on the second Monday in October. It is a holiday for some people. Banks and the post office are closed. Some schools are closed, as well as government offices. Allison is going to the sale at the mall.
   - Ⓐ Columbus Day is a holiday for some people.
   - Ⓑ Banks and the post office are closed.
   - Ⓒ Some schools are closed, as well as government offices.
   - Ⓓ Allison is going to the sale at the mall.

Name Date

Paragraphs

Directions: Read the paragraph carefully. Then answer each question.

(1) Basketball was invented by James Naismith in 1891. (2) He was a physical education teacher. (3) His boss asked him to invent a team sport that could be played indoors in the winter. (4) He used a soccer ball. (5) It was large enough to be caught easily. (6) For hoops he used two peach baskets that were hung from the balcony railing in the gym. (7) The referee is in charge of the game. (8) The first game was played between students in his P.E. classes.

6. Which sentence could be added to the paragraph?

Ⓕ After the experimental game, Naismith created the first 13 rules for basketball.
Ⓖ In 1894 larger balls replaced soccer balls.
Ⓗ Hank Liusetti made the one-handed shot popular.
Ⓙ The 10-second rule was added in 1932.

7. Which sentence does not belong in the paragraph?

Ⓐ Basketball was invented by James Naismith.
Ⓑ He used a soccer ball.
Ⓒ For hoops he used two peach baskets that were hung from the balcony railing in the gym.
Ⓓ The referee is in charge of the game.

8. How could sentences 4 and 5 best be combined without changing the meaning?

Ⓕ He used a soccer ball so it could be large enough to be caught easily.
Ⓖ He used a soccer ball because it was large enough to be caught easily.
Ⓗ It was large enough to be caught easily, so he used a soccer ball.
Ⓙ He used a soccer ball, and it was large enough to be caught easily.

9. What is the best title for this paragraph?

Ⓐ Uses for Peach Baskets
Ⓑ How Basketball Was Invented
Ⓒ James Naismith
Ⓓ An Indoor Sport

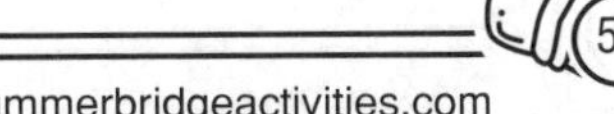

Name Date

Study Skills

Directions: Look at each pair of words. Then choose the pair of words that go together in the same way.

Example:

A. foot, shoe

Ⓐ coat, sweater Ⓑ sock, hat
● hand, glove Ⓓ shirt, skirt

1. apple, tree

Ⓐ flower, pot Ⓑ grape, vine
Ⓒ carrot, bush Ⓓ cow, barn

2. picture, album

Ⓕ story, chapter Ⓖ book, shelf
Ⓗ map, car Ⓙ recipe, cookbook

3. tree, green

Ⓐ apple, sweet
Ⓑ lemon, yellow
Ⓒ cookie, chocolate
Ⓓ ice cream, cold

4. tiny, ant

Ⓕ tall, giraffe
Ⓖ furry, kitten
Ⓗ spotted, leopard
Ⓙ wild, lion

5. egg, hen

Ⓐ money, purse
Ⓑ meat, freezer
Ⓒ cereal, box
Ⓓ milk, cow

Directions: Choose the best answer for each question.

6. Where would you find the meaning of parasite?

Ⓕ dictionary Ⓖ thesaurus
Ⓗ index Ⓙ atlas

7. Where would you look for a synonym for happy?

Ⓐ almanac Ⓑ *The Birthday Book*
Ⓒ thesaurus Ⓓ atlas

8. Where would you look for a map of Australia?

Ⓕ cookbook Ⓖ atlas
Ⓗ dictionary Ⓙ thesaurus

9. Where would you look to learn how to pronounce rodent?

Ⓐ atlas Ⓑ thesaurus
Ⓒ almanac Ⓓ dictionary

Name Date

Study Skills

Directions: For B and items 10–14, choose the word that would be found on the dictionary page with each pair of guide words.

Example:

B. improve, issue

Ⓕ illegal Ⓖ italics
● into Ⓙ identify

10. echo, effort

Ⓕ elephant Ⓖ ear
Ⓗ error Ⓙ education

11. better, bicycle

Ⓐ beautiful Ⓑ beverage
Ⓒ basketball Ⓓ bit

12. walnut, wander

Ⓕ wait Ⓖ walrus
Ⓗ way Ⓙ west

13. paragraph, pat

Ⓐ part Ⓑ pal
Ⓒ pamper Ⓓ potato

14. hurry, icy

Ⓕ if Ⓖ humble
Ⓗ idol Ⓙ hustle

Directions: For C and items 15–19, choose the word that would come first in alphabetical order.

Example:

C.

Ⓐ candle Ⓑ card
Ⓒ call ● café

15.

Ⓐ western Ⓑ wagon
Ⓒ worry Ⓓ windmill

16.

Ⓕ alphabet Ⓖ argue
Ⓗ amber Ⓙ axle

17.

Ⓐ jelly Ⓑ jerk
Ⓒ jewel Ⓓ jeans

18.

Ⓕ story Ⓖ stem
Ⓗ stare Ⓙ stiff

19.

Ⓐ dog Ⓑ daffodil
Ⓒ deaf Ⓓ dirt

Name Date

Study Skills

Directions: Look at the table of contents and the index. Choose the best answer to each question.

Table of Contents

Index

Remember that the table of contents tells the names or topics of chapters or sections. The index tells the location of specific information.

Practice

20. Where would you find information about baby birds?

Ⓕ How Birds Find Food
Ⓖ The Importance of Feathers
Ⓗ Raising the Young
Ⓙ All about Owls

21. On what page would you find information about the call of an owl?

Ⓐ 222
Ⓑ 229
Ⓒ 287
Ⓓ 228

22. Where would you look for information about ostriches?

Ⓕ Birds: Built for Flight
Ⓖ The Importance of Feathers
Ⓗ Building a Nest
Ⓙ The Biggest Birds

23. Information about owls can be found on all of these pages except:

Ⓐ 222
Ⓑ 228
Ⓒ 229
Ⓓ 287

STOP

Name Date

Language Expression: Sample Test

Directions: For items 1–10, choose the word that fits best in the blank.

1. _____ hit a home run.

Ⓐ His
Ⓑ Him
Ⓒ He
Ⓓ Them

2. Please give Marie _____ medicine at 3:00.

Ⓕ it's
Ⓖ its
Ⓗ her
Ⓙ him

3. The boys lost _____ money at the carnival.

Ⓐ them
Ⓑ they
Ⓒ its
Ⓓ their

4. Help _____ find my coat.

Ⓕ we
Ⓖ it
Ⓗ me
Ⓙ his

5. My aunt _____ staying with my family for a week.

Ⓐ is
Ⓑ are
Ⓒ can't
Ⓓ will

6. Kenny feels _____ today than he felt yesterday.

Ⓕ best
Ⓖ better
Ⓗ bested
Ⓙ bestest

7. The four _____ dresses are on the first clothes rack.

Ⓐ prettier
Ⓑ prettiest
Ⓒ more pretty
Ⓓ most prettiest

8. The faucet dripped _____ all night.

Ⓕ slower
Ⓖ slow
Ⓗ slowing
Ⓙ slowly

9. Richard _____ the ball game to the bitter end.

Ⓐ watch
Ⓑ is watched
Ⓒ watched
Ⓓ watching

10. _____ have the same dress on today.

Ⓕ I and Connie
Ⓖ Connie and me
Ⓗ Me and Connie
Ⓙ Connie and I

GO ON

Name Date

Language Expression: Sample Test

Directions: For items 11–16, mark the answer choice that has a mistake. If there are no mistakes, mark "No mistakes." For items 17–22, mark the answer choice that is not a sentence.

11.
- Ⓐ Our soccer team must play
- Ⓑ more better if we expect
- Ⓒ to win any games this year.
- Ⓓ No mistakes

12.
- Ⓕ Harriet has wore her new
- Ⓖ brown shoes to school
- Ⓗ every day this week.
- Ⓙ No mistakes

13.
- Ⓐ Please chew your food slowly.
- Ⓑ You can't have no more sweets.
- Ⓒ Mother eats several vegetables.
- Ⓓ No mistakes

14.
- Ⓕ Whose car keys are these?
- Ⓖ My mother is really funny.
- Ⓗ Them red apples are good.
- Ⓙ No mistakes

15.
- Ⓐ She chooses her words carefully.
- Ⓑ Valerie is talking very quietly.
- Ⓒ These books were on sale.
- Ⓓ No mistakes

16.
- Ⓕ Thomas is running two miles.
- Ⓖ He is really good.
- Ⓗ The band played beautiful.
- Ⓙ No mistakes

17.
- Ⓐ It is such a beautiful day.
- Ⓑ The blue skies and white clouds.
- Ⓒ Can we walk to the park?
- Ⓓ No mistakes

18.
- Ⓕ A rhinoceros is a huge animal.
- Ⓖ It has very thick skin.
- Ⓗ Appears to lie in folds.
- Ⓙ No mistakes

19.
- Ⓐ The children were very patient.
- Ⓑ After what seemed like hours.
- Ⓒ Sarah and I laughed a lot.
- Ⓓ No mistakes

20.
- Ⓕ Dinner was almost ready.
- Ⓖ Matt and Marie helped set the table.
- Ⓗ With candles and flowers on the table.
- Ⓙ No mistakes

21.
- Ⓐ Tony whispered to Jennifer.
- Ⓑ Speaking softly into the phone.
- Ⓒ Tony said, "I'll call you later."
- Ⓓ No mistakes

22.
- Ⓕ An index is part of a book.
- Ⓖ It lists topics in alphabetical order.
- Ⓗ Also lists page numbers.
- Ⓙ No mistakes

Name Date

Language Expression: Sample Test

Directions: Read the paragraph carefully. Then answer each question.

A clock is an instrument that tells time. The first clock did not have hands or a face but told time by ringing a bell. The word clock probably comes from French and German words that mean "bell". There are two kinds of clocks: face clocks and digital clocks. The *works*, or movement, which is the inside of a clock, provides power and keeps time. An electrical clock gets power from electricity or batteries. A mechanical clock gets power from being wound up. Almost all mechanical clocks have faces, while many electrical clocks are digital.

23. Where would you look for the meaning of digital?

Ⓐ almanac
Ⓑ thesaurus
Ⓒ dictionary
Ⓓ *The Clock Book*

24. What guide words would be on the page with mechanical?

Ⓕ medicine, merry
Ⓖ lump, medical
Ⓗ marshmallow, meat
Ⓙ meet, melt

25. Where would you look to find more information about clocks?

Ⓐ encyclopedia
Ⓑ dictionary
Ⓒ atlas
Ⓓ thesaurus

26. Where would you look for a synonym for instrument?

Ⓕ almanac
Ⓖ atlas
Ⓗ encyclopedia
Ⓙ thesaurus

27. Mark the word that would come last in alphabetical order.

Ⓐ digital
Ⓑ deal
Ⓒ French
Ⓓ electrical

28. Which one would not have information about when the clock was invented?

Ⓕ thesaurus
Ⓖ encyclopedia
Ⓗ *The History of Clocks*
Ⓙ the Internet

29. Where would you find an antonym for mechanical?

Ⓐ almanac
Ⓑ encyclopedia
Ⓒ thesaurus
Ⓓ index

Name Date

Numeration

Directions: Read each question carefully. Then choose the best answer.

Examples:

A. In 4,762, what digit is in the tens place?

Ⓐ 4 Ⓑ 7
● 6 Ⓓ 2

B. Which number is less than 17?

Ⓕ 19 ● 15
Ⓗ 21 Ⓙ 38

Be sure to read the question carefully. Pay attention to key words.

Practice

1. In 3,961, what digit is in the hundreds place?

Ⓐ 3
Ⓑ 9
Ⓒ 6
Ⓓ 1

2. Written correctly, two thousand seven hundred thirty-four would be ____.

Ⓕ 20,734
Ⓖ 270,034
Ⓗ 2,734
Ⓙ 2,070,034

3. Which number is less than 357?

Ⓐ 375
Ⓑ 537
Ⓒ 360
Ⓓ 325

4. 8 tens and 3 ones is the same as ____.

Ⓕ 803
Ⓖ 83
Ⓗ 830
Ⓙ 38

5. Read correctly, 4,920 is

Ⓐ forty-nine thousand twenty.
Ⓑ four hundred ninety-two.
Ⓒ four thousand nine hundred twenty.
Ⓓ four thousand ninety-two hundred.

6. Which one shows the numbers arranged correctly from least to greatest?

Ⓕ 100; 101; 110; 1,001
Ⓖ 100; 1,001; 101; 110
Ⓗ 110; 101; 1,001; 100
Ⓙ 100; 110; 101; 1,001

GO ON

Name Date

7. Which number belongs in the blank in this series of numbers?
15, 25, 35, ___, 55, 65
Ⓐ 4.5
Ⓑ 40
Ⓒ 45
Ⓓ 50

8. How many of these numbers are smaller than 316?
301, 310, 320, 312
Ⓕ 1
Ⓖ 3
Ⓗ 4
Ⓙ Not given

9. During the storm, between 2.5 and 3.5 inches of rain fell. Which one could be the actual amount of rainfall?
Ⓐ 3.6 inches
Ⓑ 3.9 inches
Ⓒ 2.9 inches
Ⓓ 2.4 inches

10. Written correctly, two thousand, eight hundred four would be _____.
Ⓕ 28,004
Ⓖ 2,008,004
Ⓗ 2,840
Ⓙ 2,804

11. Read correctly, 9,017 would be
Ⓐ nine thousand seventeen.
Ⓑ ninety hundred seventeen.
Ⓒ nine hundred seventeen.
Ⓓ nine thousand one hundred seventy.

12. Which number belongs in the blank on the number line shown?

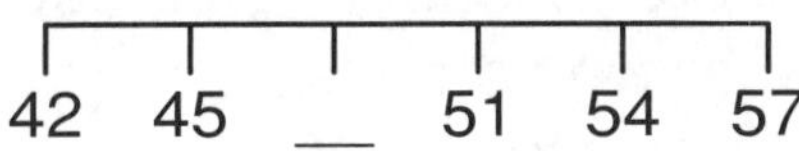

Ⓕ 47
Ⓖ 50
Ⓗ 49
Ⓙ 48

13. If the number shown is read one thousand two hundred fifty-three, what numeral belongs in the blank? 1,2__3
Ⓐ 5
Ⓑ 50
Ⓒ 05
Ⓓ 3

14. Which numbers are greater than 172?
Ⓕ 174, 175, 170
Ⓖ 165, 175, 185
Ⓗ 174, 175, 180
Ⓙ 171, 170, 173

GO ON

Name Date

15. Which shows two equal sets?

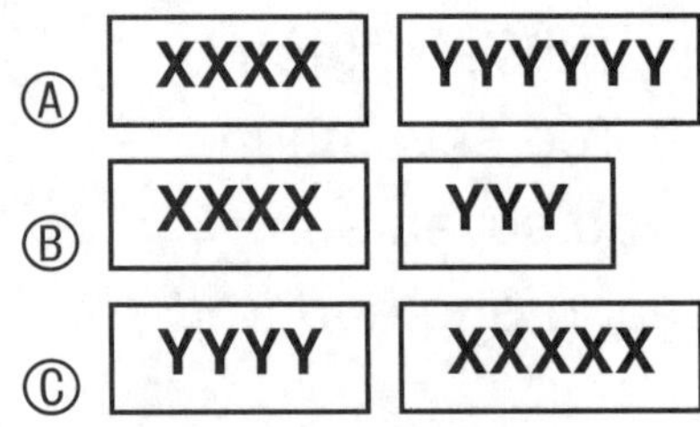

Ⓐ XXXX YYYYYY

Ⓑ XXXX YYY

Ⓒ YYYY XXXXX

Ⓓ YYY XXX

16. Arranged in order, least to greatest, which number would be last?

3,010 3,001 1,003 3,100

Ⓕ 3,001
Ⓖ 3,100
Ⓗ 1,003
Ⓙ 3,010

17. What digit is in the hundreds place in 5,076?

Ⓐ 5
Ⓑ 6
Ⓒ 7
Ⓓ 0

18. What is another name for 732?

Ⓕ 7 hundreds, 3 tens, 2 ones
Ⓖ 7 hundreds, 3 ones, 2 tens
Ⓗ 2 hundreds, 3 tens, 7 ones
Ⓙ 3 hundreds, 7 tens, 2 ones

19. Which of these shows the same number of flowers and bees?

Ⓐ 

Ⓑ 

Ⓒ 

Ⓓ 

20. Which number belongs in the blank in this series?

2, 4, 8, __, 32, 64

Ⓕ 24
Ⓖ 20
Ⓗ 16
Ⓙ 18

21. Which numbers are less than 239?

Ⓐ 245, 242, 232
Ⓑ 237, 247, 200
Ⓒ 225, 230, 235
Ⓓ 230, 238, 241

STOP

Name Date

Number Concepts

Directions: Read each question carefully. Then choose the best answer.

Examples:

A. Which of these is an even number?

Ⓐ 3 Ⓑ 7
● 10 Ⓓ 15

B. Which of these is fifty-seven?

● 57 Ⓖ 507
Ⓗ 570 Ⓙ 75

Remember to read the questions carefully. Pay close attention to key words.

Practice

1. Which of these is seventy-eight?

Ⓐ 780
Ⓑ 708
Ⓒ 87
Ⓓ 78

2. What number is represented by the chart?

Hundreds	Tens	Ones
III	II	IIIII

Ⓕ 3,205
Ⓖ 523
Ⓗ 300,205
Ⓙ 325

3. Which of these is an odd number?

Ⓐ 6
Ⓑ 11
Ⓒ 2
Ⓓ 18

4. Which number has a 6 in the tens place?

Ⓕ 6,230 Ⓖ 4,761
Ⓗ 5,876 Ⓙ 2,683

5. Find the one that shows 18 pieces of gum.

Ⓐ 

Ⓑ 

Ⓒ 

Ⓓ 

6. Which one is one thousand seventy-five?

Ⓕ 175 Ⓖ 1,750
Ⓗ 1,075 Ⓙ 100,075

 www.summerbridgeactivities.com

Name Date

7. Which shows even numbers?

Ⓐ 2, 6, 10, 13
Ⓑ 3, 6, 9, 12
Ⓒ 10, 20, 32, 47
Ⓓ 12, 18, 24, 36

8. What number is missing from this sequence?

4, __, 12, 16

Ⓕ 10
Ⓖ 8
Ⓗ 11
Ⓙ 6

9. What number is shown in the chart?

Thousands	Hundreds	Tens	Ones
IIIII	II	I	IIII

Ⓐ 500,020,014
Ⓑ 5,214
Ⓒ 2,514
Ⓓ 50,214

10. Which shows 10 cookies?

Ⓕ 

Ⓖ 

Ⓗ 

Ⓙ 

11. 4 hundreds, 6 tens, and 3 ones equals ____.

Ⓐ 40,063
Ⓑ 4,603
Ⓒ 463
Ⓓ 4,630

12. Which are odd numbers?

Ⓕ 23, 26, 32, 37
Ⓖ 15, 17, 19, 22
Ⓗ 31, 39, 57, 65
Ⓙ 10, 19, 27, 34

13. Which is two hundred twenty?

Ⓐ 202
Ⓑ 2,002
Ⓒ 2,200
Ⓓ 220

14. Which has 7 in the thousands place?

Ⓕ 7,396
Ⓖ 3,796
Ⓗ 9,376
Ⓙ 70,376

15. Which has 4 in the hundreds place?

Ⓐ 4,032
Ⓑ 432
Ⓒ 342
Ⓓ 3,042

GO ON

Name Date

Number Concepts

Directions: Read each question carefully. Then choose the best answer.

Examples:

C. How much of this figure is shaded?

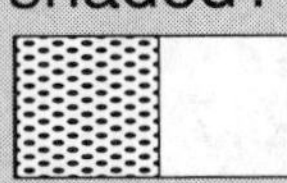

● $\frac{1}{2}$ Ⓑ $\frac{1}{3}$
Ⓒ $\frac{1}{4}$ Ⓓ Not given

D. Which sign makes the number sentence true?

3 + 6 ○ 6 + 3

Ⓕ > Ⓖ <
● = Ⓙ Not given

Be sure to read the questions carefully and pay attention to details.

Practice

16. Which one shows $\frac{1}{4}$ of the figure shaded?

Ⓕ 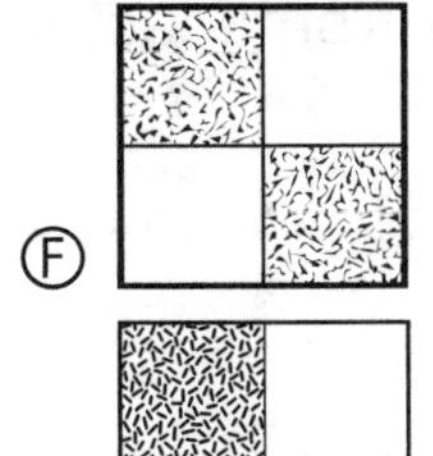

Ⓖ 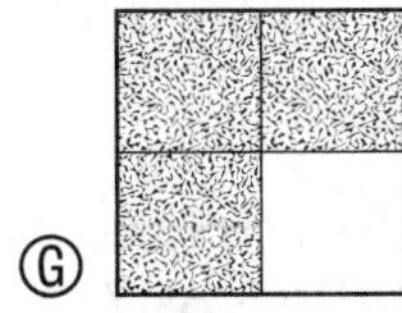

Ⓗ 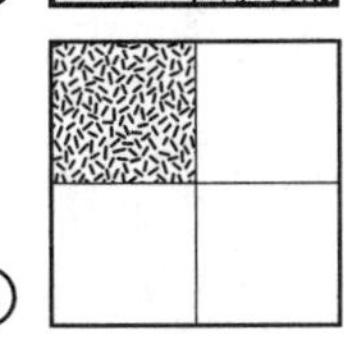

Ⓙ 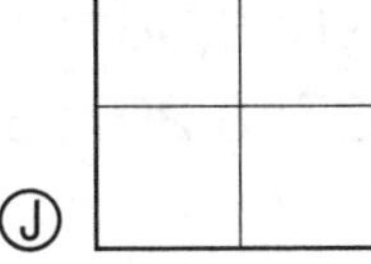

17. Which one shows $\frac{1}{3}$ of the figure shaded?

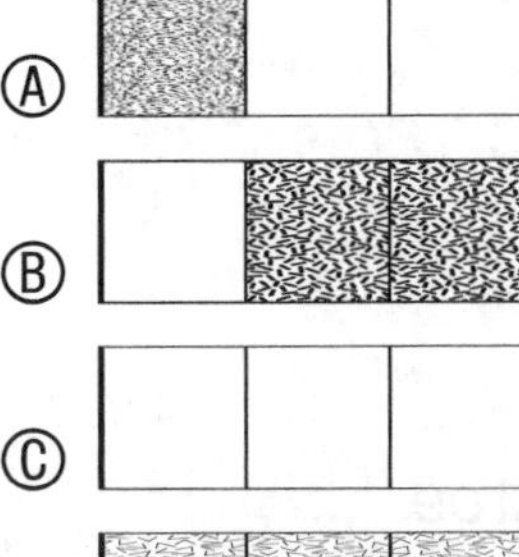

Ⓐ
Ⓑ
Ⓒ
Ⓓ

18. To show the fraction $\frac{2}{5}$, how many sections of the figure should be shaded?

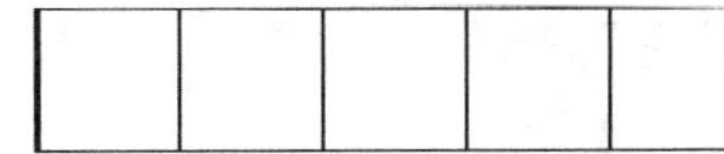

Ⓕ 1
Ⓖ 2
Ⓗ 3
Ⓙ 4

19. Which symbol makes the number sentence correct?

4 + 7 ○ 3 + 9

Ⓐ >
Ⓑ <
Ⓒ =
Ⓓ Not given

20. Which number sentence says six plus seven is greater than three plus four?

Ⓕ 6 + 7 < 3 + 4
Ⓖ 3 + 4 > 6 + 7
Ⓗ 6 + 7 > 3 + 4
Ⓙ Not given

Name Date

Number Concepts

Directions: Read each question carefully. Then choose the best answer.

Examples:

E. In 36,285, the 5 is in which place?
- Ⓐ tens
- ● ones
- Ⓒ thousands
- Ⓓ hundreds

F. Which has the greatest value?
- Ⓕ 3,027
- Ⓖ 3,247
- Ⓗ 3,274
- ● 3,427

21. In 25,076, the 0 is in which place?
- Ⓐ ones
- Ⓑ tens
- Ⓒ hundreds
- Ⓓ ten thousands

22. Which number has 7 in the thousands place?
- Ⓕ 27,351
- Ⓖ 23,751
- Ⓗ 73,251
- Ⓙ 32,751

23. Which number has 0 in the tens place?
- Ⓐ 3,026
- Ⓑ 1,590
- Ⓒ 90,756
- Ⓓ 1,706

24. Which digit completes the number three thousand two hundred fifty-nine?
3,2__9
- Ⓕ 0
- Ⓖ 5
- Ⓗ 1
- Ⓙ 60

25. Which number shows twenty-five thousand two hundred eighty?
- Ⓐ 25,280
- Ⓑ 2,520,080
- Ⓒ 25,002,080
- Ⓓ 25,208

26. Which group is in order from least to greatest?
- Ⓕ 4,762; 4,672; 4,276
- Ⓖ 5,789; 5,897; 5,798
- Ⓗ 3,196; 3,961; 1,936
- Ⓙ 8,027; 8,207; 8,270

27. Arranged from greatest to least, which number fits in the blank?
2,870; ______; 2,708
- Ⓐ 2,087
- Ⓑ 2,780
- Ⓒ 2,078
- Ⓓ Not given

28. How is 4,136 read?
- Ⓕ forty-one sixty-three
- Ⓖ forty-one thousand thirty-six
- Ⓗ four thousand one hundred thirty-six
- Ⓙ Not given

STOP

Name Date

Properties

Directions: Read each question carefully. Then choose the best answer.

Examples:

A. Which sign makes the number sentence true?

3 ◯ 6 = 9

Ⓐ ÷ Ⓑ x
Ⓒ – ● +

B. Which one shows how to find the total number of cars?

● 2 x 4 Ⓖ 4 + 2
Ⓗ 2 + 4 Ⓙ 4 ÷ 2

If you are not sure of the answer, try reading the number sentence quietly to yourself.

Practice

1. Which sign makes both number sentences true?

2 ◯ 7 = 14; 3 ◯ 4 = 12

Ⓐ +
Ⓑ –
Ⓒ x
Ⓓ ÷

2. Which pair of number sentences mean the same thing?

Ⓕ 3 x 2; 2 + 2 + 2
Ⓖ 4 x 7; 7 + 4
Ⓗ 5 + 5; 5 x 5
Ⓙ 1 + 4; 1 + 1 + 1 + 1

3. Which pair of number sentences tells how to find the number of flowers?

Ⓐ 6 x 2; 6 ÷ 2
Ⓑ 3 + 2; 2 x 3
Ⓒ 3 x 2; 2 + 2 + 2
Ⓓ Not given

4. Which sign makes both number sentences true?

12 ◯ 9 = 3; 18 ◯ 9 = 9

Ⓕ +
Ⓖ –
Ⓗ x
Ⓙ ÷

5. What numeral belongs in the circle?

$\frac{1}{2} = \frac{2}{◯}$

Ⓐ 1
Ⓑ 2
Ⓒ 3
Ⓓ 4

6. Which number completes both number sentences?

3 x ◯ = 21; 11 – 4 = ◯

Ⓕ 6
Ⓖ 7
Ⓗ 8
Ⓙ 9

GO ON

Name Date

Properties

Directions: Read each question carefully. Then choose the best answer.

Examples:

C. Rounded to the nearest ten, 38 would be _____.

Ⓐ 30 Ⓑ 35
● 40 Ⓓ 25

D. Rounded to the nearest hundred, 475 would be _____.

Ⓕ 400 Ⓖ 450
Ⓗ 470 ● 500

7. Rounded to the nearest ten, which numbers would be 40?

Ⓐ 35, 42
Ⓑ 33, 42
Ⓒ 37, 48
Ⓓ 31, 49

8. Rounded to the nearest hundred, 181 would be _____.

Ⓕ 180
Ⓖ 200
Ⓗ 100
Ⓙ Not given

9. How many of these would be 60 if rounded to the nearest 10?
51, 55, 57, 65, 62

Ⓐ 0
Ⓑ 1
Ⓒ 2
Ⓓ 3

10. Which one is closest to 350?

Ⓕ 352
Ⓖ 347
Ⓗ 358
Ⓙ 341

11. 0.6 = _____

Ⓐ $\frac{1}{6}$
Ⓑ $\frac{6}{10}$
Ⓒ $\frac{6}{100}$
Ⓓ $\frac{10}{6}$

12. 0.9 = _____

Ⓕ $\frac{10}{9}$
Ⓖ $\frac{9}{100}$
Ⓗ $\frac{9}{10}$
Ⓙ $\frac{1}{9}$

13. $\frac{1}{2} = \frac{\square}{10}$

What does □ equal?

Ⓐ 1
Ⓑ 2
Ⓒ 4
Ⓓ 5

STOP

Name Date

Math Concepts: Sample Test

Directions: Read each question carefully. Pay close attention to details. Then choose the best answer.

Examples:

A. What is another name for four hundreds, seven tens, and three ones?

Ⓐ 437 Ⓑ 347
● 473 Ⓓ 743

B. Rounded to the nearest ten, 279 would be _____.

● 280 Ⓖ 270
Ⓗ 275 Ⓙ 285

1. Which sign makes the number sentence correct?

10 – 6 _____ 3 + 9

Ⓐ >
Ⓑ =
Ⓒ <
Ⓓ Not given

2. Which sign fits in both sentences?

3 ◯ 2 = 6 5 ◯ 4 = 20

Ⓕ +
Ⓖ –
Ⓗ x
Ⓙ ÷

3. Which number has 0 in the ones place?

Ⓐ 4,701
Ⓑ 4,710
Ⓒ 4,071
Ⓓ 407

4. What numeral is in the hundreds place in 5,632?

Ⓕ 5
Ⓖ 6
Ⓗ 3
Ⓙ 2

5. What number is shown in the chart?

Thousands	Hundreds	Tens	Ones
IIIIII	II	I	IIIII

Ⓐ 6,207
Ⓑ 620,016
Ⓒ 5,216
Ⓓ 6,215

6. Joe and Jim each have 5 packs of baseball cards. Which shows how many packs they have together?

Ⓕ 2 + 5 = 7
Ⓖ 2 + 2 = 4
Ⓗ 2 x 5 = 10
Ⓙ 5 x 5 = 25

GO ON

Name

Date

7. Count by twos. What numbers are missing?

12, 14, 16, ___, 20, ___, 24

Ⓐ 15, 17 Ⓑ 17, 18
Ⓒ 18, 22 Ⓓ 18, 21

8. Which number is greater than 4,795?

Ⓕ 4,800 Ⓖ 4,700
Ⓗ 4,790 Ⓙ 4,759

9. Rounded to the nearest hundred, 4,281 would be _____.

Ⓐ 4,280 Ⓑ 4,200
Ⓒ 4,000 Ⓓ 4,300

10. Which number is two thousand two hundred seventy-six?

Ⓕ 22,076 Ⓖ 2,276
Ⓗ 22,706 Ⓙ 22,276

11. What fraction is shown?

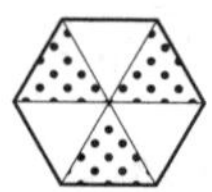

Ⓐ $\frac{1}{6}$ Ⓑ $\frac{3}{5}$
Ⓒ $\frac{3}{6}$ Ⓓ $\frac{5}{6}$

12. Read correctly, 1,050 is _____.

Ⓕ one hundred five
Ⓖ one hundred fifty
Ⓗ one thousand five
Ⓙ one thousand fifty

13. What sign makes the number sentence correct?

2 x 6 ◯ 10 + 2

Ⓐ > Ⓑ <
Ⓒ = Ⓓ Not given

14. Written another way, 531 is

Ⓕ 5 hundreds, 30 tens, 1 one.
Ⓖ 5 thousands, 3 tens, 1 one.
Ⓗ 5 hundreds, 31 tens.
Ⓙ Not given

15. In 3,095, what numeral is in the hundreds place?

Ⓐ 3 Ⓑ 0
Ⓒ 9 Ⓓ 5

16. Which pair of number sentences tell how to find the number of pets?

Ⓕ 2 x 5; 5 + 5
Ⓖ 10 – 5; 10 + 5
Ⓗ 10 ÷ 2; 10 ÷ 5
Ⓙ 5 x 1; 1 + 5

GO ON

Name Date

17. Arranged from least to greatest, which one would be last?

1,000; 1,001; 1,010; 1,100

Ⓐ 1,000
Ⓑ 1,001
Ⓒ 1,010
Ⓓ 1,100

18. Rounded to the nearest ten, 4,563 would be ______.

Ⓕ 4,560
Ⓖ 4,570
Ⓗ 4,500
Ⓙ 4,000

19. To show $\frac{3}{4}$, how many sections should be shaded?

Ⓐ 1
Ⓑ 2
Ⓒ 3
Ⓓ 4

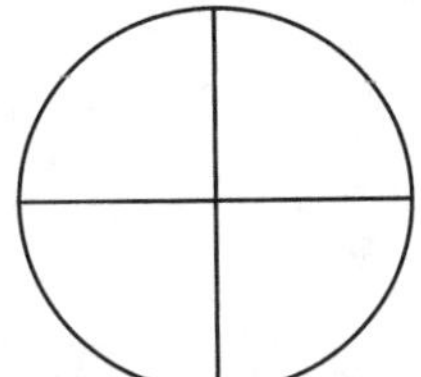

20. Matthew's math test had 25 questions. He missed 3. Which number sentence shows how many correct answers he had?

Ⓕ 25 + 3
Ⓖ 25 – 3
Ⓗ 25 ÷ 3
Ⓙ Not given

21. Which sign makes the number sentence correct?

12 ○ 3 = 2 + 2

Ⓐ +
Ⓑ –
Ⓒ x
Ⓓ ÷

22. Which number has 2 in the tens place?

Ⓕ 2,036
Ⓖ 3,206
Ⓗ 2,360
Ⓙ Not given

23. After Halloween, Mr. Graham had 18 pieces of candy left over. He gave an equal number of pieces to Allison, Karen, and John. Which number sentence shows how many pieces of candy each child received?

Ⓐ 18 – 3 = 15
Ⓑ 18 + 3 = 21
Ⓒ 18 ÷ 3 = 6
Ⓓ Not given

24. Which number would be 3,100 rounded to the nearest hundred?

Ⓕ 3,158
Ⓖ 3,137
Ⓗ 3,203
Ⓙ 3,049

STOP

Name Date

Math Computation: Addition

Directions: For each addition problem, mark the choice for the correct answer. If the correct answer is not given, mark the space "Not given."

Examples:

A. 11
+ 7

Ⓐ 16
Ⓑ 8
● 18
Ⓓ 28
Ⓔ Not given

B. 17 + 6 =

Ⓕ 20
Ⓖ 11
Ⓗ 21
Ⓙ 26
● Not given

If the correct answer is not given, mark the space for "Not given."

Practice

1. 33 + 7 =

Ⓐ 40
Ⓑ 39
Ⓒ 26
Ⓓ 30
Ⓔ Not given

2. 362
+ 57

Ⓕ 329
Ⓖ 419
Ⓗ 319
Ⓙ 305
Ⓚ Not given

3. 21 + 6 + 4 =

Ⓐ 29
Ⓑ 27
Ⓒ 31
Ⓓ 47
Ⓔ Not given

4. 17
12
+ 15

Ⓕ 45
Ⓖ 39
Ⓗ 34
Ⓙ 44
Ⓚ Not given

5. 70
40
+ 20

Ⓐ 110
Ⓑ 120
Ⓒ 130
Ⓓ 140
Ⓔ Not given

6. 299
+ 167

Ⓕ 436
Ⓖ 352
Ⓗ 356
Ⓙ 466
Ⓚ Not given

GO ON

Name Date

7. $6.36 + $2.57 =

Ⓐ $7.93
Ⓑ $8.93
Ⓒ $3.78
Ⓓ $2.78
Ⓔ Not given

8. 8.2 + 0.45

Ⓕ 8.25
Ⓖ 8.45
Ⓗ 8.65
Ⓙ 8.85
Ⓚ Not given

9. 1,383 + 1,605

Ⓐ 2,988
Ⓑ 3,988
Ⓒ 2,908
Ⓓ 3,908
Ⓔ Not given

10. 3.6 + 5.8 =

Ⓕ 2.2
Ⓖ 7.4
Ⓗ 8.6
Ⓙ 9.6
Ⓚ Not given

11. 50 10 + 60

Ⓐ 100
Ⓑ 110
Ⓒ 120
Ⓓ 130
Ⓔ Not given

12. $0.22 + $0.69

Ⓕ $0.71
Ⓖ $0.81
Ⓗ $0.91
Ⓙ $0.87
Ⓚ Not given

13. 62 + 10 + 5 =

Ⓐ 77
Ⓑ 72
Ⓒ 67
Ⓓ 82
Ⓔ Not given

14. 500 + 200

Ⓕ 7
Ⓖ 70
Ⓗ 700
Ⓙ 300
Ⓚ Not given

15. $3.28 + $5.73

Ⓐ $8.55
Ⓑ $8.91
Ⓒ $8.99
Ⓓ $9.01
Ⓔ Not given

16. 199 + 333

Ⓕ 432
Ⓖ 422
Ⓗ 532
Ⓙ 522
Ⓚ Not given

17. 6.9 + 6.8 =

Ⓐ 11.9
Ⓑ 13.7
Ⓒ 13.9
Ⓓ 12.7
Ⓔ Not given

18. 122 37 + 40

Ⓕ 299
Ⓖ 159
Ⓗ 189
Ⓙ 99
Ⓚ Not given

STOP

Name Date

Math Computation: Subtraction

Directions: For each subtraction problem, mark the space for the correct answer. Mark "Not given" if the correct answer is not given.

Examples:

A. 25 − 8

- Ⓐ 7
- ● 17
- Ⓒ 27
- Ⓓ 33
- Ⓔ Not given

B. 51 − 19 =

- Ⓕ 70
- Ⓖ 42
- ● 32
- Ⓙ 22
- Ⓚ Not given

If you are not sure of an answer, check your answer by adding.

Practice

1. 81 − 17 =

- Ⓐ 98
- Ⓑ 68
- Ⓒ 66
- Ⓓ 54
- Ⓔ Not given

2. 99 − 43

- Ⓕ 56
- Ⓖ 66
- Ⓗ 65
- Ⓙ 64
- Ⓚ Not given

3. \$5.64 − \$0.42 =

- Ⓐ \$5.40
- Ⓑ \$4.42
- Ⓒ \$4.22
- Ⓓ \$5.22
- Ⓔ Not given

4. 318 − 232

- Ⓕ 186
- Ⓖ 86
- Ⓗ 114
- Ⓙ 550
- Ⓚ Not given

5. 470 − 80 =

- Ⓐ 550
- Ⓑ 450
- Ⓒ 410
- Ⓓ 390
- Ⓔ Not given

6. 674 − 213

- Ⓕ 462
- Ⓖ 451
- Ⓗ 467
- Ⓙ 561
- Ⓚ Not given

GO ON

Name Date

7. 106 – 27 =

Ⓐ 89
Ⓑ 79
Ⓒ 133
Ⓓ 123
Ⓔ Not given

8. 234 – 128

Ⓕ 116
Ⓖ 112
Ⓗ 104
Ⓙ 122
Ⓚ Not given

9. \$6.64 – \$6.42

Ⓐ \$1.22
Ⓑ \$0.40
Ⓒ \$0.42
Ⓓ \$0.22
Ⓔ Not given

10. 5,000 – 235 =

Ⓕ 5,765
Ⓖ 5,725
Ⓗ 5,775
Ⓙ 5,765
Ⓚ Not given

11. 522 – 481

Ⓐ 41
Ⓑ 51
Ⓒ 141
Ⓓ 161
Ⓔ Not given

12. 62 – 37

Ⓕ 39
Ⓖ 35
Ⓗ 26
Ⓙ 25
Ⓚ Not given

13. $\frac{4}{7} - \frac{1}{7} =$

Ⓐ $\frac{1}{7}$
Ⓑ $\frac{5}{7}$
Ⓒ $\frac{3}{7}$
Ⓓ $\frac{4}{14}$
Ⓔ Not given

14. 815 – 78

Ⓕ 863
Ⓖ 837
Ⓗ 747
Ⓙ 737
Ⓚ Not given

15. \$0.62 – \$0.34 =

Ⓐ \$0.24
Ⓑ \$0.28
Ⓒ \$0.32
Ⓓ \$0.38
Ⓔ Not given

16. 76 – 37

Ⓕ 37
Ⓖ 49
Ⓗ 43
Ⓙ 41
Ⓚ Not given

17. 300 – 126 =

Ⓐ 184
Ⓑ 174
Ⓒ 284
Ⓓ 274
Ⓔ Not given

18. 294 – 71

Ⓕ 233
Ⓖ 223
Ⓗ 213
Ⓙ 225
Ⓚ Not given

STOP

Name Date

Math Computation: Multiplication and Division

Directions: For each multiplication or division problem, mark the space for the correct answer. Mark *Not given* if the correct answer is not given.

Examples:

A. 8 x 7 =

Ⓐ 48
● 56
Ⓒ 64
Ⓓ 15
Ⓔ Not given

B. 21 ÷ 3 =

Ⓕ 9
Ⓖ 8
● 7
Ⓙ 6
Ⓚ Not given

Be sure to pay close attention to each problem. Watch the sign.

Practice

1. 2 x 9 =

Ⓐ 16
Ⓑ 18
Ⓒ 19
Ⓓ 11
Ⓔ Not given

2. 54 ÷ 6 =

Ⓕ 8
Ⓖ 9
Ⓗ 9 R1
Ⓙ 8 R5
Ⓚ Not given

3. 53 x 3 =

Ⓐ 86
Ⓑ 156
Ⓒ 159
Ⓓ 1,509
Ⓔ Not given

4. $9\overline{)45}$

Ⓕ 7
Ⓖ 6
Ⓗ 5
Ⓙ 4
Ⓚ Not given

5. 12 x 8 =

Ⓐ 90
Ⓑ 96
Ⓒ 106
Ⓓ 20
Ⓔ Not given

6. 351 ÷ 25 =

Ⓕ 14 R1
Ⓖ 14
Ⓗ 25
Ⓙ 25 R1
Ⓚ Not given

7. 320 x 3 =

Ⓐ 650
Ⓑ 963
Ⓒ 1,060
Ⓓ 1,063
Ⓔ Not given

8. 3,900 ÷ 40 =

Ⓕ 96
Ⓖ 96 R30
Ⓗ 97
Ⓙ 97 R20
Ⓚ Not given

GO ON

Name Date

9. 60 x 90 =

Ⓐ 540
Ⓑ 480
Ⓒ 4,800
Ⓓ 5,400
Ⓔ Not given

10. $4\overline{)68}$

Ⓕ 14
Ⓖ 19
Ⓗ 17
Ⓙ 21
Ⓚ Not given

11. 26 x 3

Ⓐ 78
Ⓑ 68
Ⓒ 84
Ⓓ 76
Ⓔ Not given

12. 12 x 12 =

Ⓕ 112
Ⓖ 144
Ⓗ 122
Ⓙ 104
Ⓚ Not given

13. 86 ÷ 2 =

Ⓐ 32
Ⓑ 42
Ⓒ 43
Ⓓ 44
Ⓔ Not given

14. $19\overline{)76}$

Ⓕ 3
Ⓖ 4
Ⓗ 5
Ⓙ 6
Ⓚ Not given

15. 36 x 7 =

Ⓐ 242
Ⓑ 213
Ⓒ 252
Ⓓ 232
Ⓔ Not given

16. $6\overline{)76}$

Ⓕ 16 R2
Ⓖ 14 R4
Ⓗ 12
Ⓙ 12 R4
Ⓚ Not given

17. 27 x 3 =

Ⓐ 71
Ⓑ 89
Ⓒ 61
Ⓓ 30
Ⓔ Not given

18. 236 ÷ 4 =

Ⓕ 49
Ⓖ 59
Ⓗ 69
Ⓙ 37
Ⓚ Not given

19. 99 x 3 =

Ⓐ 193
Ⓑ 197
Ⓒ 293
Ⓓ 297
Ⓔ Not given

20. $6\overline{)654}$

Ⓕ 101
Ⓖ 108
Ⓗ 109
Ⓙ 96
Ⓚ Not given

GO ON

Name

Date

21. 70 x 30 =

Ⓐ 210
Ⓑ 2,100
Ⓒ 1,000
Ⓓ 100
Ⓔ Not given

22. $3\overline{)52}$

Ⓕ 17
Ⓖ 17 R1
Ⓗ 14
Ⓙ 14 R1
Ⓚ Not given

23. 37 x 5

Ⓐ 155
Ⓑ 165
Ⓒ 175
Ⓓ 185
Ⓔ Not given

24. 11 x 11 =

Ⓕ 112
Ⓖ 121
Ⓗ 122
Ⓙ 110
Ⓚ Not given

25. 64 ÷ 3 =

Ⓐ 21 R2
Ⓑ 21
Ⓒ 21 R1
Ⓓ 22
Ⓔ Not given

26. $15\overline{)45}$

Ⓕ 3
Ⓖ 4
Ⓗ 5
Ⓙ 6
Ⓚ Not given

27. 43 x 5 =

Ⓐ 210
Ⓑ 215
Ⓒ 218
Ⓓ 208
Ⓔ Not given

28. $4\overline{)90}$

Ⓕ 25
Ⓖ 21 R3
Ⓗ 22
Ⓙ 22 R2
Ⓚ Not given

29. 47 x 4 =

Ⓐ 182
Ⓑ 184
Ⓒ 188
Ⓓ 181
Ⓔ Not given

30. 357 ÷ 5 =

Ⓕ 72
Ⓖ 71 R2
Ⓗ 72 R2
Ⓙ 71
Ⓚ Not given

31. 86 x 6 =

Ⓐ 526
Ⓑ 516
Ⓒ 512
Ⓓ 532
Ⓔ Not given

32. $3\overline{)727}$

Ⓕ 142
Ⓖ 209
Ⓗ 242
Ⓙ 241
Ⓚ Not given

GO ON

Name Date

33. 29 x 20 =

Ⓐ 418
Ⓑ 480
Ⓒ 518
Ⓓ 580
Ⓔ Not given

34. $4\overline{)275}$

Ⓕ 68 R3
Ⓖ 68
Ⓗ 68 R4
Ⓙ 67 R3
Ⓚ Not given

35. $\begin{array}{r} 23 \\ \underline{\times\ 6} \end{array}$

Ⓐ 138
Ⓑ 130
Ⓒ 128
Ⓓ 129
Ⓔ Not given

36. 13 x 15 =

Ⓕ 185
Ⓖ 175
Ⓗ 195
Ⓙ 108
Ⓚ Not given

37. 84 ÷ 4 =

Ⓐ 88
Ⓑ 40
Ⓒ 21
Ⓓ 22
Ⓔ Not given

38. $16\overline{)640}$

Ⓕ 64
Ⓖ 44
Ⓗ 24
Ⓙ 42
Ⓚ Not given

39. 89 x 4 =

Ⓐ 356
Ⓑ 353
Ⓒ 256
Ⓓ 366
Ⓔ Not given

40. $6\overline{)96}$

Ⓕ 11 R1
Ⓖ 13
Ⓗ 16
Ⓙ 21
Ⓚ Not given

41. 22 x 14 =

Ⓐ 318
Ⓑ 308
Ⓒ 288
Ⓓ 316
Ⓔ Not given

42. 209 ÷ 3 =

Ⓕ 73 R2
Ⓖ 69
Ⓗ 69 R2
Ⓙ 71
Ⓚ Not given

43. 80 x 10 =

Ⓐ 910
Ⓑ 800
Ⓒ 90
Ⓓ 810
Ⓔ Not given

44. $4\overline{)526}$

Ⓕ 131 R2
Ⓖ 131
Ⓗ 132 R2
Ⓙ 142
Ⓚ Not given

STOP

Name Date

Math Computation: Sample Test

Directions: Read each problem carefully, noticing the correct operation. Mark the correct answer choice. If the correct answer is not given, choose "Not given."

1. 25 – 12 =

Ⓐ 12
Ⓑ 13
Ⓒ 14
Ⓓ 3
Ⓔ Not given

2. 7 x 4 =

Ⓕ 11
Ⓖ 14
Ⓗ 21
Ⓙ 28
Ⓚ Not given

3. $\begin{array}{r} 89 \\ \underline{+\ 69} \end{array}$

Ⓐ 148
Ⓑ 158
Ⓒ 168
Ⓓ 20
Ⓔ Not given

4. $3\overline{)93}$

Ⓕ 20
Ⓖ 30
Ⓗ 21
Ⓙ 31
Ⓚ Not given

5. \$0.37 + \$0.54 =

Ⓐ \$0.91
Ⓑ \$0.93
Ⓒ \$0.81
Ⓓ \$0.83
Ⓔ Not given

6. 400 + 200 =

Ⓕ 60
Ⓖ 600
Ⓗ 6
Ⓙ 200
Ⓚ Not given

7. $\begin{array}{r} 734 \\ \underline{-\ 699} \end{array}$

Ⓐ 135
Ⓑ 134
Ⓒ 35
Ⓓ 34
Ⓔ Not given

8. 502 x 3 =

Ⓕ 1,606
Ⓖ 1,660
Ⓗ 1,560
Ⓙ 1,506
Ⓚ Not given

9. \$5.64 + \$0.42 =

Ⓐ \$4.22
Ⓑ \$4.42
Ⓒ \$5.12
Ⓓ \$5.40
Ⓔ Not given

10. $7\overline{)219}$

Ⓕ 31
Ⓖ 31 R2
Ⓗ 30
Ⓙ 30 R7
Ⓚ Not given

GO ON

Name Date

11. $\frac{1}{9} + \frac{6}{9} =$

Ⓐ $\frac{4}{9}$
Ⓑ $\frac{5}{9}$
Ⓒ $\frac{7}{9}$
Ⓓ $\frac{7}{18}$
Ⓔ Not given

12. 11 + 7 + 5 =

Ⓕ 18
Ⓖ 23
Ⓗ 12
Ⓙ 24
Ⓚ Not given

13. 549 + 81 =

Ⓐ 620
Ⓑ 630
Ⓒ 720
Ⓓ 730
Ⓔ Not given

14. 200 – 164 =

Ⓕ 36
Ⓖ 46
Ⓗ 136
Ⓙ 146
Ⓚ Not given

15. $\frac{4}{7} - \frac{1}{7} =$

Ⓐ $\frac{1}{7}$
Ⓑ $\frac{5}{7}$
Ⓒ $\frac{3}{7}$
Ⓓ $\frac{4}{14}$
Ⓔ Not given

16. $6\overline{)76}$

Ⓕ 16 R2
Ⓖ 14 R4
Ⓗ 12
Ⓙ 12 R4
Ⓚ Not given

17. $4\overline{)48}$

Ⓐ 14
Ⓑ 13
Ⓒ 12
Ⓓ 8
Ⓔ Not given

18. $\begin{array}{r} 5.42 \\ \underline{+\ 1.73} \end{array}$

Ⓕ 6.15
Ⓖ 7.15
Ⓗ 7.05
Ⓙ 6.05
Ⓚ Not given

19. $\begin{array}{r} 18 \\ 12 \\ \underline{+\ 3} \end{array}$

Ⓐ 21
Ⓑ 31
Ⓒ 23
Ⓓ 33
Ⓔ Not given

20. 460 x 3 =

Ⓕ 790
Ⓖ 1,383
Ⓗ 1,380
Ⓙ 1,180
Ⓚ Not given

21. \$637 + \$75 =

Ⓐ \$712
Ⓑ \$702
Ⓒ \$652
Ⓓ \$612
Ⓔ Not given

22. 92 – 54 =

Ⓕ 48
Ⓖ 38
Ⓗ 42
Ⓙ 44
Ⓚ Not given

GO ON

Name Date

23. $\begin{array}{r} 2{,}283 \\ +\ 1{,}506 \\ \hline \end{array}$

Ⓐ 2,709
Ⓑ 3,709
Ⓒ 2,789
Ⓓ 3,789
Ⓔ Not given

24. 93 ÷ 3 =

Ⓕ 30
Ⓖ 31
Ⓗ 20
Ⓙ 21
Ⓚ Not given

25. 322 x 2 =

Ⓐ 644
Ⓑ 544
Ⓒ 744
Ⓓ 944
Ⓔ Not given

26. 78 – 9 =

Ⓕ 67
Ⓖ 68
Ⓗ 69
Ⓙ 87
Ⓚ Not given

27. $\begin{array}{r} 257 \\ 397 \\ +\ 603 \\ \hline \end{array}$

Ⓐ 1,157
Ⓑ 1,247
Ⓒ 1,147
Ⓓ 1,347
Ⓔ Not given

28. $5\overline{)475}$

Ⓕ 90
Ⓖ 85
Ⓗ 75
Ⓙ 95
Ⓚ Not given

29. $\begin{array}{r} \$0.31 \\ \$0.78 \\ +\ \$0.22 \\ \hline \end{array}$

Ⓐ $1.31
Ⓑ $1.41
Ⓒ $1.32
Ⓓ $2.31
Ⓔ Not given

30. 17 x 61 =

Ⓕ 78
Ⓖ 1,036
Ⓗ 1,037
Ⓙ 937
Ⓚ Not given

31. 643 ÷ 3 =

Ⓐ 96
Ⓑ 108
Ⓒ 107
Ⓓ 109
Ⓔ Not given

32. $\frac{1}{3} + \frac{1}{3} =$

Ⓕ $\frac{1}{2}$
Ⓖ $\frac{2}{3}$
Ⓗ 1
Ⓙ $\frac{1}{6}$
Ⓚ Not given

33. $\begin{array}{r} 1{,}010 \\ +\ 2{,}727 \\ \hline \end{array}$

Ⓐ 3,723
Ⓑ 3,727
Ⓒ 3,737
Ⓓ 3,637
Ⓔ Not given

34. 58 x 3 =

Ⓕ 61
Ⓖ 174
Ⓗ 171
Ⓙ 231
Ⓚ Not given

STOP

Name Date

Math Applications: Telling Time

Directions: Read each question carefully. Pay attention to details. Choose the best answer.

Examples:

A. What time is showing on the clock?

● 2:15
Ⓑ 2:10
Ⓒ 2:25
Ⓓ 2:45

B. Sarah started her homework at 4:10. She worked until 5:15. How long did Sarah work?

Ⓕ 1 hour, 15 minutes
● 1 hour, 5 minutes
Ⓗ 55 minutes
Ⓙ Not given

Look carefully at the clock to determine the time. If necessary, work the problem on a sheet of paper.

Practice

1. What time is showing on the clock?

Ⓐ 7:25
Ⓑ 7:35
Ⓒ 7:55
Ⓓ 7:05

2. What time is showing on the clock?

Ⓕ 12:00
Ⓖ 12:10
Ⓗ 12:30
Ⓙ 6:00

3. What time is showing on the clock?

Ⓐ 4:15
Ⓑ 4:30
Ⓒ 4:45
Ⓓ 4:50

4. Joe is going to a 7:20 movie. It takes him 20 minutes to get to the theater. What time should he leave home to make sure he gets there in plenty of time?

Ⓕ 7:05
Ⓖ 7:40
Ⓗ 7:20
Ⓙ 6:50

5. Michele arrives home from school at 3:45. Her piano lesson is at 5:30. How long does she have before going to piano?

Ⓐ 2 hours, 15 minutes
Ⓑ 1 hour, 45 minutes
Ⓒ 1 hour, 30 minutes
Ⓓ 2 hours

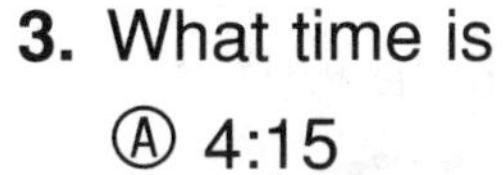

Name Date

Math Applications: Telling Time

Directions: Read each question carefully. Pay attention to details. Choose the best answer.

6. How much time has passed between the starting and ending times on the clocks?

Start

End

Ⓕ 2 hours, 25 minutes
Ⓖ 2 hours
Ⓗ 1 hour, 30 minutes
Ⓙ 3 hours

7. Margie went to baby-sit at 7:00. She came home 3 hours and 15 minutes later. What time did she come home?

Ⓐ 10:15
Ⓑ 9:15
Ⓒ 10:30
Ⓓ 10:00

8. In 45 minutes from the time shown on the clock, what time will it be?

Ⓕ 1:45
Ⓖ 12:45
Ⓗ 1:00
Ⓙ 12:30

9. Which of the following clocks shows 8:23?

Ⓐ

Ⓑ

Ⓒ

Ⓓ

10. Look at the clock. Jeffrey must be at school at 8:00. How long does he have before he is late?

Ⓕ 7 minutes
Ⓖ 8 minutes
Ⓗ 4 minutes
Ⓙ 10 minutes

11. Look at the clock. What time was it 15 minutes ago?

Ⓐ 5:00
Ⓑ 4:55
Ⓒ 4:50
Ⓓ 5:10

STOP

Name Date

Math Applications: Estimation

Directions: Read the question carefully. Choose the best answer. Work the problem on paper if necessary.

Examples:

A. Mark's lunch cost $1.00. He also wants to get ice cream for 50 cents. About how much money does Mark need to take to school?

Ⓐ $0.50
● $2.00
Ⓒ $0.75
Ⓓ $5.00

B. The closest estimate of 473 plus 105 is _____.

Ⓕ 500
Ⓖ 300
● 600
Ⓙ 400

Remember to look for the one that is "closest" to the exact answer.

Practice

1. John is going to the movies with two friends. Their tickets cost $6.25 each. The three tickets will cost about _____.

Ⓐ $15.00
Ⓑ $20.00
Ⓒ $17.50
Ⓓ Not given

2. Mary's family is going to the mountains for the weekend. The trip takes two hours. If they leave at 3:00, about what time will they arrive?

Ⓕ 6:00
Ⓖ 6:25
Ⓗ 2:30
Ⓙ 5:00

3. The closest estimate of 315 minus 190 is _____.

Ⓐ 100
Ⓑ 140
Ⓒ 130
Ⓓ 150

4. Molly earned $10.50 taking care of her neighbor's dog and $7.25 picking up the newspapers for a week. About how much did she earn?

Ⓕ $17.00
Ⓖ $18.00
Ⓗ $19.00
Ⓙ Not given

Name Date

Math Applications: Estimation

Directions: Read the problem carefully. Choose the best answer.

5. Which is the best estimate of the height of an 8-year-old child?

Ⓐ 4 yards
Ⓑ 4 feet
Ⓒ 4 inches
Ⓓ 4 kilometers

6. Ms. Brown is setting up her second grade classroom for the first day of school. What is the best estimate of the number of desks she needs?

Ⓕ 5
Ⓖ 50
Ⓗ 105
Ⓙ 25

7. John must practice violin for 30 minutes and do his math and science homework. What is the best estimate of how long this will take?

Ⓐ 30 minutes
Ⓑ 5 hours
Ⓒ $1\frac{1}{2}$ hours
Ⓓ 45 minutes

8. The cafeteria seats 250 children. There are about 25 children in each class. What is the best estimate of the number of classes that can eat at the same time?

Ⓕ 10
Ⓖ 25
Ⓗ 250
Ⓙ Not given

9. What is the best estimate of the weight of an 8-year-old child?

Ⓐ 50 ounces
Ⓑ 50 pounds
Ⓒ 50 grams
Ⓓ Not given

10. A large pizza serves 8. About how many pizzas should be ordered for the class party if there are 20 children in the class?

Ⓕ 8
Ⓖ 1
Ⓗ 20
Ⓙ 3

11. The teacher is collecting money from her students for a service project. The class wants to donate at least $20. If there are 18 children in the class, what is the best estimate of the amount each child should bring?

Ⓐ $1
Ⓑ $5
Ⓒ $0.25
Ⓓ $0.50

12. What is the best estimate for weekly allowance for an 8-year-old child?

Ⓕ $50
Ⓖ $100
Ⓗ $5
Ⓙ $25

Name Date

Math Applications: Estimation

Directions: Read the problem carefully. Choose the best answer.

13. What is 572 rounded to the nearest 10?

Ⓐ 500
Ⓑ 570
Ⓒ 575
Ⓓ Not given

14. What is 572 rounded to the nearest 100?

Ⓕ 600
Ⓖ 500
Ⓗ 570
Ⓙ Not given

15. What is 1,762 rounded to the nearest 100?

Ⓐ 1,760
Ⓑ 1,700
Ⓒ 1,600
Ⓓ Not given

16. What is 3,289 rounded to the nearest 10?

Ⓕ 3,200
Ⓖ 3,300
Ⓗ 3,290
Ⓙ Not given

17. What is $3.92 rounded to the nearest dollar?

Ⓐ $3.00
Ⓑ $4.00
Ⓒ $3.90
Ⓓ Not given

18. What is $0.38 rounded to the nearest ten cents?

Ⓕ $0.30
Ⓖ $3.00
Ⓗ $4.00
Ⓙ Not given

19. What is $4,299 rounded to the nearest hundred dollars?

Ⓐ $4,200
Ⓑ $4,290
Ⓒ $4,300
Ⓓ Not given

20. What is $4.61 rounded to the nearest dollar?

Ⓕ $5.00
Ⓖ $4.60
Ⓗ $4.00
Ⓙ Not given

21. What is 9,478 rounded to the nearest 1,000?

Ⓐ 9,000
Ⓑ 9,400
Ⓒ 10,000
Ⓓ Not given

22. What is $5.43 rounded to the nearest ten cents?

Ⓕ $5.50
Ⓖ $5.40
Ⓗ $5.00
Ⓙ Not given

Name Date

Math Applications: Estimation

Directions: Read the problem carefully. Choose the best answer.

23. What is the best estimate of the weight of Gary's birthday cake?

Ⓐ 2 feet
Ⓑ 2 ounces
Ⓒ 2 pounds
Ⓓ Not given

24. What is the best estimate of the number of cupcakes needed for Lisa's choir party if there are 40 people in the choir?

Ⓕ 4
Ⓖ 4 dozen
Ⓗ 4 pounds
Ⓙ 4 cups

25. Party favors cost $0.20 each. Estimated to the nearest dollar, how much will 20 party favors cost?

Ⓐ $20.20
Ⓑ $44.00
Ⓒ $4.00
Ⓓ Not given

26. What is one dozen rounded to the nearest 10?

Ⓕ 12
Ⓖ 10
Ⓗ 1
Ⓙ Not given

27. Clay has 13 dimes. Rounded to the nearest dollar, how much money does he have?

Ⓐ $1.00
Ⓑ $1.30
Ⓒ $2.00
Ⓓ Not given

28. Rob has 139 pennies in a jar. Rounded to the nearest ten cents, how much money does he have?

Ⓕ $1.39
Ⓖ $139
Ⓗ $1.30
Ⓙ Not given

29. At Lynn's school, there are 75 kindergartners, 294 students in the first through third grades, and 188 fourth and fifth graders. About how many students attend Lynn's school?

Ⓐ 1,000
Ⓑ 400
Ⓒ 600
Ⓓ Not given

30. What is the best estimate of the amount of paint Jay needs to paint his bedroom?

Ⓕ one gallon
Ⓖ one quart
Ⓗ one pint
Ⓙ one pound

STOP

Name Date

Math Applications: Geometry

Directions: Read each question carefully. Then choose the best answer.

Examples:

A. A four-sided figure could be a ______.

Ⓐ circle
Ⓑ triangle
Ⓒ hexagon
● rectangle

B. If each square in this figure is a square foot, what is the area of the shaded part?

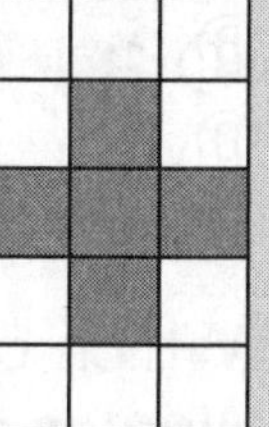

● 5 square feet
Ⓖ 10 square feet
Ⓗ 3 square feet
Ⓙ Not given

Look at the figures carefully, and pay attention to details.

Practice

1. This shape is a(n) ____.

Ⓐ circle
Ⓑ hexagon
Ⓒ pentagon
Ⓓ octagon

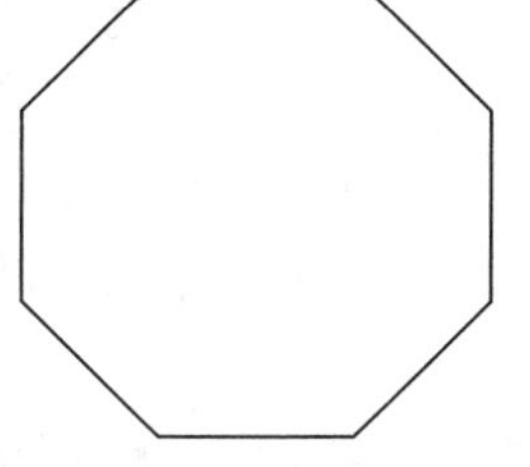

2. Congruent figures have the same shape and size as one another. Which figure is not congruent?

Ⓕ

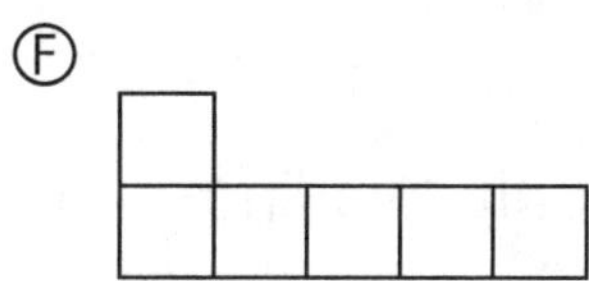

Ⓖ

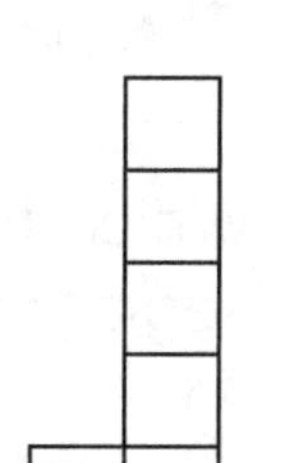

Ⓗ

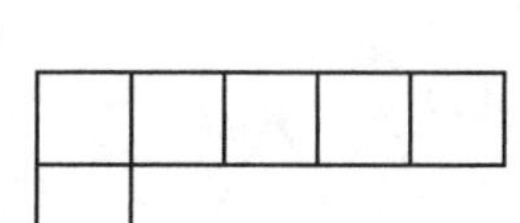

Ⓙ

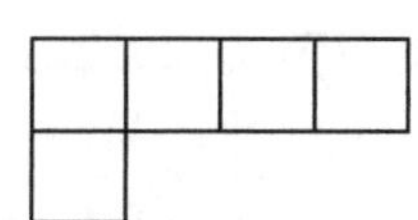

3. Which shape could be folded along the dotted line so the parts match?

Ⓐ

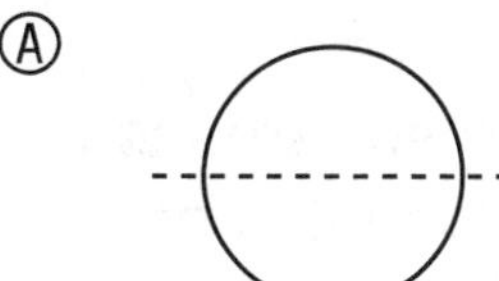

Ⓑ

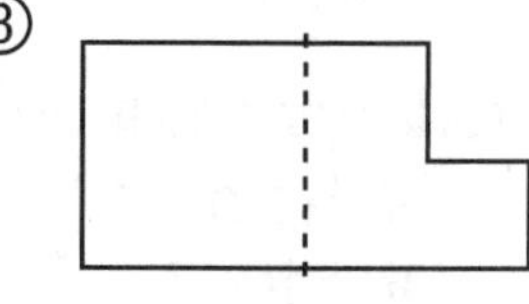

Ⓒ Ⓓ

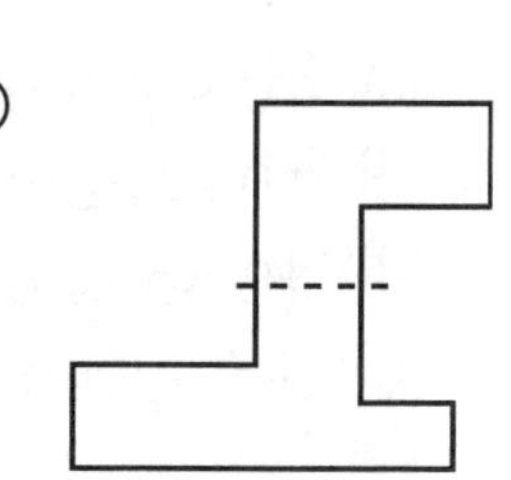

4. What is the perimeter of this figure?

Ⓕ 13 inches
Ⓖ 36 inches
Ⓗ 25 inches
Ⓙ 49 inches

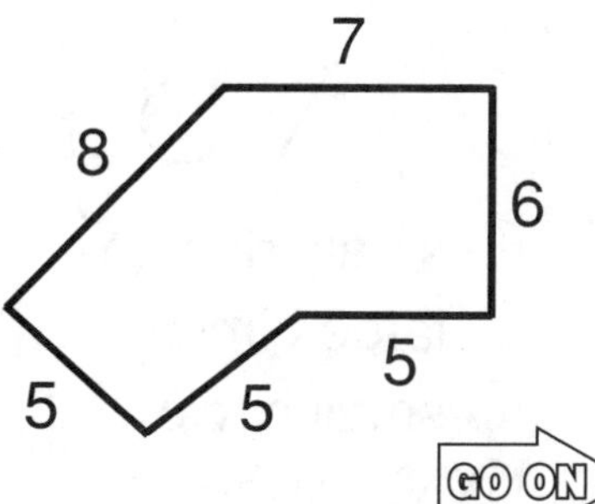

GO ON

Name Date

Math Applications: Geometry

Directions: Read each question carefully. Look at the diagram. Then choose the best answer.

5. Which letter is symmetrical?

Ⓐ P
Ⓑ Q
Ⓒ R
Ⓓ T

6. Which one has the same shape and size as the shaded figure?

Ⓕ
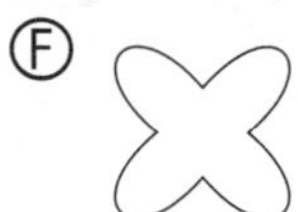

Ⓖ

Ⓗ

Ⓙ Not given

7. If each square is one square inch, what is the area of the part that is not shaded?

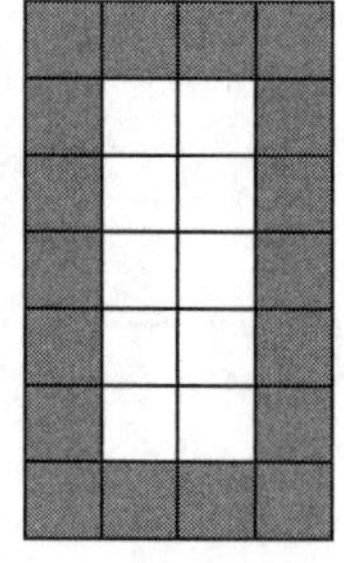

Ⓐ 10 square feet
Ⓑ 10 square inches
Ⓒ 18 square feet
Ⓓ Not given

8. What shape is to the left of the small square?

Ⓕ small triangle
Ⓖ large circle
Ⓗ small circle
Ⓙ Not given

Use the figure to answer questions 9 and 10. Each box equals 1 square foot.

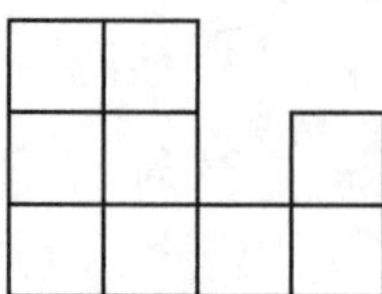

9. What is the perimeter of the figure?

Ⓐ 6 feet
Ⓑ 12 feet
Ⓒ 9 feet
Ⓓ 16 feet

10. What is the area of the figure?

Ⓕ 6 square feet
Ⓖ 16 square feet
Ⓗ 12 square feet
Ⓙ 9 square feet

11. Which one has the shape of a cylinder?

Ⓐ a tin can
Ⓑ a cardboard box
Ⓒ a rubber ball
Ⓓ Not given

12. Which figure has only two line segments?

Ⓕ
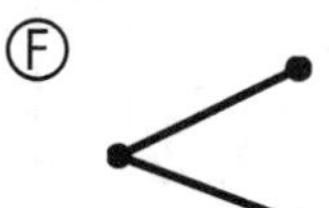

Ⓖ

Ⓗ
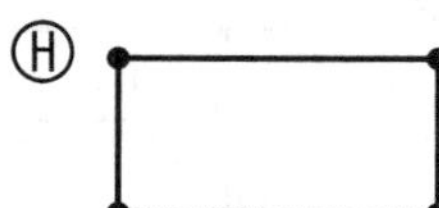

Ⓙ

Name Date

Math Applications: Geometry

Directions: Read each question carefully. Look at the diagram. Then choose the best answer.

13. Which figure shows parallel lines?

(A)

(B)
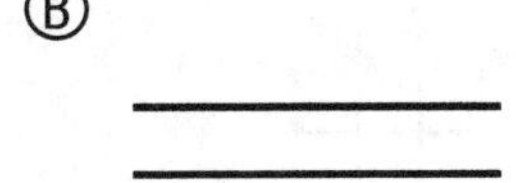

(C)
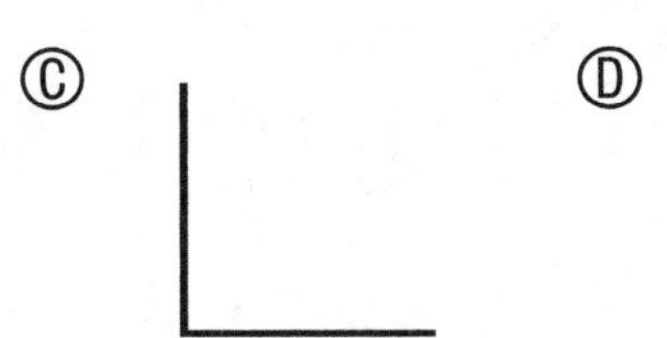

(D)
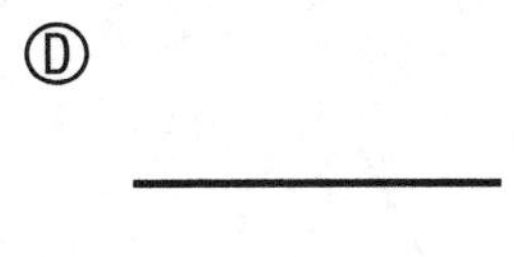

14. Which one is not symmetrical?

(F)
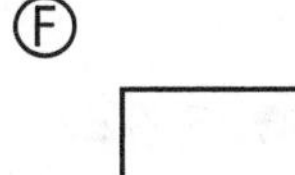

(G)
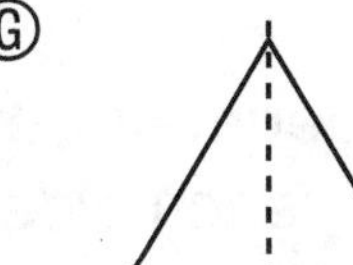

(H)
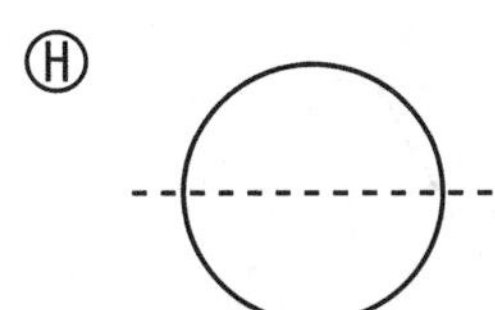

(J)
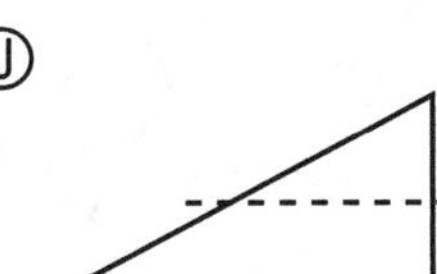

15. Which figure has lines that form a right angle?

(A)
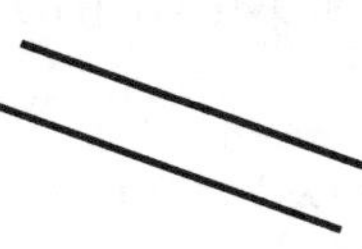

(B)
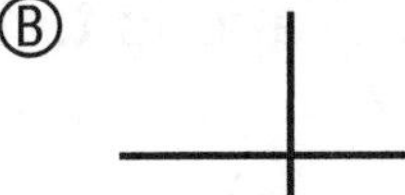

(C)
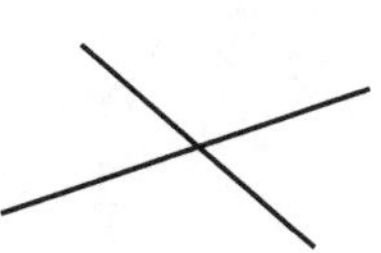

(D)
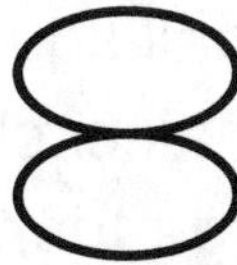

16. A five-sided figure is a(n) _____.

(F) octagon
(G) square
(H) pentagon
(J) cylinder

17. A nickel is what shape?

(A) prism
(B) circle
(C) sphere
(D) cone

18. What is the area of the shaded portion?

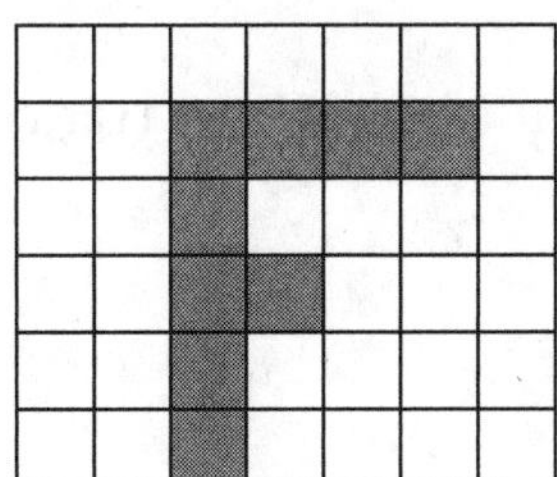

(F) 9 square units
(G) 42 square units
(H) 31 square units
(J) 32 square units

19. Which figure is divided into four squares?

(A)
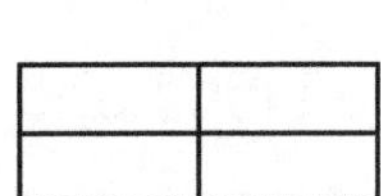

(B)
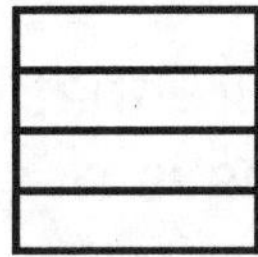

(C)
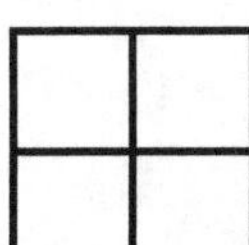

(D)

GO ON

Name Date

Math Applications: Geometry

Directions: Read each question carefully. Look at the diagram. Then choose the best answer.

Use the figure to answer questions 20 and 21.

20. Which shape is used only one time?

Ⓕ circle
Ⓖ triangle
Ⓗ square
Ⓙ diamond

21. How many circles are used in the figure?

Ⓐ 2
Ⓑ 3
Ⓒ 4
Ⓓ 5

22. A four-sided figure could be a(n) _____.

Ⓕ hexagon
Ⓖ octagon
Ⓗ rectangle
Ⓙ triangle

23. A figure that has three sides and three angles is a _____.

Ⓐ triangle
Ⓑ pentagon
Ⓒ square
Ⓓ Not given

24. Which figures are congruent?

Ⓕ 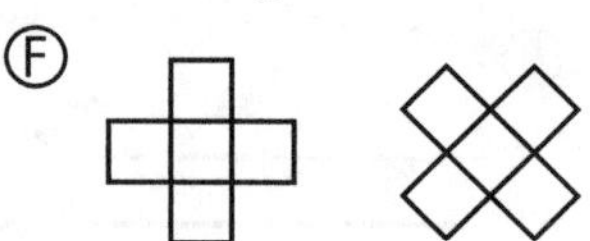

Ⓖ 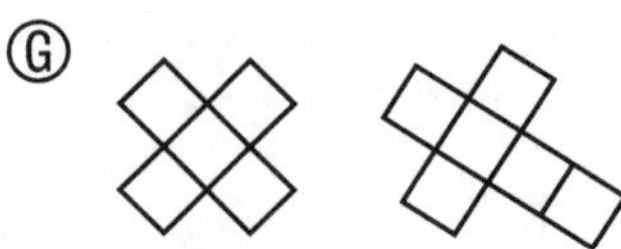

Ⓗ 

Ⓙ 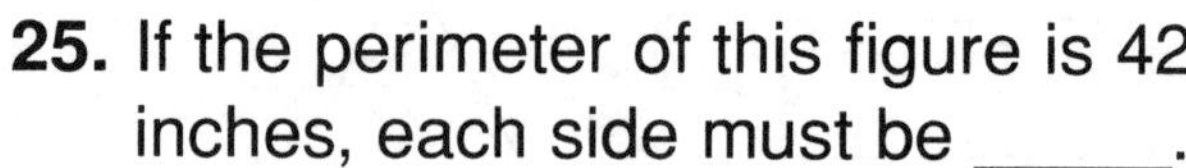

25. If the perimeter of this figure is 42 inches, each side must be _____.

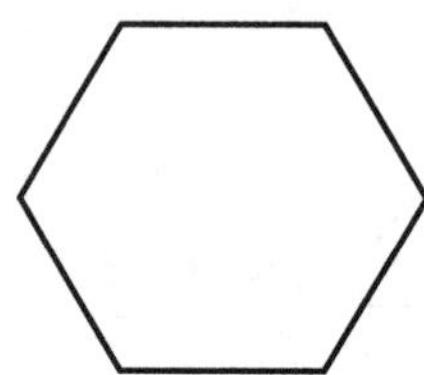

Ⓐ 42 inches long
Ⓑ 4 inches long
Ⓒ 6 inches long
Ⓓ 7 inches long

26. What shape is to the right of the large circle?

Ⓕ small square
Ⓖ small circle
Ⓗ large triangle
Ⓙ large square

Name Date

Math Applications: Measurement

Directions: Read each question carefully. Then choose the best answer.

Examples:

A. Melanie has been on a diet. What unit of measurement would be used to tell how much weight she has lost?

Ⓐ ounce Ⓑ kilometer
● pound Ⓓ gram

B. Which statement is true?

Ⓕ 12 inches = 1 yard
Ⓖ 36 inches = 1 meter
● 1 foot = 12 inches
Ⓙ Not given

Pay careful attention to details. Work the problems on scratch paper if you need to.

Practice

1. Which is the same as $5.38?

Ⓐ 5 one-dollar bills, 3 nickels, 8 pennies
Ⓑ 5 one-dollar bills, 3 dimes, 8 nickels
Ⓒ 5 one-dollar bills, 30 pennies, 8 nickels
Ⓓ 5 one-dollar bills, 3 dimes, 8 pennies

2. This thermometer shows the temperature when Molly came home from school. When she went to bed, the temperature had dropped 13°. What was the temperature at bedtime?

Ⓕ 49°
Ⓖ 50°
Ⓗ 47°
Ⓙ 55°

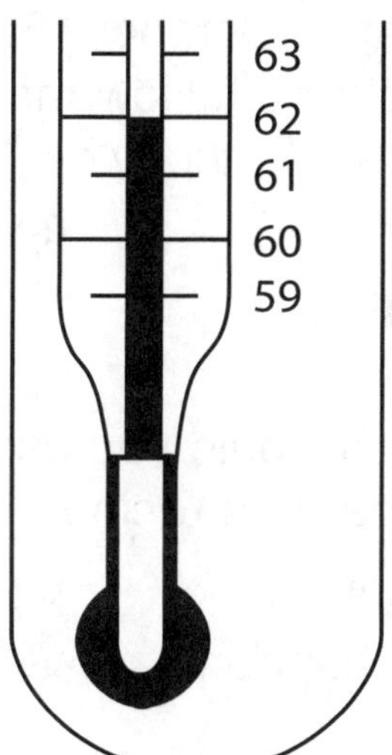

3. About how long is this pencil?

Ⓐ 3 inches
Ⓑ $3\frac{1}{4}$ inches
Ⓒ $3\frac{3}{4}$ inches
Ⓓ $2\frac{1}{4}$ inches

4. Matt and his dad ran a race together. What unit of measurement should be used to tell how far they ran?

Ⓕ inches
Ⓖ centimeters
Ⓗ meters
Ⓙ Not given

5. Which is the same as a kilometer?

Ⓐ one mile
Ⓑ 10 meters
Ⓒ 100 feet
Ⓓ 1,000 meters

Name Date

Applications: Measurement

Directions: Read each question carefully. Then choose the best answer.

6. Jeff always drinks a glass of milk for breakfast. Which one most likely tells how much milk he drinks?

Ⓕ one pint
Ⓖ one ounce
Ⓗ one gallon
Ⓙ one liter

7. What would you use to measure the length of the hall in your school?

Ⓐ a ruler
Ⓑ a liter
Ⓒ a yardstick
Ⓓ Not given

8. Hattie bought a candy bar. She gave the clerk $1.00. Her change is shown below. How much did the candy bar cost?

Ⓕ $0.45
Ⓖ $0.55
Ⓗ $0.50
Ⓙ $0.60

9. Which is longest?

Ⓐ 1 meter
Ⓑ 1 yard
Ⓒ 1 millimeter
Ⓓ 1 inch

Use this calendar to answer questions 10–12.

October

Sunday	Monday	Tuesday	Wednesday	Thursday	Friday	Saturday
				1	2	3
4	5	6	7	8	9	10
11	12	13	14	15	16	17
18	19	20	21	22	23	24
25	26	27	28	29	30	31

10. How many Saturdays does this month have?

Ⓕ 4 Ⓖ 5
Ⓗ 6 Ⓙ Not given

11. On what day is Halloween, October 31?

Ⓐ Thursday Ⓑ Friday
Ⓒ Saturday Ⓓ Monday

12. Today is October 15. Jamie's birthday is October 24. How many days until Jamie's birthday?

Ⓕ 7 Ⓖ 8
Ⓗ 9 Ⓙ 10

13. Which would you use to measure pepper in a recipe?

Ⓐ cup Ⓑ pint
Ⓒ teaspoon Ⓓ liter

GO ON

Name Date

Math Applications: Measurement

Directions: Read each question carefully. Then choose the best answer.

Use this thermometer to answer questions 14–16.

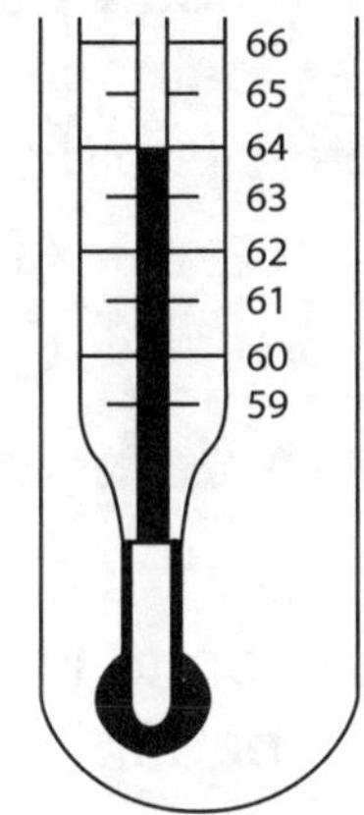

14. What temperature is shown on the thermometer?

Ⓕ 60°
Ⓖ 63°
Ⓗ 64°
Ⓙ Not given

15. The temperature has risen 7 degrees in the last 2 hours. What was the temperature 2 hours ago?

Ⓐ 54°
Ⓑ 71°
Ⓒ 53°
Ⓓ Not given

16. The high temperature for the day is predicted to be 72°. How many degrees must the temperature rise to meet the prediction?

Ⓕ 8°
Ⓖ 10°
Ⓗ 9°
Ⓙ 7°

17. Which is correct?

Ⓐ 8 ounces = 1 pint
Ⓑ 2 cups = 1 quart
Ⓒ 4 quarts = 1 liter
Ⓓ 8 ounces = 1 cup

Use this calendar to answer questions 18–20.

December

Sunday	Monday	Tuesday	Wednesday	Thursday	Friday	Saturday
		1	2	3	4	5
6	7	8	9	10	11	12
13	14	15	16	17	18	19
20	21	22	23	24	25	26
27	28	29	30	31		

18. What date is the second Monday in December?

Ⓕ 7 Ⓖ 14
Ⓗ 15 Ⓙ 27

19. On what day does December 23 come?

Ⓐ Tuesday Ⓑ Wednesday
Ⓒ Thursday Ⓓ Friday

20. There are 5 of which days in this month?

Ⓕ Tuesday, Thursday
Ⓖ Monday, Wednesday
Ⓗ Wednesday, Friday
Ⓙ Saturday, Sunday

Name Date

Math Applications: Problem Solving

Directions: Read each problem carefully. Then choose the best answer.

Examples:

A. There are 17 students in Marie's third grade class, 16 in Philip's, and 15 in Mason's. How many students are in the third grade?

Ⓐ 45 ● 48
Ⓒ 50 Ⓓ 53

B. Ms. May gave all the students in her class 2 new pencils. If there are 18 students in her class, how many pencils did she need?

Ⓕ 18 ÷ 3 = __ Ⓖ 18 ÷ 2 = __
● 18 x 2 = __ Ⓙ 18 + 2 = __

Be sure to read the problem carefully. Pay attention to key words, signs, and charts. If you need to, work the problem on paper.

Practice

1. Hal bought new soccer shoes for $39.95 and two pairs of socks for $5.00 each. How much did he spend?

Ⓐ $49.95
Ⓑ $44.95
Ⓒ $54.95
Ⓓ $41.95

2. Mike needs school supplies. Notebook paper costs $1.79, pencils $0.99, markers $2.98, and folders $1.49. Which is the best estimate of how much money he needs to take to the store?

Ⓕ $6.00
Ⓖ $10.00
Ⓗ $5.00
Ⓙ $8.00

3. Sam's family is driving to visit his sister at college. The drive usually takes about 6 hours. If they leave at 9:30 a.m., about what time should they arrive?

Ⓐ 9:30 p.m.
Ⓑ 3:30 p.m.
Ⓒ 3:30 a.m.
Ⓓ 6:00 p.m.

4. Jake's mother bought 3 dozen cookies for his band party. Twelve children came to the party. How many cookies did each child get?

Ⓕ 36 ÷ 3 = ______
Ⓖ 36 x 12 = ______
Ⓗ 36 ÷ 12 = ______
Ⓙ 12 + 36 = ______

GO ON

Name Date

Use the graph to answer numbers 5–8.

Pet Ownership in Ms. Smith's Class

cat	☺☺☺
dog	☺☺☺☺☺☺☺
birds	☺
fish	☺☺

☺ = 1 child

5. How many children in Ms. Smith's first grade have pets?

Ⓐ 10
Ⓑ 9
Ⓒ 7
Ⓓ 13

6. How many children have a pet that is not a dog?

Ⓕ 6
Ⓖ 7
Ⓗ 3
Ⓙ 13

7. How many children in Ms. Smith's class have pet fish?

Ⓐ 2
Ⓑ 1
Ⓒ 3
Ⓓ Not given

8. If there are 17 children in Ms. Smith's class, how many do not have a pet?

Ⓕ 6
Ⓖ 3
Ⓗ 4
Ⓙ Not given

Use the clock to answer numbers 9–12.

9. What time will it be in one hour?

Ⓐ 6:00
Ⓑ 5:30
Ⓒ 7:00
Ⓓ 4:00

10. Tony gets home from school at 3:30. How long has he been home?

Ⓕ 1 hour
Ⓖ 2 hours, 30 minutes
Ⓗ 1 hour, 30 minutes
Ⓙ 2 hours

11. Tony has 3 hours, 30 minutes before bedtime. What is Tony's bedtime?

Ⓐ 8:00
Ⓑ 8:30
Ⓒ 9:00
Ⓓ 7:30

12. Tony practices his cello for a half hour. If he starts at 5:15, what time will he finish?

Ⓕ 5:30
Ⓖ 5:45
Ⓗ 5:25
Ⓙ 6:00

GO ON

Name Date

13. Sarah bought a soda and popcorn at the movie. The popcorn was $2.50, and the soda was $1.50. How much change should she get from $5.00?

Ⓐ $2.00
Ⓑ $1.50
Ⓒ $0.50
Ⓓ $1.00

14. Amy bought a soda for $1.50 and a candy bar for $0.75. How much did she spend?

Ⓕ $2.25
Ⓖ $0.75
Ⓗ $2.00
Ⓙ $2.75

15. Art's mother was doing errands. She drove 2.75 miles to the grocery, 1 mile to the cleaner's, 1.75 miles to the video store, and 3 miles home. Which is the best estimate of how far she drove?

Ⓐ 3 miles
Ⓑ 9 miles
Ⓒ 5 miles
Ⓓ 7 miles

16. Barry's mother is making a costume for the school play. She needs 3 yards of fabric that costs $7.95 per yard. About how much will the costume cost?

Ⓕ $21
Ⓖ $24
Ⓗ $30
Ⓙ $20

Use the chart to answer questions 17–19.

Rental Fees

VHS	$3.00 per day
DVD	$4.00 per day
Game	$3.50 per day

17. Frances has $6.00. How many VHS tapes can she rent?

Ⓐ 3
Ⓑ 1
Ⓒ 2
Ⓓ 0

18. If Nick rents a VHS, a DVD, and a game for one day, how much will it cost?

Ⓕ $9.75
Ⓖ $11.00
Ⓗ $10.00
Ⓙ $10.50

19. If Kathi rents a VHS and a DVD for 2 days, how much will it cost?

Ⓐ $10.50
Ⓑ $14.00
Ⓒ $7.00
Ⓓ $15.00

20. Missy is making her dad's birthday cake. She needs $\frac{1}{3}$ cup of oil and $1\frac{1}{3}$ cups of water. How much liquid is in the cake?

Ⓕ $1\frac{1}{3}$ cups
Ⓖ 1 cup
Ⓗ 2 cups
Ⓙ $1\frac{2}{3}$ cups

Name Date

Use the thermometers to answer questions 21 and 22.

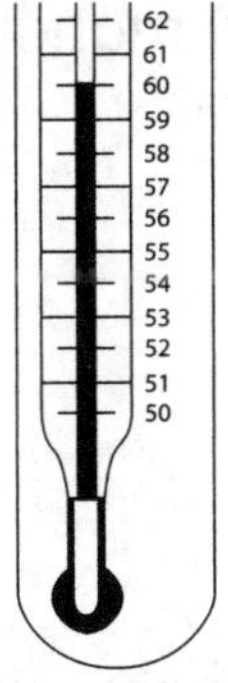

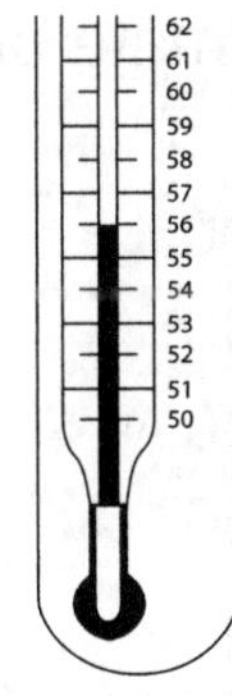

Monday **Tuesday**

21. The thermometers show the high temperature for 2 days. What was the high on Monday?

Ⓐ 45°

Ⓑ 50°

Ⓒ 55°

Ⓓ 60°

22. How much warmer was Monday than Tuesday?

Ⓕ 5°

Ⓖ 7°

Ⓗ 4°

Ⓙ 3°

23. Paul's school was selling wrapping paper to raise money. His grandmother bought 5 rolls, and his aunt bought 4. If the paper cost $7.00 per roll, how much did Paul raise?

Ⓐ $63.00

Ⓑ $9.00

Ⓒ $35.00

Ⓓ $28.00

Use the diagram of Joel's garden to answer questions 24–27.

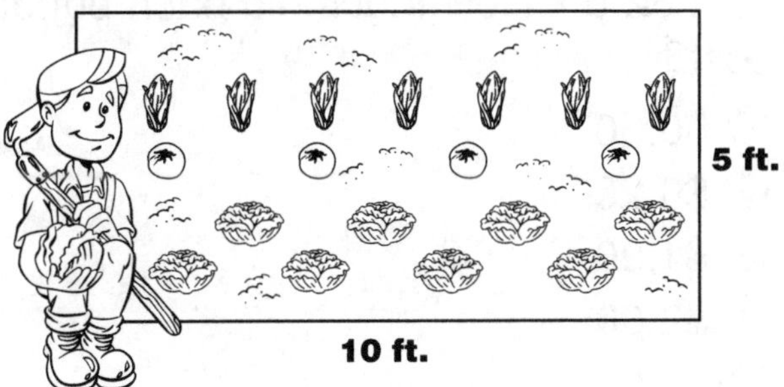

24. How much fencing does Joel need to go around the outside of his garden?

Ⓕ 10 feet

Ⓖ 15 feet

Ⓗ 20 feet

Ⓙ 30 feet

25. How many more corn plants did Joel plant than tomatoes?

Ⓐ 7

Ⓑ 4

Ⓒ 3

Ⓓ Not given

26. If Joel planted 4 rows of cabbage instead of 2 rows, how many cabbages would he have?

Ⓕ 8

Ⓖ 14

Ⓗ 12

Ⓙ Not given

27. If rabbits ate half of Joel's cabbages, how many cabbages would be left?

Ⓐ 8

Ⓑ 4

Ⓒ 6

Ⓓ 2

Name Date

28. Brad lost a button from his sweater. He had to buy a package of 4 buttons that cost $2.00. How much did each button cost?

Ⓕ $0.50
Ⓖ $0.25
Ⓗ $1.00
Ⓙ $2.00

Use the chart to answer questions 29–32.

Book Fair

Paperbacks	$2.95
Hardcovers	$10.95
Puzzle Books	$3.75
Bookmarks	$0.95
Posters	$6.50

29. Rebecca bought 2 paperbacks, a bookmark, and a poster. How much did she spend?

Ⓐ $13.25
Ⓑ $14.00
Ⓒ $13.35
Ⓓ $13.50

30. Robert wants a hardcover book, a poster, and a bookmark. He has $15.00. How much more money does he need?

Ⓕ $4.50
Ⓖ $5.00
Ⓗ $3.50
Ⓙ $3.40

31. Kirk wants to buy a hardcover book, a puzzle book, and a poster. Which is the best estimate of how much money he needs?

Ⓐ $14.00
Ⓑ $22.00
Ⓒ $15.00
Ⓓ $18.00

32. Kay earns $2.50 per hour baby-sitting. How many hours would she need to baby-sit in order to buy a hardcover book and a bookmark?

Ⓕ 5 hours
Ⓖ 4 hours
Ⓗ 6 hours
Ⓙ 3 hours

Use the clock to answer questions 33–34.

33. Mr. Carr's class goes to lunch at 12:45. How much longer is it until their lunchtime?

Ⓐ 1 hour
Ⓑ 30 minutes
Ⓒ 15 minutes
Ⓓ 3 minutes

34. School starts at 8:00. How long have Mr. Carr's students been in school before they go to lunch?

Ⓕ 5 hours, 45 minutes
Ⓖ 4 hours, 45 minutes
Ⓗ 4 hours, 30 minutes
Ⓙ 5 hours

Name Date

The graph shows how many minutes some students in Ms. Johnson's class read during the week. Use the graph to answer questions 35–40.

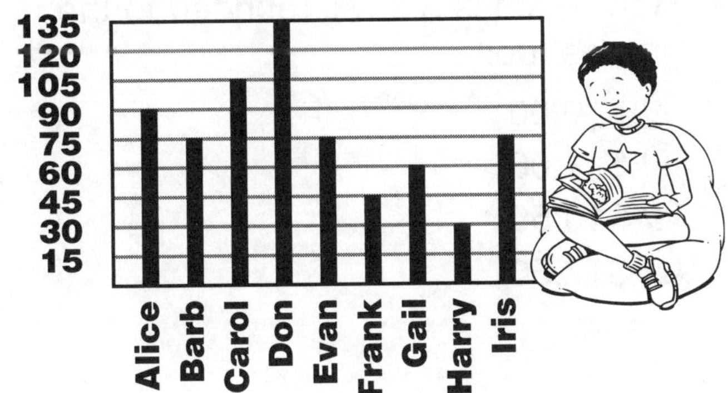

35. Which student read the most?

Ⓐ Iris
Ⓑ Don
Ⓒ Harry
Ⓓ Carol

36. Which students read the same amount?

Ⓕ Alice, Evan, Gail
Ⓖ Barb, Evan, Gail
Ⓗ Frank, Harry
Ⓙ Barb, Evan, Iris

37. How many minutes did Carol and Don read altogether?

Ⓐ 225
Ⓑ 200
Ⓒ 125
Ⓓ 240

38. How many more minutes did Frank read than Harry?

Ⓕ 45 minutes
Ⓖ 30 minutes
Ⓗ 15 minutes
Ⓙ Not given

39. Which student read exactly 1 hour?

Ⓐ Alice
Ⓑ Barb
Ⓒ Don
Ⓓ Gail

40. If Iris read the same number of minutes each night for 5 nights, how many minutes did she read each night?

Ⓕ 10 minutes
Ⓖ 15 minutes
Ⓗ 20 minutes
Ⓙ 25 minutes

41. Mr. Black used his cell phone for 990 minutes in August, 1,050 minutes in September, and 1,100 minutes in October. Which plan should he have so he does not have to pay extra for the minutes he uses?

Ⓐ 1,000 minutes per month
Ⓑ 1,200 minutes per month
Ⓒ 1,500 minutes per month
Ⓓ 3,000 minutes per month

42. Ms. Black's cell phone plan allows her to use 1,000 minutes per month. If she uses more, she must pay $0.35 per minute. If she used 1,027 minutes last month, how much extra did she pay?

Ⓕ 1,000 x $0.35 = ______
Ⓖ 1,027 x $0.35 = ______
Ⓗ 27 x $0.35 = ______
Ⓙ Not given

STOP

Name Date

Math Applications: Sample Test

Directions: Read each problem carefully. Pay close attention to details, figures, and signs. Choose the best answer.

1. There are 50 items on the spelling test. Students have 25 minutes to finish the test. Which number sentence shows how long they have for each item?

Ⓐ 25 ÷ 50 = ______
Ⓑ 50 + 25 = ______
Ⓒ 25 x 50 = ______
Ⓓ Not given

2. Which figure is a rectangle?

Ⓕ 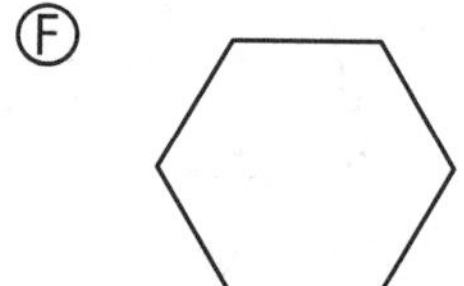

Ⓖ 

Ⓗ 

Ⓙ 

3. Which figure does not have parallel sides?

Ⓐ 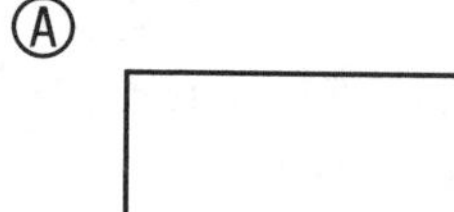

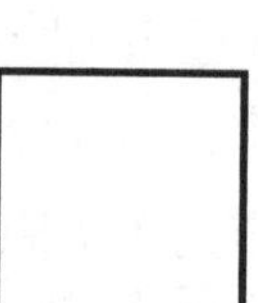

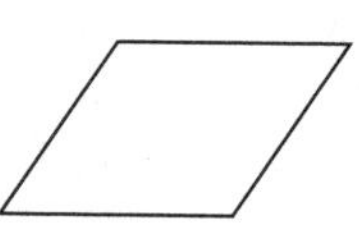

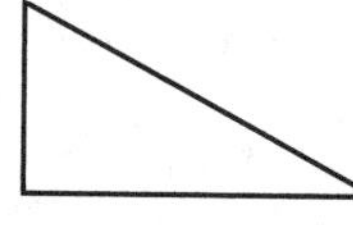

4. How much is $10.75 rounded to the nearest dollar?

Ⓕ $10.00
Ⓖ $11.00
Ⓗ $10.50
Ⓙ $17.50

5. Jody sorted the coins in her bank. She has 4 quarters, 10 dimes, 5 nickels, and 7 pennies. How much money does she have?

Ⓐ $2.57
Ⓑ $2.32
Ⓒ $2.37
Ⓓ Not given

6. Amy is making biscuits for dinner. Which will she need?

Ⓕ ruler
Ⓖ meter stick
Ⓗ cup
Ⓙ Not given

7. What is 569 + 103 rounded to the nearest hundred?

Ⓐ 700
Ⓑ 672
Ⓒ 600
Ⓓ 670

GO ON

Name Date

Use the clock to answer questions 8–11.

8. What time does the clock show?

Ⓕ 5:00
Ⓖ 12:25
Ⓗ 5:12
Ⓙ 12:05

9. What time will it be in 1 hour and 20 minutes?

Ⓐ 5:20
Ⓑ 5:30
Ⓒ 6:00
Ⓓ 6:20

10. What time was it a half hour ago?

Ⓕ 12:00
Ⓖ 4:30
Ⓗ 4:45
Ⓙ 5:15

11. What time was it 45 minutes ago?

Ⓐ 5:00
Ⓑ 5:45
Ⓒ 4:45
Ⓓ 4:15

Use the chart to answer questions 12–14.

Movie	Feature Time	Feature Time
Big Bear	4:25	7:45
Funny Cartoons	4:45	9:10
Scary Feature	3:30	6:20
Football Heroes	5:00	7:05

12. How many movies are playing at this theater?

Ⓕ 5
Ⓖ 8
Ⓗ 12
Ⓙ 4

13. Jan and Carol get out of school at 3:30. Which movie could they not see after school?

Ⓐ *Big Bear*
Ⓑ *Funny Cartoons*
Ⓒ *Scary Feature*
Ⓓ *Football Heroes*

14. Harry and Bob tried to see *Big Bear* at 4:25, but they didn't get there in time. How long do they have to wait before the next showing of *Big Bear*?

Ⓕ 3 hours, 15 minutes
Ⓖ 2 hours, 45 minutes
Ⓗ 3 hours, 20 minutes
Ⓙ 2 hours, 20 minutes

GO ON

Name Date

Math Applications: Sample Test

Directions: Read each question carefully. Pay close attention to details, figures, and signs. Choose the best answer.

15. Which shape is not used in the drawing?

- Ⓐ circle
- Ⓑ triangle
- Ⓒ rectangle
- Ⓓ octagon

16. How many circles are in the drawing?

- Ⓕ 3
- Ⓖ 4
- Ⓗ 5
- Ⓙ 6

17. Which shape is used most often in the drawing?

- Ⓐ square
- Ⓑ circle
- Ⓒ triangle
- Ⓓ rectangle

18. What is the best estimation of the length of a football field?

- Ⓕ 100 centimeters
- Ⓖ 100 meters
- Ⓗ 100 kilometers
- Ⓙ 100 inches

19. Congruent figures have the same _____.

- Ⓐ shape and color
- Ⓑ size and color
- Ⓒ shape and size
- Ⓓ Not given

20. Which one shows figures that are congruent?

Ⓕ

Ⓖ
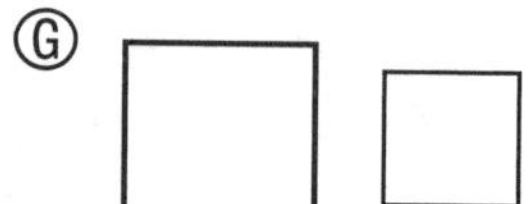

Ⓗ

Ⓙ

21. What is the best estimation of the area of the top of Patrick's bedside table?

- Ⓐ 144 square feet
- Ⓑ 144 square yards
- Ⓒ 144 square inches
- Ⓓ Not given

GO ON

Name Date

Math Applications: Sample Test

Directions: Read each question carefully. Pay close attention to details, figures, and signs. Choose the best answer.

James runs 25 miles each week. Use his running chart to answer questions 22–24.

Day	Miles
Sunday	4 miles
Monday	3 miles
Tuesday	3 miles
Wednesday	5 miles
Thursday	2 miles
Friday	______
Saturday	______

22. How many more miles must James run on Friday or Saturday to meet his 25-mile goal?

Ⓕ 6 miles
Ⓖ 7 miles
Ⓗ 8 miles
Ⓙ 9 miles

23. If James divides the rest of his miles equally between Friday and Saturday, how many miles must he run each day?

Ⓐ 8 miles
Ⓑ 3 miles
Ⓒ 5 miles
Ⓓ 4 miles

24. On which day did James run the most miles?

Ⓕ Sunday
Ⓖ Wednesday
Ⓗ Thursday
Ⓙ Monday

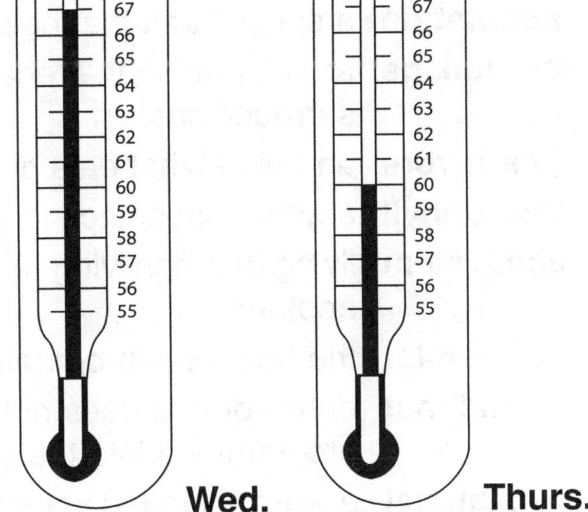

25. What is the difference between the temperatures shown on the thermometers?

Ⓐ 5°
Ⓑ 10°
Ⓒ 4°
Ⓓ 7°

26. What is \$5.89 plus \$39.95 rounded to the nearest \$10?

Ⓕ \$45.84
Ⓖ \$40.00
Ⓗ \$45.00
Ⓙ \$50.00

27. Laura is in school 6 hours. If school starts at 8:00, what time does Laura get out of school?

Ⓐ 3:00
Ⓑ 2:00
Ⓒ 4:00
Ⓓ Not given

Name Date

Science: Life Science

Directions: Use the glossary to answer each question. Choose the best answer.

adaptation	a special trait that helps an organism survive
camouflage	an adaptation that enables an animal to hide by blending in to its surroundings
carnivore	an animal that eats only meat
chlorophyll	a green substance in plants that traps the sun's energy to help make food
ecosystem	living and nonliving things in an environment and their interactions with one another
habitat	the home of an organism
instinct	behavior that does not require an animal to think because it is programmed into the animal's brain
mammal	a warm-blooded vertebrate with hair or fur; females produce milk to feed babies
omnivore	an animal that eats both plants and animals
vertebrate	an animal with a backbone

1. The green color of a frog is an example of _____.

Ⓐ habitat
Ⓑ chlorophyll
Ⓒ instinct
Ⓓ camouflage

2. Which one is not a mammal?

Ⓕ snake
Ⓖ rabbit
Ⓗ kangaroo
Ⓙ gorilla

3. An example of an instinct is _____.

Ⓐ a dog learning to sit
Ⓑ a parrot talking
Ⓒ a mother feeding her young
Ⓓ a child reading a story

4. The hard shell and large claws of a lobster are examples of _____.

Ⓕ camouflage
Ⓖ adaptation
Ⓗ ecosystem
Ⓙ carnivore

5. Which one is necessary for a plant to grow?

Ⓐ omnivore
Ⓑ ecosystem
Ⓒ chlorophyll
Ⓓ instinct

STOP

Name Date

Science: Life Science

Directions: Read the paragraph and look at the diagram about ecosystems and food webs to answer each question. Choose the best answer.

Ecosytems and Food Webs

All the parts of nature fit together, and every living thing has its place in nature. Plants and animals can be divided into different groups according to their role in nature. Plants use the sun's energy to produce new growth, so they are called producers; animals eat plants and other animals, so they are called consumers. All the plants and animals that live in one area and feed off each other make up a community. A diagram of the relationships between the plants and animals in a community is called a food web or food chain. In a food web, an herbivore (plant eater) eats plants. A carnivore (meat eater) or an omnivore (plant and meat eater) then eats the herbivore.

Ocean Food Chain

1. A food web includes producers and
   Ⓐ plants.
   Ⓑ consumers.
   Ⓒ energy.
   Ⓓ communities.

2. What do plants need in order to grow?
   Ⓕ other plants
   Ⓖ the food web
   Ⓗ herbivores
   Ⓙ the sun's energy

3. Omnivores and carnivores are
   Ⓐ consumers.
   Ⓑ producers.
   Ⓒ communities.
   Ⓓ animals.

4. After a plant grows and is eaten by an herbivore, what happens next in the food chain?
   Ⓕ A community forms.
   Ⓖ The plants and animals are divided.
   Ⓗ An omnivore or carnivore eats the herbivore.
   Ⓙ The sun's energy causes the plant to grow.

Name Date

Science: Life Science

Directions: Use the diagram and the paragraph about the life cycle of a flowering plant to answer each question. Choose the best answer.

Life Cycle of a Flowering Plant

Flowering plants reproduce by making seeds in flowers. The flowers have a female part that makes eggs and a male part that creates pollen. Pollen is carried to the eggs by the wind, insects such as bees, or birds. When the eggs and pollen come together, seeds are formed. The flowers then turn into fruit that contains the seeds, and some of these seeds grow into new plants. From these plants, the cycle starts again.

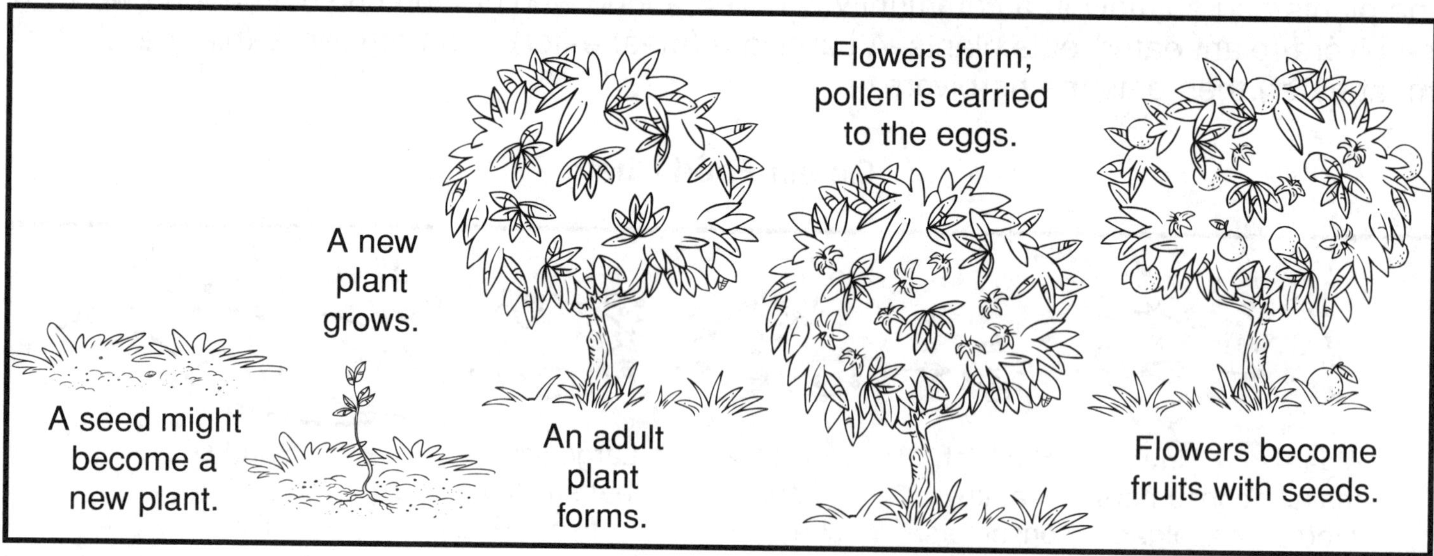

1. Pollen is carried to eggs by all of these except
   Ⓐ birds.
   Ⓑ insects.
   Ⓒ people.
   Ⓓ the wind.

2. Which plant would not reproduce in the way described in this diagram and paragraph?
   Ⓕ an apple tree
   Ⓖ a peach tree
   Ⓗ a tomato plant
   Ⓙ a carrot plant

3. Which sequence is correct for a flowering plant?
   Ⓐ eggs, seeds, flowers, fruit
   Ⓑ seeds, eggs, fruit, flowers
   Ⓒ fruit, eggs, seeds, flowers
   Ⓓ Not given

4. In a flowering plant, the female part of the flower creates eggs, and the male part creates
   Ⓕ flowers.
   Ⓖ pollen.
   Ⓗ leaves.
   Ⓙ Not given

STOP

Name Date

Science: Life Science

Directions: Read the paragraph, and answer each question. Choose the best answer.

Animals in the Swamp

The home of an animal is its **habitat**. A swamp is a fascinating habitat. One of the largest swamps is the Okefenokee Swamp in Georgia. The ground there is very wet because it was once part of the ocean floor. It is also so soft that you can make a tree shake just by stomping your foot. The natives who lived in the area named it Okefenokee because in their language that word meant "land of the trembling earth." One of the interesting animals that lives in this swamp is the bowfin fish. It can swim near the surface of the water and breathe air, which is helpful since the murky swamp water does not contain much oxygen. The alligator snapping turtle is another curious creature. It catches its prey by tricking them. It lies covered in water; then it opens its mouth and wiggles its pink tongue. Other animals think the tongue is a worm, and when they swim in to eat it, the snapping turtle gets them! Another odd animal is the star-nosed mole. This animal is nearly blind, so it uses its star-shaped nose to help it sense its surroundings. The nose is only one-half inch wide, but it has eleven "fingers" that stick out from it, with over 25,000 sensors. The mole is a great swimmer. Another great swimmer is the otter, thanks to its webbed feet. It can swim for one-fourth of a mile before coming up for air.

1. The word <u>habitat</u> means

Ⓐ an animal's diet.
Ⓑ an animal's home.
Ⓒ an animal's mate.
Ⓓ Not given

2. When an alligator snapping turtle catches prey by using its tongue that looks like a worm, this is an example of

Ⓕ heredity.
Ⓖ instinct.
Ⓗ mimicry.
Ⓙ camouflage.

3. The bowfin fish has adapted to the swamp by

Ⓐ having sharp fins.
Ⓑ having a pink tongue.
Ⓒ being able to stay near the surface and breathe air.
Ⓓ being almost blind.

4. Which is probably <u>not</u> a part of the diet of an animal in this habitat?

Ⓕ cactus
Ⓖ fish
Ⓗ water plants
Ⓙ other water animals

Name Date

Science: Earth Science

Directions: Read each sentence. Then choose the correct word to fit in the blank.

1. The gases that surround the earth are called the _____.
   Ⓐ anemometer
   Ⓑ atmosphere
   Ⓒ precipitation
   Ⓓ environment

2. A _____ rock is one that forms when sand, mud, and pebbles at the bottom of oceans, rivers, and lakes pile up.
   Ⓕ marble
   Ⓖ textured
   Ⓗ sedimentary
   Ⓙ opaque

3. A substance that occurs naturally and is neither a plant nor an animal is _____.
   Ⓐ matter
   Ⓑ an igneous rock
   Ⓒ groundwater
   Ⓓ a mineral

4. Jupiter and Neptune are examples of _____.
   Ⓕ outer planets
   Ⓖ inner planets
   Ⓗ new moons
   Ⓙ tundra

5. _____ is a mixture of tiny particles of rock, minerals, and decayed animal and plant materials.
   Ⓐ Metamorphic rock
   Ⓑ Igneous rock
   Ⓒ Soil
   Ⓓ Pollution

6. The imprint of a fish skeleton in a rock is an example of _____.
   Ⓕ erosion
   Ⓖ a fossil
   Ⓗ an element
   Ⓙ fungi

7. A _____ is a violent storm with heavy rain and strong wind.
   Ⓐ tornado
   Ⓑ volcano
   Ⓒ windlass
   Ⓓ hurricane

8. An anemometer, a barometer, and a thermometer are all instruments used to measure _____.
   Ⓕ constellations
   Ⓖ rock formations
   Ⓗ weather
   Ⓙ landforms

STOP

Name Date

Science: Earth Science

Directions: Read the paragraph about fossils. Then answer each question. Choose the best answer.

Fossils

A **fossil** is the remains of a plant or animal that lived in the prehistoric past. Fossils are formed when animals or plants die and the hard parts of them remain. Sometimes, for example, minerals seep into teeth, bones, or shells and preserve them like rocks. **Imprints** form when plants or animals die and are pressed into material that later becomes rock.

One of the best places to study fossils is the La Brea Tar Pits in California. Animals would come to drink water that had accumulated on top of the tar and become stuck in it and die. Fossilized coyotes, saber-toothed cats, camels, and condors are just a few of the millions of fossil remains found there.

Scientists study fossils to learn more about the earth as it was millions of years ago. They have found fossils of seashells high in the Andes Mountains and palm tree fossils in Greenland. This helps explain how the earth has changed over millions of years.

1. Scientists study fossils to learn
- Ⓐ how the earth might be in the future.
- Ⓑ how the earth has changed over millions of years.
- Ⓒ where tar comes from.
- Ⓓ what life is like in Greenland.

2. Fossils formed at the La Brea Tar Pits when animals
- Ⓕ drowned.
- Ⓖ killed each other.
- Ⓗ froze.
- Ⓙ got stuck in the tar.

3. A rock with a leaf pattern pressed into it is an example of
- Ⓐ a mold.
- Ⓑ a mineral.
- Ⓒ an imprint.
- Ⓓ Not given

4. What parts of plants and animals remain to create fossils?
- Ⓕ the hard parts such as bones and teeth
- Ⓖ the soft parts such as skin
- Ⓗ only the ears and feet
- Ⓙ Not given

Name Date

Science: Earth Science

Directions: Use the table about the solar system to answer each question. Choose the best answer.

Planet	Diameter	Dist. from Sun	Rotation	Orbit	No. Satellites
Mercury	3,000 mi.	36 million mi.	59 days	88 days	0
Venus	7,550 mi.	67 million mi.	243 days	225 days	0
Earth	7,926 mi.	93 million mi.	24 hours	365 days	1
Mars	4,200 mi.	142 million mi.	25 hours	687 days	2
Jupiter	88,700 mi.	484 million mi.	10 hours	12 years	15
Saturn	74,000 mi.	891 million mi.	11 hours	29 years	21
Uranus	29,000 mi.	1.8 billion mi.	18 hours	84 years	5
Neptune	28,000 mi.	2.8 billion mi.	18 hours	165 years	2
Pluto	1,500 mi.	3.7 billion mi.	6 days	248 years	1

1. Which planets rotate on their axes at the same rate?

Ⓐ Venus and Earth
Ⓑ Saturn and Uranus
Ⓒ Uranus and Neptune
Ⓓ Earth and Mars

2. Which planet has the most satellites?

Ⓕ Jupiter
Ⓖ Saturn
Ⓗ Mercury
Ⓙ Uranus

3. Which planet has the shortest orbit?

Ⓐ Mercury
Ⓑ Uranus
Ⓒ Jupiter
Ⓓ Saturn

4. Which planet is closest in diameter to Earth?

Ⓕ Pluto
Ⓖ Neptune
Ⓗ Venus
Ⓙ Mars

5. Which planet takes about the same time to orbit the sun as it takes to rotate on its axis?

Ⓐ Mercury
Ⓑ Earth
Ⓒ Pluto
Ⓓ Venus

6. Arranged in order from smallest to largest, which planet would come first?

Ⓕ Mercury
Ⓖ Venus
Ⓗ Earth
Ⓙ Pluto

Name Date

Science: Earth Science

Directions: Read the paragraph about the water cycle, and answer each question. Choose the best answer.

The Water Cycle

Plants and animals use water every day. The water they use comes from some part of the water cycle, which is nature's way of recycling. Water is constantly moving from the earth to the atmosphere through **evaporation** and **condensation**. When water accumulates in the ground, it is called **groundwater**. When it falls to the earth from clouds, it is called **precipitation**, and it can be in the form of rain, snow, sleet, or hail. In the water cycle, the sun's heat warms water in the oceans and on the ground and causes it to evaporate. As the water vapor rises, it cools and changes back into water droplets and forms clouds. This is condensation. When enough water has condensed, it falls to the ground as precipitation. Some precipitation flows into rivers, lakes, and oceans; some falls directly into these bodies of water; and some soaks into the ground.

1. The water cycle consists of evaporation, condensation, and
- Ⓐ precipitation.
- Ⓑ clouds.
- Ⓒ lakes, river, and seas.
- Ⓓ Not given

2. The process through which clouds are formed from water droplets is
- Ⓕ precipitation.
- Ⓖ condensation.
- Ⓗ accumulation.
- Ⓙ recycling.

3. What causes water to evaporate from oceans, lakes, and rivers?
- Ⓐ water vapor
- Ⓑ condensation
- Ⓒ clouds
- Ⓓ the sun's heat

4. Which is <u>not</u> correct?
- Ⓕ Clouds consist of water droplets.
- Ⓖ Water evaporates and condenses constantly.
- Ⓗ Heat causes clouds to form.
- Ⓙ Some precipitation becomes groundwater.

5. The movement of water from the earth to the atmosphere is called a <u>cycle</u> because
- Ⓐ it happens once in a while.
- Ⓑ it has three stages like a tricycle.
- Ⓒ it happens the same way over and over.
- Ⓓ Not given

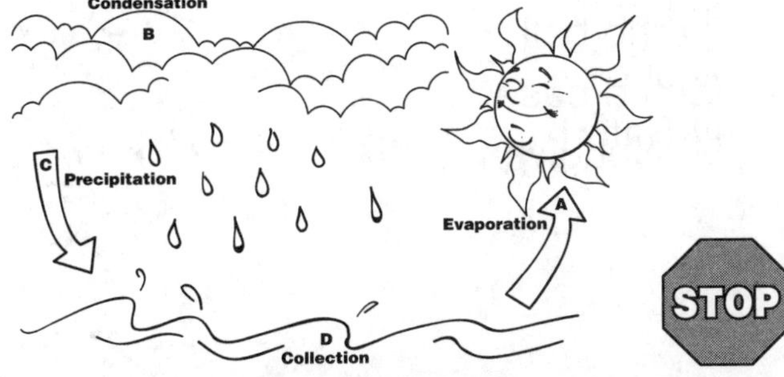

STOP

 www.summerbridgeactivities.com

Name Date

Science: Physical Science

Directions: Read the paragraph about machines, and answer the questions. Choose the best answer.

Simple and Compound Machines

The word **work** means the *force that changes the motion of an object.* Machines make work easier for us to do. **Simple machines** have few or no moving parts. One example of a simple machine is a lever, which has three parts: the load, the fulcrum, and the force. The load is the object that is being moved, the force is the pull or push that moves the lever, and the fulcrum is the point where the lever turns. A seesaw is a lever where the fulcrum is the middle of the seesaw, and the force and load are the people on each end. Another simple machine is a wheel and axle where a wheel turns on a post, which is the axle. A doorknob is an example of a wheel and axle. A pulley is a simple machine that uses a wheel and a rope. The way a bucket is lowered into a well to get water is an example of a pulley. Other simple machines include an inclined plane, a screw, and a wedge. **Compound machines** are created when two or more simple machines are put together. A pair of scissors is a compound machine made of a lever and a wedge. So is a water faucet, which is made of a wheel and axle and a screw.

1. Which simple machine would you use if you walked up a ramp?

Ⓐ lever
Ⓑ inclined plane
Ⓒ wedge
Ⓓ screw

2. When a person hits a ball with a baseball bat, the bat acts as a lever. What is the fulcrum?

Ⓕ the person
Ⓖ the ball
Ⓗ the base
Ⓙ Not given

3. Which is an example of a compound machine made from a wheel and axle and a screw?

Ⓐ a bicycle
Ⓑ a water faucet
Ⓒ scissors
Ⓓ Not given

4. When you use force to change the motion of an object, you are

Ⓕ doing magic.
Ⓖ doing exercises.
Ⓗ doing work.
Ⓙ doing nothing.

STOP

Name Date

Science: Physical Science

Directions: Read the paragraph, and then answer each question. Choose the best answer.

Motion is a change in the position of an object. What causes motion? Motion is caused when the forces that act on an object are not equal. For example, in a tug-of-war, as long as you and the other person pulling on the rope are pulling with equal force, the center of the rope does not move. But if one of you pulls harder than the other, the rope moves. This is motion.

Isaac Newton was an English scientist who observed and described three laws of motion. The first one is that if an object is still, it will stay still, and if an object is moving, it will usually continue to move unless a force pushes or pulls it. Newton's second law says that a force can change the speed of an object, and the greater the force, the greater the change that occurs. His third law states that a force in one direction creates an equal force in the opposite direction.

Two forces that can create motion are pushes and pulls. The unit used to measure pushes and pulls is the **newton**. Another force that changes the way an object moves is **friction**. Friction occurs when one object rubs against another.

1. The name of the unit used to measure pushes and pulls probably came from
- Ⓐ Isaac Newton.
- Ⓑ a kind of cookie.
- Ⓒ a ton of pushes or pulls.
- Ⓓ Not given

2. Which one would not result in motion?
- Ⓕ two children the same size and weight pushing on a door from opposite sides
- Ⓖ an adult pushing a small child in a wagon
- Ⓗ a small child kicking a ball
- Ⓙ two children the same size and weight pushing on a door from the same side

3. Which one is not an example of friction changing the way an object moves?
- Ⓐ the brakes on a bicycle
- Ⓑ sliding a book across the table to someone
- Ⓒ the blades on a fan coming to a stop
- Ⓓ ice falling out of a dispenser

4. Which one best illustrates Newton's first law of motion?
- Ⓕ someone throwing a ball
- Ⓖ an airplane flying overhead
- Ⓗ a book sitting on a shelf
- Ⓙ Not given

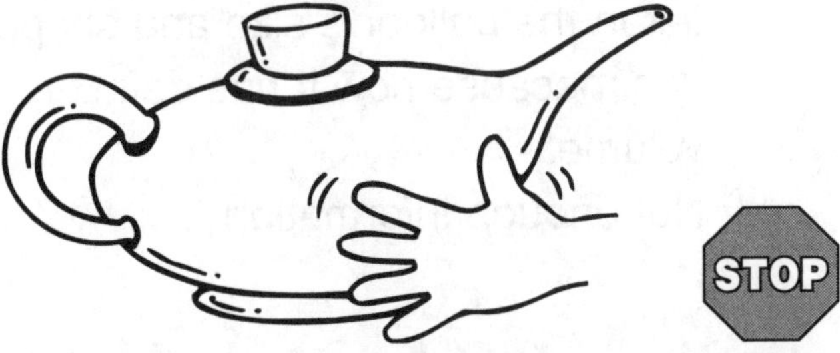

STOP

Name Date

Science: Physical Science

Directions: Read the paragraph, and look at the chart about the states of matter. Then answer each question. Choose the best answer.

Matter is anything that takes up space and has mass. Matter can occur in three states. The state in which matter occurs is determined by the amount of space there is between the particles from which it is made.

States of Matter

State	Properties	Examples	Space between Particles
Solid	has definite size and shape	book, table	very close together
Liquid	has definite volume	water, milk	farther apart
Gas	has no definite shape or volume	air, helium	very far apart

1. A substance with no definite shape or volume is a

Ⓐ solid.
Ⓑ liquid.
Ⓒ gas.
Ⓓ Not given

2. When a balloon is blown up, does the air inside change states?

Ⓕ Yes, because now it has a definite size and shape.
Ⓖ No, because it still does not have a definite size and shape. It has only taken the balloon's size and shape.
Ⓗ Yes, because now it has definite volume.
Ⓙ Not enough information

3. Which one describes changing the state of a piece of paper?

Ⓐ cutting it into four pieces
Ⓑ tearing it into many small pieces
Ⓒ folding it in half
Ⓓ Not given

4. When water boils and changes to a gas, what happens to the water particles?

Ⓕ They get farther apart.
Ⓖ They stay the same distance apart.
Ⓗ They get closer together.
Ⓙ Not given

STOP

Name Date

Science: Physical Science

Directions: Read the paragraph, and answer the questions. Choose the best answer.

Light and sound are both forms of energy. Light rays travel from their source in a straight line. Light can travel through some materials but not through others. **Opaque** materials block light from passing through them, but **transparent** materials such as glass allow light to pass through. Light **reflects**, or "bounces," off some objects such as mirrors. When light passes through other materials, it **refracts**, or bends. The lenses in a person's eyeglasses bend light and focus it so that the person can see better. Sound travels in waves, and it can pass through solids, liquids, and gases but not through a space with no air, called a vacuum. Sound is created when an object **vibrates**, or moves very quickly. Sometimes you can see the object vibrating, but other times it moves so quickly that you cannot see it moving. A sound can be described by its **pitch** and **volume**. Pitch is how high or low the sound is, and volume is how loud it is.

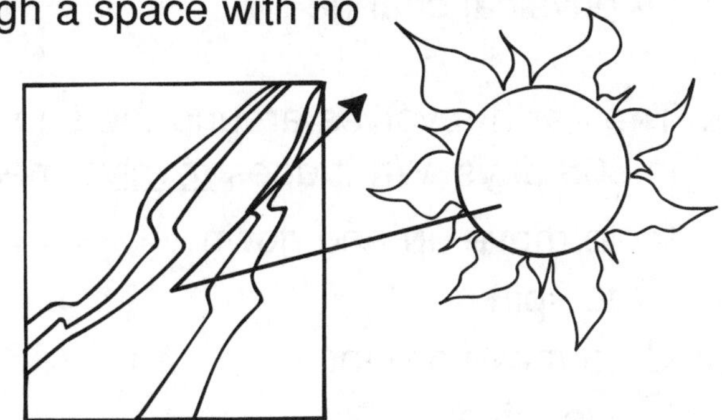

1. Sound waves can travel through solid objects, but ______ cannot.

Ⓐ pitch
Ⓑ reflection
Ⓒ light
Ⓓ energy

2. When light passes through a prism, the light is bent and separated into different colors. This is an example of

Ⓕ vibration.
Ⓖ refraction.
Ⓗ reflection.
Ⓙ volume.

3. Vibrate means

Ⓐ to bend.
Ⓑ to bounce off.
Ⓒ to move very quickly.
Ⓓ to block.

4. Why does sound not travel through outer space?

Ⓕ It is too far.
Ⓖ It is too cold.
Ⓗ It is dark.
Ⓙ It is a vacuum.

5. If you are told to reduce the volume of your radio, someone thinks it is too

Ⓐ loud.
Ⓑ quiet.
Ⓒ low.
Ⓓ Not given

6. Two forms of energy are

Ⓕ pitch and volume.
Ⓖ reflection and refraction.
Ⓗ light and sound.
Ⓙ waves and rays.

Name Date

Science: Sample Test

Directions: Read each question carefully. Then choose the best answer.

1. The polar bear's white fur is an example of _____.

Ⓐ adaptation.
Ⓑ amphibian.
Ⓒ reproduction.
Ⓓ physical change.

2. The earth revolves around the sun once in 365 days. What does revolve mean?

Ⓕ to move up and down
Ⓖ to spin
Ⓗ to move around
Ⓙ Not given

3. Light and sound are both forms of

Ⓐ precipitation.
Ⓑ tissue.
Ⓒ work.
Ⓓ energy.

4. Matter exists in _____ states.

Ⓕ all
Ⓖ three
Ⓗ seven
Ⓙ solid

5. You can see yourself in a mirror because of

Ⓐ refraction.
Ⓑ reproduction.
Ⓒ recycling.
Ⓓ reflection.

6. The _____ of a flowering plant contains both male and female parts.

Ⓕ flower
Ⓖ stem
Ⓗ root
Ⓙ leaf

7. Two examples of inner planets are

Ⓐ Venus and Saturn.
Ⓑ Earth and Pluto.
Ⓒ Uranus and Neptune.
Ⓓ Mars and Mercury.

8. Sawing a board into three pieces is an example of

Ⓕ physical change.
Ⓖ chemical change.
Ⓗ change of state.
Ⓙ a decomposer.

9. Two instruments that are used to measure weather are

Ⓐ a producer and a consumer.
Ⓑ an anemometer and a barometer.
Ⓒ a ray and a wave.
Ⓓ a thermometer and a simple machine.

GO ON

Name _______________ Date _______________

Science: Sample Test

Directions: Read each question carefully. Then choose the best answer.

10. Air, water, soil, and other organisms are all part of the _____ in which an organism lives.

Ⓕ forest Ⓖ ocean
Ⓗ environment Ⓙ tundra

11. The roots of plants grow underground and help hold the plant in the ground. They also

Ⓐ take in water and minerals.
Ⓑ make food from chlorophyll.
Ⓒ help the plant get air.
Ⓓ Not given

12. Plants and people look like their parents because of

Ⓕ germination. Ⓖ observation.
Ⓗ camouflage. Ⓙ heredity.

13. Lungs and gills are ways that animals take in

Ⓐ food. Ⓑ oxygen.
Ⓒ light. Ⓓ carbon dioxide.

14. In the winter, some animals migrate, while others

Ⓕ shed their fur.
Ⓖ take a vacation.
Ⓗ get cold.
Ⓙ Not given

15. Which one does not change by metamorphosis?

Ⓐ a butterfly
Ⓑ a human baby
Ⓒ a frog
Ⓓ a cricket

16. Human tissue is a group of cells that are all alike. An organ is a group of tissues that work together to do a job. A _____ is a group of organs that work together.

Ⓕ stomach
Ⓖ solution
Ⓗ spore
Ⓙ system

17. Animals are classified as vertebrates or invertebrates according to whether they have

Ⓐ a backbone.
Ⓑ a tail.
Ⓒ four legs.
Ⓓ lungs or gills.

18. A reptile is a cold-blooded animal that has a waterproof skin and lives on land. Which one is not a reptile?

Ⓕ snake
Ⓖ lizard
Ⓗ turtle
Ⓙ salamander

GO ON

Name Date

Science: Sample Test

Directions: Read each question carefully. Then choose the best answer.

19. Predators hunt for food, but ______ eat animals that are already dead.

Ⓐ prey
Ⓑ scavengers
Ⓒ meat eaters
Ⓓ Not given

20. A parasite lives inside or on another organism. Which one is not a parasite?

Ⓕ a flea
Ⓖ a tapeworm
Ⓗ head lice
Ⓙ a baby opossum

21. All organisms need space, water, and food. When one organism works against another to get what it needs, this is called

Ⓐ team sports.
Ⓑ survival.
Ⓒ a niche.
Ⓓ competition.

22. All of the following can change an ecosystem except

Ⓕ people.
Ⓖ drought or flood.
Ⓗ volcanic eruption.
Ⓙ an eclipse.

23. The smallest particle of matter is

Ⓐ an atom.
Ⓑ a cell.
Ⓒ an element.
Ⓓ Not given

24. A compound forms when two or more elements are combined chemically. Which is a compound?

Ⓕ dirt
Ⓖ lemonade
Ⓗ rust
Ⓙ carbon

25. Burning, forming new colors, and bubbling are all signs of

Ⓐ physical change.
Ⓑ mixtures forming.
Ⓒ metamorphosis.
Ⓓ chemical change.

26. Warm clothes that you wear to play in the snow are examples of

Ⓕ insulators.
Ⓖ conductors.
Ⓗ hibernation.
Ⓙ camouflage.

27. Electricity is a form of energy that travels in a

Ⓐ wave.
Ⓑ ray.
Ⓒ circuit.
Ⓓ vacuum.

Name Date

Social Studies: Geography

Directions: Read the question carefully. Choose the best answer.

Examples: **A.** A compass rose shows

Ⓐ distances.
● directions.
Ⓒ capitals.
Ⓓ highways.

Always read the question carefully. If you are not sure, first eliminate as many of the wrong answers as you can.

Practice

1. Which of the following are <u>not</u> physical features?

Ⓐ boundaries and state lines
Ⓑ islands and rivers
Ⓒ mountains and valleys
Ⓓ plains and hills

2. Which of these names a model of the earth?

Ⓕ compass rose
Ⓖ world map
Ⓗ globe
Ⓙ pictograph

3. Which of the following names a physical feature?

Ⓐ boat
Ⓑ bridge
Ⓒ river
Ⓓ factory

4. Which is the best description of a continent?

Ⓕ a point on a map
Ⓖ valleys, streams, and mountains
Ⓗ a physical globe
Ⓙ a large land mass

5. The imaginary line around the center of the earth is called the

Ⓐ hemisphere.
Ⓑ zone.
Ⓒ equator.
Ⓓ pole.

6. A body of land completely surrounded by water is a(n)

Ⓕ mountain.
Ⓖ river.
Ⓗ lake.
Ⓙ island.

Name Date

Social Studies: Geography

Directions: Read the question carefully. Choose the best answer.

7. A large body of salt water is a(n)

Ⓐ volcano.
Ⓑ ocean.
Ⓒ river.
Ⓓ equator.

8. Which one of the following is not a continent?

Ⓕ Australia
Ⓖ Africa
Ⓗ Asia
Ⓙ Alabama

9. An area of low land between mountains or hills is called a(n)

Ⓐ river.
Ⓑ volcano.
Ⓒ ocean.
Ⓓ valley.

10. A high landform with steep sides and a peak is called a(n)

Ⓕ mountain.
Ⓖ valley.
Ⓗ island.
Ⓙ plateau.

11. Which one of the following is not a country?

Ⓐ Canada
Ⓑ Mexico
Ⓒ Chicago
Ⓓ Germany

12. Which country is a neighbor of the United States to the south?

Ⓕ Canada
Ⓖ Mexico
Ⓗ China
Ⓙ Greenland

13. A high, flat-topped landform that rises steeply above surrounding land is called a(n)

Ⓐ island.
Ⓑ mountain.
Ⓒ desert.
Ⓓ plateau.

14. Which country is a neighbor of the United States to the north?

Ⓕ Canada
Ⓖ Mexico
Ⓗ China
Ⓙ Brazil

Name Date

Social Studies: Geography

Directions: Use the map of Crestville to choose the best answer to each question.

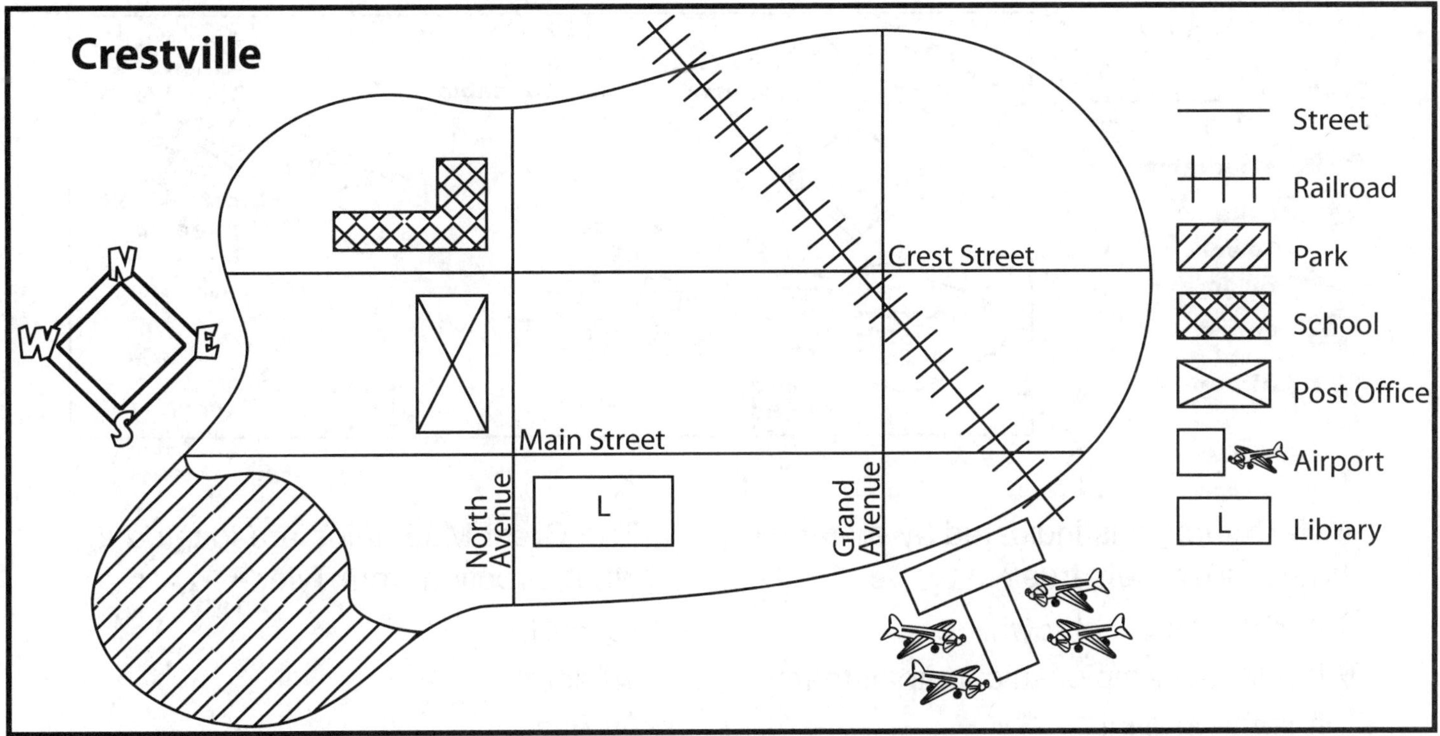

1. What is the name of the town on the map?
   Ⓐ Crest Street
   Ⓑ Grand Avenue
   Ⓒ Crestville
   Ⓓ North Avenue

2. In what direction would you travel to get from the school to the post office?
   Ⓕ north Ⓖ south
   Ⓗ east Ⓙ west

3. In what direction would you travel to get from the town park to the airport?
   Ⓐ north Ⓑ south
   Ⓒ east Ⓓ west

4. The school is located on what two streets?
   Ⓕ Crest Street and Grand Avenue
   Ⓖ North Avenue and Crest Street
   Ⓗ Crest Street and Main Street
   Ⓙ Main Street and Grand Avenue

5. The railroad crosses all of these streets <u>except</u>
   Ⓐ Crest Street.
   Ⓑ Main Street.
   Ⓒ Grand Avenue.
   Ⓓ North Avenue.

6. If you were at the school, what direction would you travel to get to the library?
   Ⓕ north Ⓖ south
   Ⓗ east Ⓙ west

Name Date

Social Studies: Geography

Directions: Study the map below. Then choose the best answer.

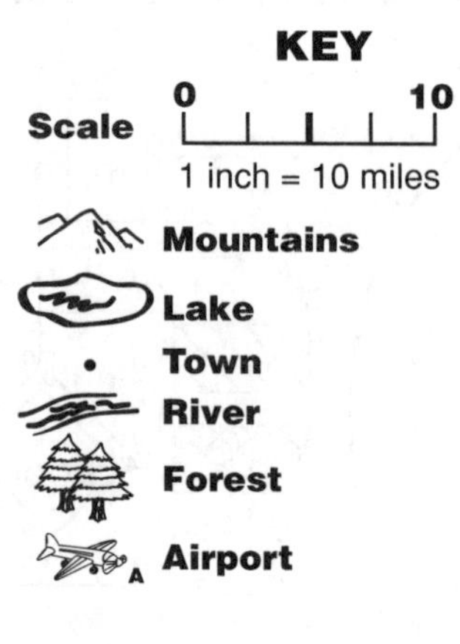

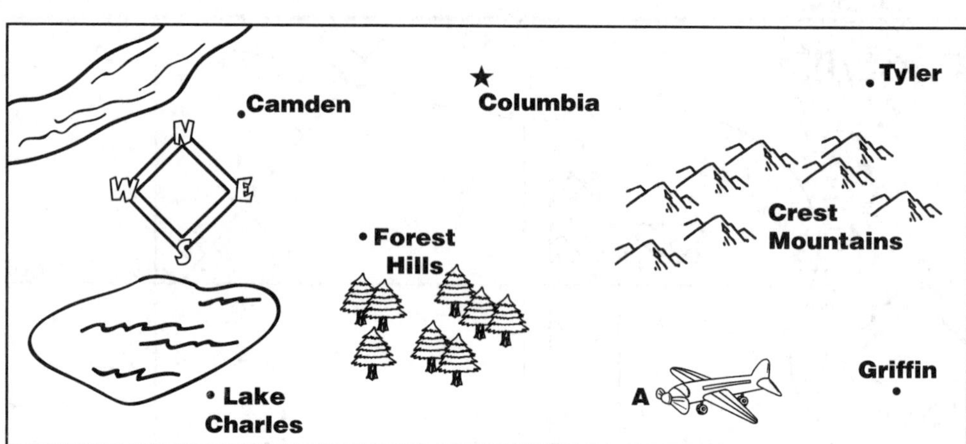

1. Since Columbia is indicated by a star, what is most likely true?
   Ⓐ It is the smallest town.
   Ⓑ It has a championship football team.
   Ⓒ It is the capital.
   Ⓓ It is the best city.

2. About how many miles is it between Camden and Forest Hills?
   Ⓕ 10 miles
   Ⓖ 15 miles
   Ⓗ 20 miles
   Ⓙ 25 miles

3. The airport is what direction from Lake Charles?
   Ⓐ north
   Ⓑ south
   Ⓒ east
   Ⓓ west

4. The Crest Mountains are located in what direction from Tyler?
   Ⓕ north
   Ⓖ south
   Ⓗ east
   Ⓙ west

5. About how many miles is it between the airport and Griffin?
   Ⓐ 10 miles
   Ⓑ 15 miles
   Ⓒ 20 miles
   Ⓓ 25 miles

6. Which town is located near water?
   Ⓕ Camden
   Ⓖ Griffin
   Ⓗ Tyler
   Ⓙ Columbia

STOP

Name Date

Social Studies: Geography

Directions: Use the map of Chessville to answer the questions. Choose the best answer.

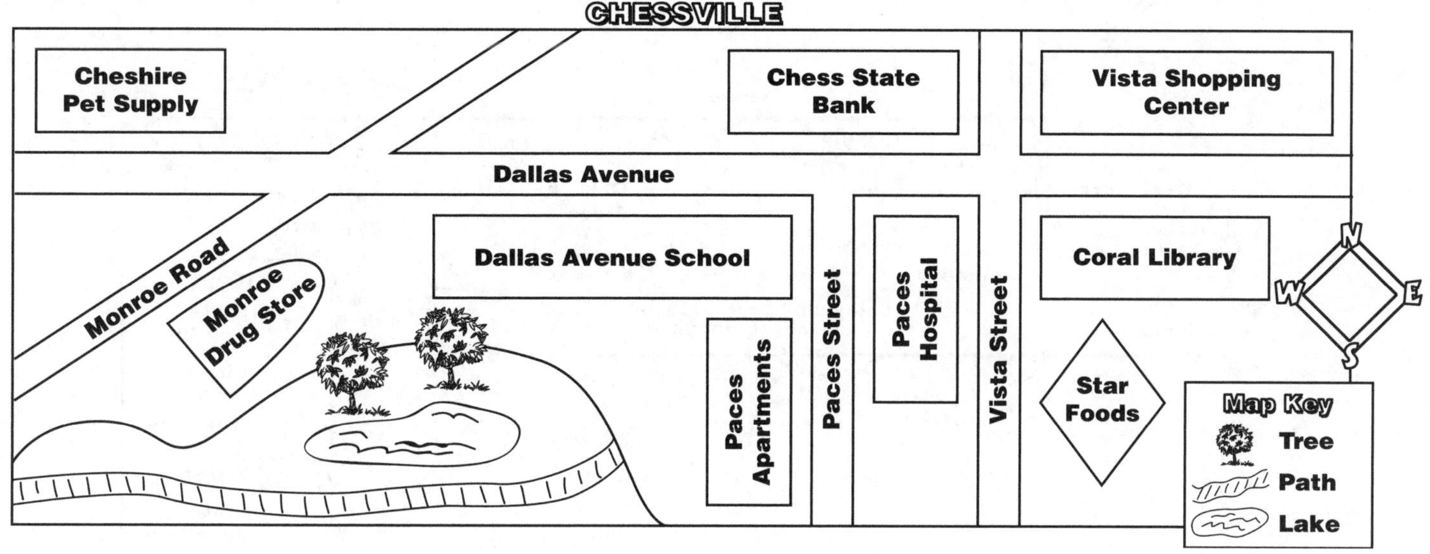

1. What is the name of the city on this map?
   Ⓐ Paces Park
   Ⓑ Chess
   Ⓒ Chessville
   Ⓓ Paces

2. What street or avenue is north of Paces Apartments?
   Ⓕ Dallas Avenue
   Ⓖ Vista Street
   Ⓗ Paces Street
   Ⓙ Not given

3. What is located directly across the street from the Coral Library?
   Ⓐ Cheshire Pet Supply
   Ⓑ Paces Apartments
   Ⓒ Dallas Avenue School
   Ⓓ Vista Shopping Center

4. What direction is Star Foods from the Coral Library?
   Ⓕ north
   Ⓖ south
   Ⓗ east
   Ⓙ west

5. Chess State Bank is located at the intersection of what two streets?
   Ⓐ Dallas Avenue and Vista Street
   Ⓑ Dallas Avenue and Monroe Road
   Ⓒ Vista Street and Paces Street
   Ⓓ Monroe Road and Paces Street

6. Cheshire Pet Supply is located on what street?
   Ⓕ Monroe Road
   Ⓖ Dallas Avenue
   Ⓗ Vista Street
   Ⓙ Paces Street

Name Date

Social Studies: Geography

Directions: Use the Tennessee map below to choose the best answer.

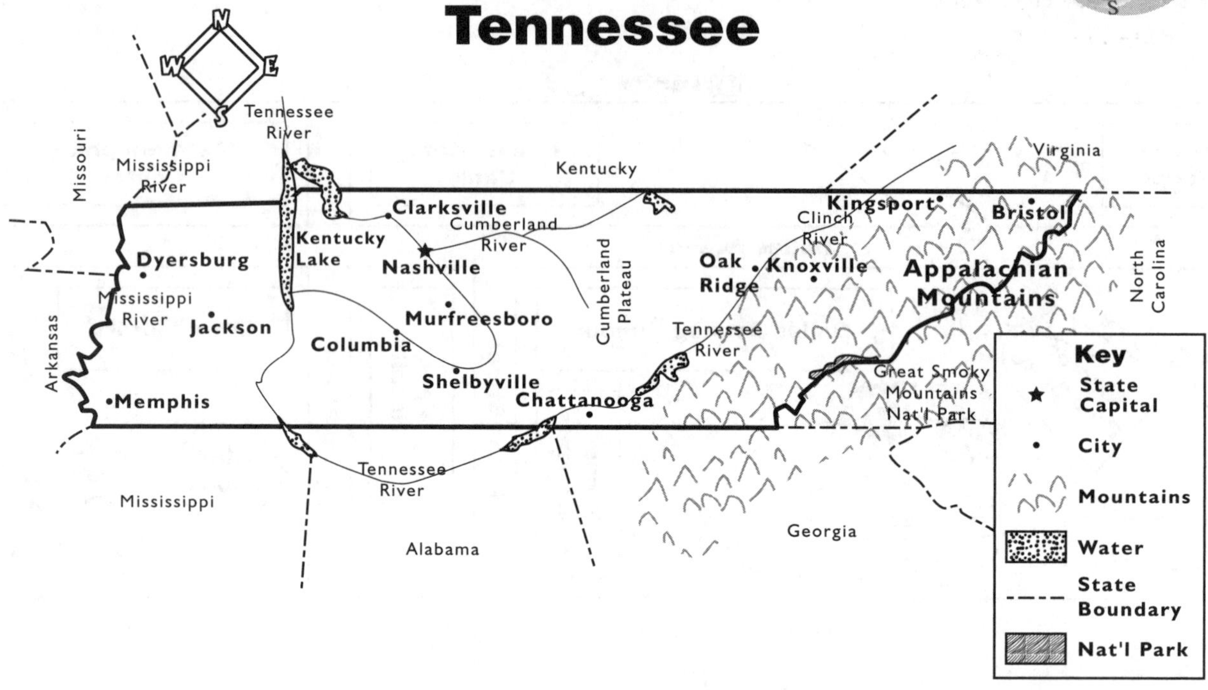

1. What is the capital city of Tennessee?

Ⓐ Chattanooga
Ⓑ Memphis
Ⓒ Knoxville
Ⓓ Nashville

2. What state is located north of Tennessee?

Ⓕ North Carolina
Ⓖ Georgia
Ⓗ Kentucky
Ⓙ Alabama

3. What is the mountain range that runs through eastern Tennessee?

Ⓐ Oak Ridge
Ⓑ Appalachian
Ⓒ Cumberland
Ⓓ Clinch

4. What state borders Tennessee on the east?

Ⓕ North Carolina
Ⓖ Missouri
Ⓗ Kentucky
Ⓙ Mississippi

5. What river forms the western border of Tennessee?

Ⓐ Cumberland
Ⓑ Mississippi
Ⓒ Kentucky
Ⓓ Clinch

6. Which direction would you go from Clarksville to Bristol?

Ⓕ north
Ⓖ south
Ⓗ east
Ⓙ west

Name Date

Social Studies: Geography

Directions: Use the map of the regions of the U.S. below to choose the best answer.

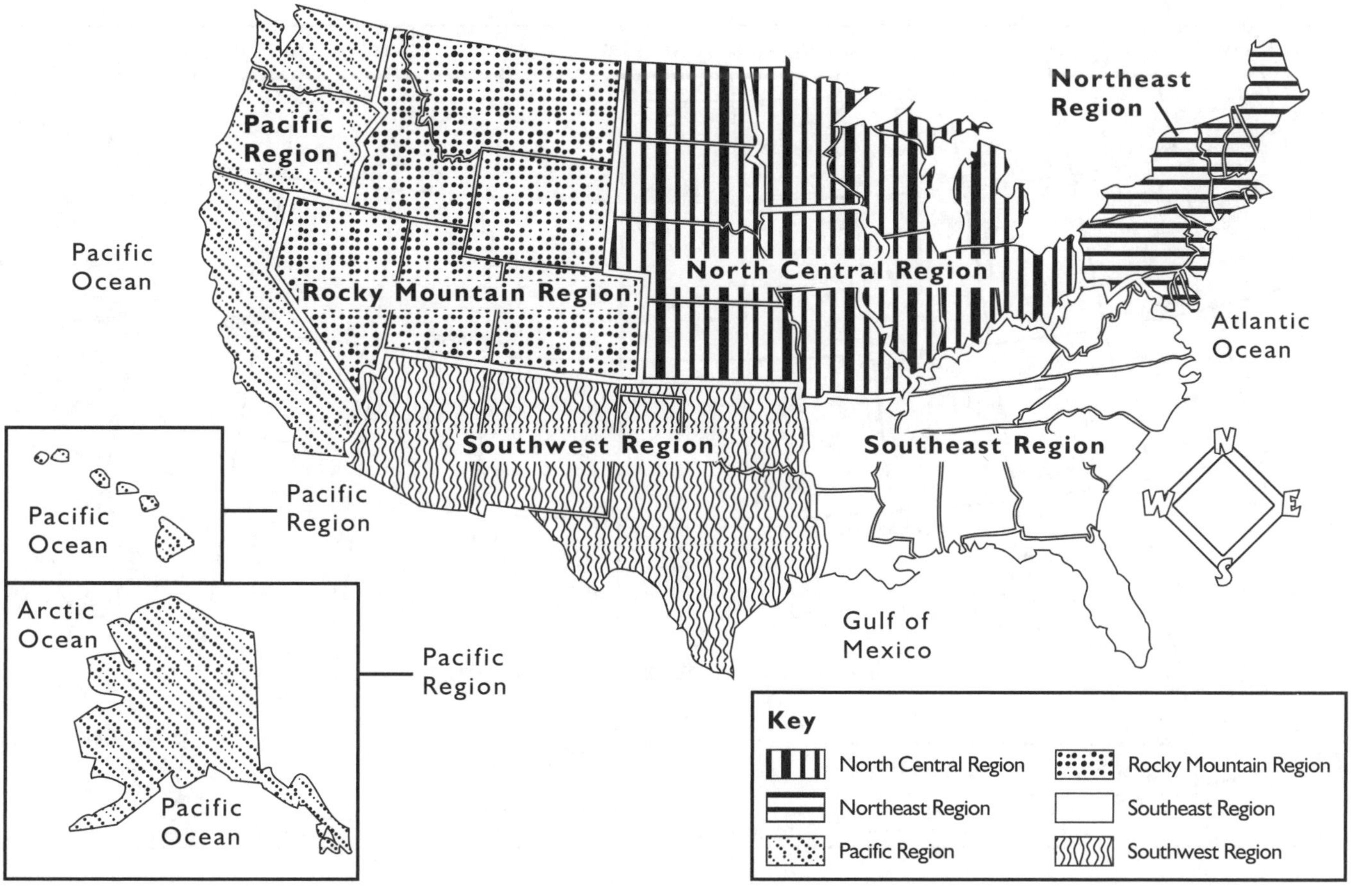

Pacific Region
Rocky Mountain Region
North Central Region
Northeast Region
Southwest Region
Southeast Region
Pacific Ocean
Atlantic Ocean
Gulf of Mexico
Arctic Ocean
N E S W

Key
- North Central Region
- Northeast Region
- Pacific Region
- Rocky Mountain Region
- Southeast Region
- Southwest Region

1. What is the largest state in the Southwest Region?
   Ⓐ Oklahoma
   Ⓑ Texas
   Ⓒ Arizona
   Ⓓ New Mexico

2. In which region is the state of Minnesota?
   Ⓕ Pacific Region
   Ⓖ Rocky Mountain Region
   Ⓗ Southwest Region
   Ⓙ North Central Region

3. How many states are in the Rocky Mountain Region?
   Ⓐ four
   Ⓑ five
   Ⓒ six
   Ⓓ seven

4. What is the smallest state in the Northeast Region?
   Ⓕ Maine
   Ⓖ Rhode Island
   Ⓗ Connecticut
   Ⓙ New Jersey

Name Date

Social Studies: Geography

Directions: Use the U.S. longitude and latitude map below to choose the best answer.

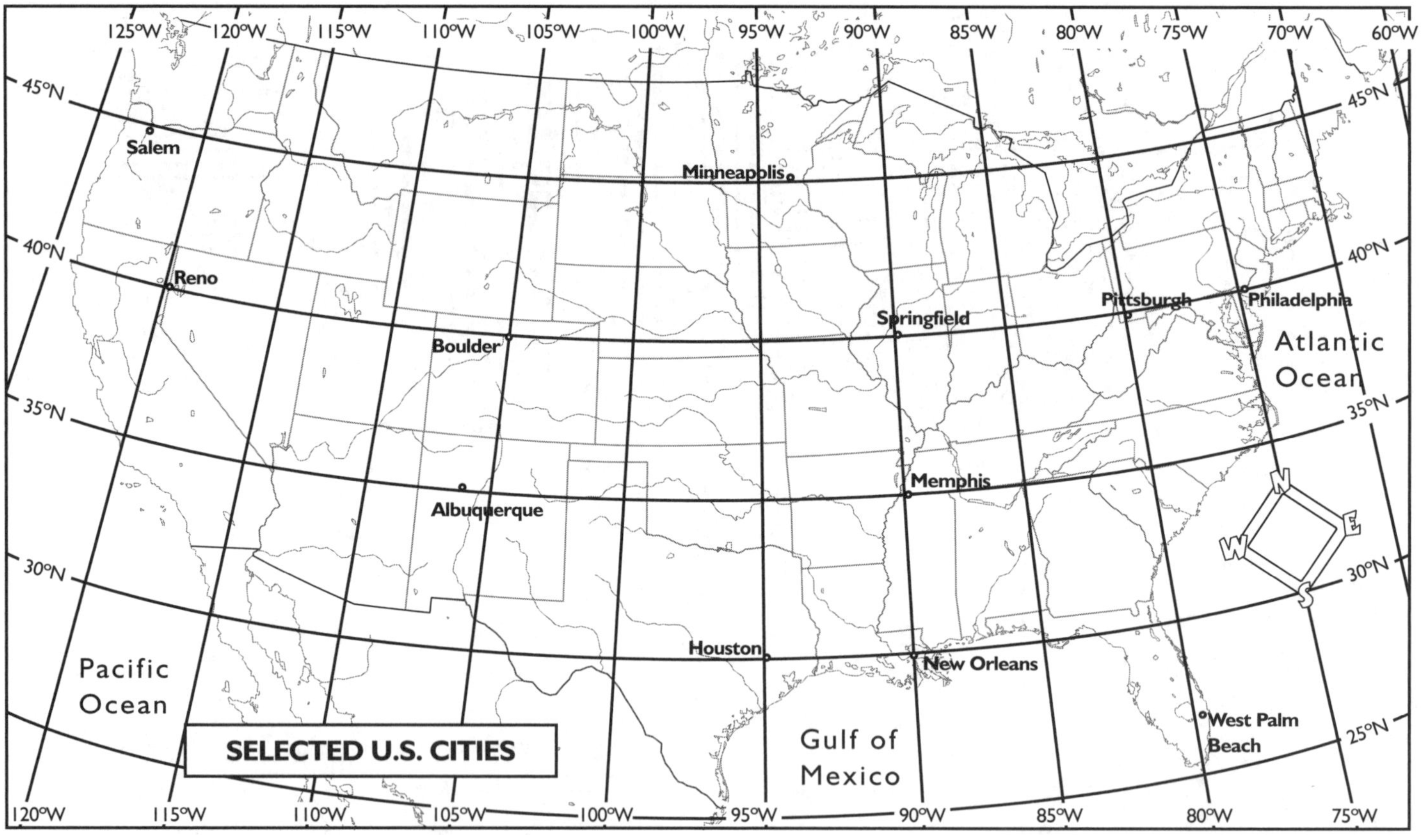

SELECTED U.S. CITIES

Salem
Minneapolis
Reno
Boulder
Springfield
Pittsburgh
Philadelphia
Albuquerque
Memphis
Houston
New Orleans
West Palm Beach
Pacific Ocean
Atlantic Ocean
Gulf of Mexico
125°W 120°W 115°W 110°W 105°W 100°W 95°W 90°W 85°W 80°W 75°W 70°W 60°W
45°N 40°N 35°N 30°N 25°N
120°W 115°W 110°W 105°W 100°W 95°W 90°W 85°W 80°W 75°W
N E S W

1. What city is located at 35°N, 90°W?

Ⓐ Albuquerque
Ⓑ Springfield
Ⓒ Memphis
Ⓓ New Orleans

2. Which two cities below are located on the line of latitude labeled 40°N?

Ⓕ Houston and New Orleans
Ⓖ Reno and Boulder
Ⓗ Albuquerque and Memphis
Ⓙ Salem and Minneapolis

3. What city is located at 40°N, 80°W?

Ⓐ Philadelphia
Ⓑ Minneapolis
Ⓒ West Palm Beach
Ⓓ Pittsburgh

4. Which two cities below are located on the line of longitude labeled 90°W?

Ⓕ New Orleans and Memphis
Ⓖ Houston and Minneapolis
Ⓗ Boulder and Albuquerque
Ⓙ New Orleans and Houston

Name Date

Social Studies: History

Directions: Carefully read each history question. Then choose the best answer.

1. The love of one's country is called what?

Ⓐ freedom
Ⓑ liberty
Ⓒ patriotism
Ⓓ government

2. A person who first explores and settles in a new area is called a

Ⓕ slave.
Ⓖ pioneer.
Ⓗ sheriff.
Ⓙ laborer.

3. The first people to live in the United States were the

Ⓐ Europeans.
Ⓑ colonists.
Ⓒ immigrants.
Ⓓ American Indians.

4. According to history, the first European who found America was

Ⓕ Ben Franklin.
Ⓖ Daniel Boone.
Ⓗ Christopher Columbus.
Ⓙ George Washington.

5. The birthday of the United States is celebrated on

Ⓐ January 1.
Ⓑ July 4.
Ⓒ September 3.
Ⓓ December 25.

6. The "Star-Spangled Banner" was written by whom?

Ⓕ Lewis and Clark
Ⓖ George Washington
Ⓗ Francis Scott Key
Ⓙ George Rogers Clark

7. The U.S. Constitution describes

Ⓐ how the city government must run its services.
Ⓑ how citizens should show their patriotism.
Ⓒ how the U.S. government is run.
Ⓓ how each state government runs its services.

8. The first president of the United States was

Ⓕ George Washington.
Ⓖ Ben Franklin.
Ⓗ Abraham Lincoln.
Ⓙ Thomas Jefferson.

Name Date

Social Studies: History

Directions: Carefully read each history question. Then choose the best answer.

9. On the U.S. flag, what symbols stand for the first 13 colonies?

Ⓐ red stripes
Ⓑ white stripes
Ⓒ stars
Ⓓ red and white stripes

10. Which was <u>not</u> one of the original 13 colonies?

Ⓕ Pennsylvania
Ⓖ Virginia
Ⓗ Ohio
Ⓙ Massachusetts

11. When was the Constitution written?

Ⓐ during the Civil War
Ⓑ after the Revolutionary War
Ⓒ before the Revolutionary War
Ⓓ Not given

12. Which bird is a symbol of the U.S. and its freedom?

Ⓕ owl
Ⓖ quail
Ⓗ turkey
Ⓙ eagle

13. Which war did the U.S. fight against Britain for independence?

Ⓐ War of 1812
Ⓑ Civil War
Ⓒ Revolutionary War
Ⓓ World War II

14. What was the first permanent English settlement in America?

Ⓕ Jamestown
Ⓖ Philadelphia
Ⓗ Boston
Ⓙ Plymouth

15. Who helped the Jamestown settlers?

Ⓐ Thomas Jefferson
Ⓑ George Washington
Ⓒ Squanto
Ⓓ Pocahontas

16. Of this list, who was U.S. president first?

Ⓕ John F. Kennedy
Ⓖ George Bush
Ⓗ Theodore Roosevelt
Ⓙ Abraham Lincoln

Name Date

Social Studies: History

Directions: Use the U.S. history timeline to answer the questions on page 134. Choose the best answer.

1492 Columbus reaches the coast of North America.

1565 St. Augustine, Florida, the oldest U.S. city, is settled.

1607 First English settlement is built in Jamestown.

1620 Pilgrims land at Plymouth Rock.

1770 Boston Massacre occurs.

1776 Declaration of Independence is written.

1789 George Washington is inaugurated.

Name Date

Social Studies: History

Directions: Use the U.S. history timeline on page 133 to answer the following questions. Choose the best answer.

1. The first English settlement in Jamestown took place in what year?

Ⓐ 1565
Ⓑ 1607
Ⓒ 1620
Ⓓ 1770

2. What year did the Pilgrims land at Plymouth Rock?

Ⓕ 1620
Ⓖ 1770
Ⓗ 1565
Ⓙ 1607

3. How many years after the Declaration of Independence was signed did Washington become president?

Ⓐ 3 years
Ⓑ 13 years
Ⓒ 23 years
Ⓓ Not given

4. According to the timeline, what year did Columbus reach the coast of North America?

Ⓕ 1492
Ⓖ 1565
Ⓗ 1620
Ⓙ 1770

5. What is considered the oldest settled city in the United States?

Ⓐ Plymouth Rock
Ⓑ Boston
Ⓒ St. Augustine
Ⓓ Jamestown

6. According to the timeline, what event happened in 1770?

Ⓕ George Washington was inaugurated.
Ⓖ The Declaration of Independence was signed.
Ⓗ The Boston Massacre occurred.
Ⓙ St. Augustine, Florida, was settled.

7. The first U.S. president, George Washington, was inaugurated in what year?

Ⓐ 1620
Ⓑ 1565
Ⓒ 1776
Ⓓ 1789

STOP

Name Date

Social Studies: History

Directions: Use the Christopher Columbus timeline to answer the questions on page 136. Choose the best answer.

1451 Born in Genoa, Italy.

1476 Shipwrecked off coast of Portugal.

1479 Married Dona Felipa; a year later son Diego was born.

1484 Asked for support for a voyage from King John II of Portugal.

1485 Went to Spain with son Diego; spent 7 years trying to get support from Queen Isabella I.

1492 Landed on an island in the Bahamas; named it San Salvador.

1493 Set sail on his second voyage to North America.

1496 Helped settle Santo Domingo, which became the first permanent European settlement in the New World.

Name Date

Social Studies: History

Directions: Use the Christopher Columbus timeline on page 135 to answer the following questions. Choose the best answer.

1. In what city was Christopher Columbus born?
   - Ⓐ San Salvador
   - Ⓑ Santo Domingo
   - Ⓒ Portugal
   - Ⓓ Genoa

2. How old was Columbus when he set sail on his second voyage?
   - Ⓕ 51 years old
   - Ⓖ 42 years old
   - Ⓗ 44 years old
   - Ⓙ 32 years old

3. From whom did Columbus try to get support for his voyages?
   - Ⓐ King John II
   - Ⓑ Dona Felipa
   - Ⓒ Santo Domingo
   - Ⓓ Diego I

4. What was the first permanent European settlement in the New World?
   - Ⓕ Genoa, Italy
   - Ⓖ Portugal
   - Ⓗ The Bahamas
   - Ⓙ Santo Domingo

5. Where was Christopher Columbus shipwrecked?
   - Ⓐ Italy
   - Ⓑ Portugal
   - Ⓒ Spain
   - Ⓓ Bahamas

6. In what year was Columbus's son born?
   - Ⓕ 1451
   - Ⓖ 1479
   - Ⓗ 1480
   - Ⓙ 1485

7. In what year was Santo Domingo settled?
   - Ⓐ 1493
   - Ⓑ 1496
   - Ⓒ 1492
   - Ⓓ 1484

8. If Columbus spent seven years trying to get support from Queen Isabella I, how old was he when she agreed to help him?
   - Ⓕ 41 years old
   - Ⓖ 43 years old
   - Ⓗ 31 years old
   - Ⓙ Not given

STOP

Name Date

Social Studies: History

Directions: Use the population graph to answer the following questions. Choose the best answer.

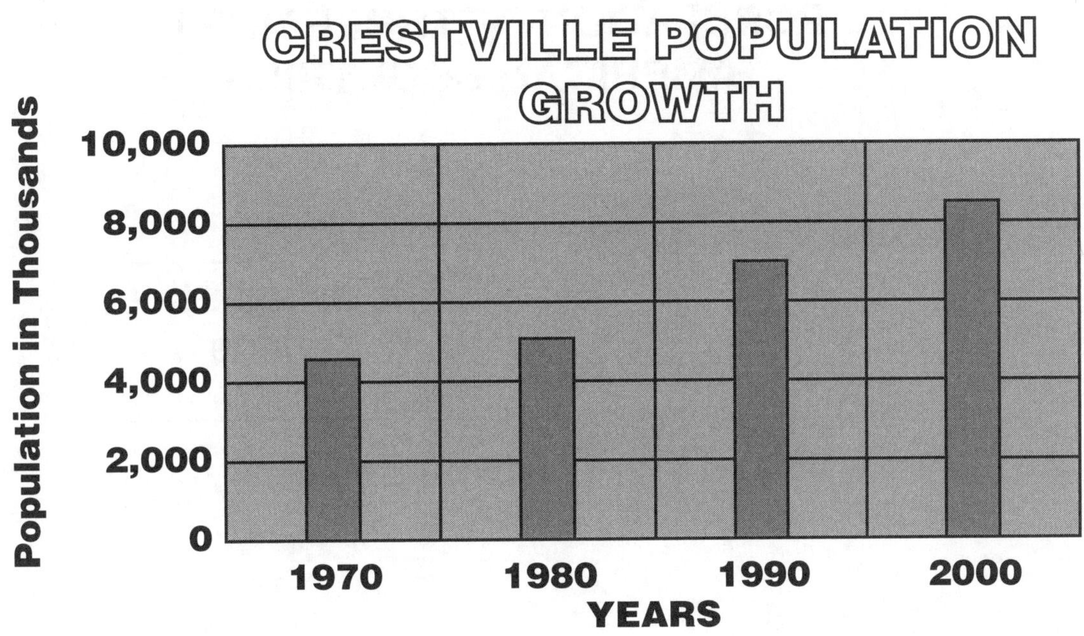

1. This population graph covers a span of how many years?
   Ⓐ 40 years
   Ⓑ 30 years
   Ⓒ 20 years
   Ⓓ Not given

2. What was the population of Crestville in 1980?
   Ⓕ 3,500
   Ⓖ 4,000
   Ⓗ 5,000
   Ⓙ 6,000

3. How much did the population grow from 1970 to 2000?
   Ⓐ 4,500
   Ⓑ 8,500
   Ⓒ 4,000
   Ⓓ Not given

4. When did the greatest population growth in Crestville occur?
   Ⓕ From 1970 to 1980
   Ⓖ From 1980 to 1990
   Ⓗ From 1990 to 2000
   Ⓙ Not given

Name Date

Social Studies: History

Directions: Use the population circle graph to answer the following questions. Choose the best answer.

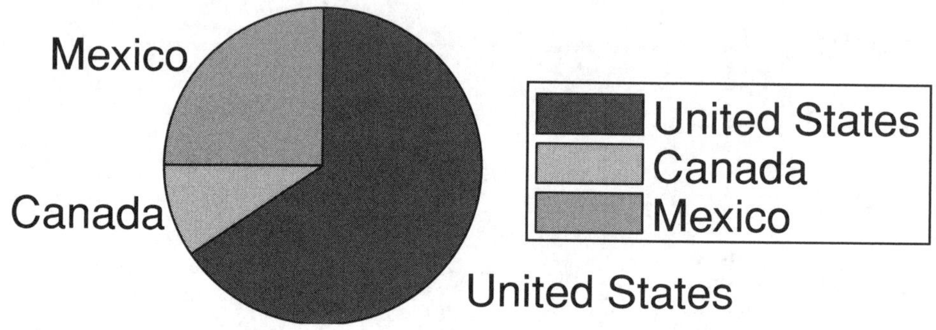

1. Of the following countries, which is not included in the circle graph?
   - Ⓐ Mexico
   - Ⓑ Greenland
   - Ⓒ United States
   - Ⓓ Canada

2. Which country has the smallest population?
   - Ⓕ Mexico
   - Ⓖ United States
   - Ⓗ Canada
   - Ⓙ Not given

3. According to the circle graph, the population of the U.S. is almost three times the population of
   - Ⓐ Mexico.
   - Ⓑ Canada.
   - Ⓒ Great Britain.
   - Ⓓ Not given

4. Listed in order from smallest to largest population, which country would come last?
   - Ⓕ Mexico
   - Ⓖ Canada
   - Ⓗ United States
   - Ⓙ Not given

STOP

Name Date

Social Studies: Government

Directions: Answer the following questions below. Choose the best answer.

1. What is the capital of the United States of America?
   Ⓐ New York City, New York
   Ⓑ Boston, Massachusetts
   Ⓒ Washington, D.C.
   Ⓓ Richmond, Virginia

2. Who is the leader of the United States?
   Ⓕ president
   Ⓖ governor
   Ⓗ mayor
   Ⓙ king

3. All of the following are major branches of the U.S. government except
   Ⓐ legislative.
   Ⓑ executive.
   Ⓒ federal.
   Ⓓ judicial.

4. Of what level are the president and Congress?
   Ⓕ national government
   Ⓖ state government
   Ⓗ local government
   Ⓙ Supreme Court

5. Why do people pay taxes?
   Ⓐ to pay for factories
   Ⓑ to pay for doctors and dentists
   Ⓒ to pay for police and schools
   Ⓓ to pay for department stores

6. A person who lives in a community is a(n)
   Ⓕ citizen.
   Ⓖ jury.
   Ⓗ forefather.
   Ⓙ army engineer.

7. How long is the U.S. president's term of office?
   Ⓐ 2 years
   Ⓑ 3 years
   Ⓒ 4 years
   Ⓓ 5 years

8. Which branch of government sees that the laws are interpreted fairly?
   Ⓕ legislative
   Ⓖ federal
   Ⓗ judicial
   Ⓙ executive

GO ON

Name Date

Social Studies: Government

Directions: Answer the questions below. Choose the best answer.

9. The head of the Army, Navy, and Air Force is
   - Ⓐ the U.S. president.
   - Ⓑ the governor of California.
   - Ⓒ the mayor of Atlanta.
   - Ⓓ the U.S. secretary of state.

10. Members of the Supreme Court are called
    - Ⓕ judges.
    - Ⓖ jurors.
    - Ⓗ justices.
    - Ⓙ senators.

11. Every state elects two ______ to the United States Congress.
    - Ⓐ mayors
    - Ⓑ governors
    - Ⓒ senators
    - Ⓓ Not given

12. United States senators are elected every ______ years.
    - Ⓕ four
    - Ⓖ five
    - Ⓗ six
    - Ⓙ eight

13. The United States Congress consists of representatives called senators and
    - Ⓐ congressmen.
    - Ⓑ electives.
    - Ⓒ citizens.
    - Ⓓ justices.

14. The main role of the United States Congress is to
    - Ⓕ make laws.
    - Ⓖ keep the peace.
    - Ⓗ conduct elections.
    - Ⓙ oversee transportation.

15. To elect a person to office means to
    - Ⓐ pay them.
    - Ⓑ vote for them.
    - Ⓒ like them.
    - Ⓓ honor them.

16. Money paid to support the government is called
    - Ⓕ interest.
    - Ⓖ fees.
    - Ⓗ fines.
    - Ⓙ taxes.

STOP

Name Date

Social Studies: Government

Directions: Use the bar graph below to answer the questions. Choose the best answer.

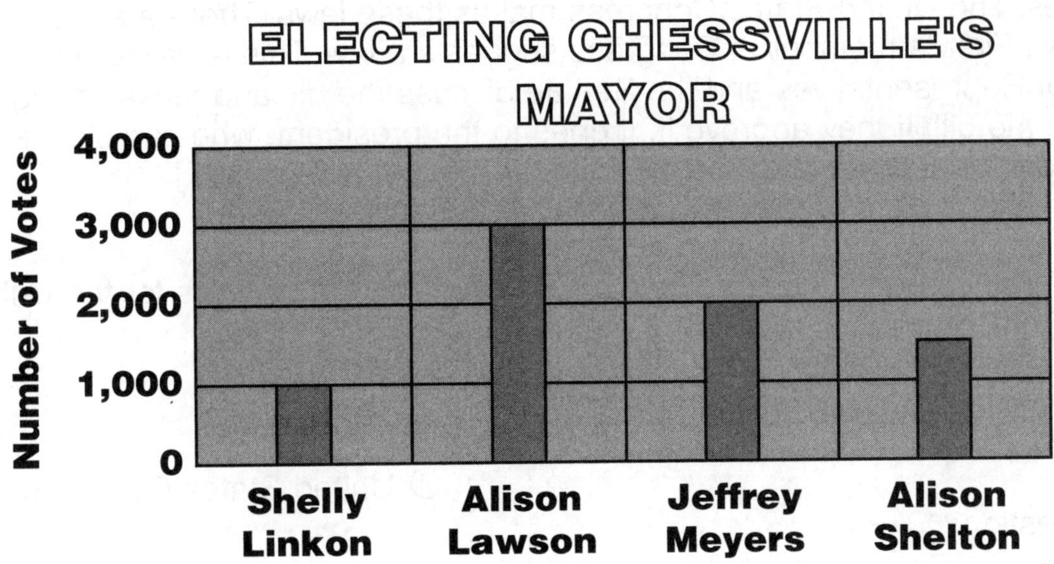

1. How many candidates ran for mayor in Chessville?
   Ⓐ four
   Ⓑ three
   Ⓒ two
   Ⓓ six

2. According to this graph, who was elected mayor of Chessville?
   Ⓕ Shelly Linkon
   Ⓖ Alison Lawson
   Ⓗ Jeffrey Meyers
   Ⓙ Alice Shelton

3. Which candidate received the second highest number of votes?
   Ⓐ Shelly Linkon
   Ⓑ Alison Lawson
   Ⓒ Alice Shelton
   Ⓓ Not given

4. How many votes did Shelly Linkon receive?
   Ⓕ 2,000
   Ⓖ 1,500
   Ⓗ 1,000
   Ⓙ 3,000

STOP

Name Date

Social Studies: Government

Directions: First, read the paragraph below. Then answer the following questions. Choose the best answer.

How Laws Are Made

Laws are made to help people know what is fair and how to act. They help keep everyone safe. Families, schools, and communities all have laws. Some laws are made for the whole United States. The United States Congress makes these laws. There are many steps to making a law. First, a member of Congress suggests a law. This is called a bill. Members of the House of Representatives and the Senate discuss the bill and make changes. Then they vote on the bill. If they approve it, it goes to the president, who can sign it into law or veto it if he does not agree with the bill.

1. A law that has been suggested by a member of Congress is called a(n)

Ⓐ act.
Ⓑ bill.
Ⓒ veto.
Ⓓ suggestion.

2. The word <u>veto</u> means

Ⓕ to approve.
Ⓖ to change.
Ⓗ to not approve.
Ⓙ to sign.

3. Who can suggest a law?

Ⓐ a school
Ⓑ a citizen
Ⓒ a member of Congress
Ⓓ a family

4. Who makes laws for the United States?

Ⓕ families
Ⓖ schools
Ⓗ communities
Ⓙ United States Congress

5. What is the last step in making a bill into a law?

Ⓐ A member of Congress suggests it.
Ⓑ The president signs it.
Ⓒ Members of Congress discuss it.
Ⓓ Members of Congress vote on it.

6. After a member of Congress suggests a law, what happens next?

Ⓕ It is voted on by Congress.
Ⓖ It is discussed by members of Congress.
Ⓗ It goes to the president.
Ⓙ Not given

Name Date

Social Studies: Economics

Directions: Answer the following questions about economic terms. Choose the best answer.

1. People who buy goods and services are called
   Ⓐ consumers.
   Ⓑ actors.
   Ⓒ producers.
   Ⓓ workers.

2. People who provide goods and services are
   Ⓕ consumers.
   Ⓖ workers.
   Ⓗ producers.
   Ⓙ competitors.

3. When one person tries to outdo another, it is called
   Ⓐ business.
   Ⓑ production.
   Ⓒ consumption.
   Ⓓ competition.

4. To buy something on credit means
   Ⓕ to pay cash.
   Ⓖ to buy it now and pay for it later.
   Ⓗ to earn it.
   Ⓙ to buy it on sale.

5. The money paid to the government to cover public services such as police and firemen is called
   Ⓐ taxes.
   Ⓑ credit.
   Ⓒ goods.
   Ⓓ resources.

6. A plan for spending money you earn is called a(n)
   Ⓕ expense.
   Ⓖ income.
   Ⓗ budget.
   Ⓙ account.

7. Money put away for emergencies is called
   Ⓐ budget.
   Ⓑ expenses.
   Ⓒ income.
   Ⓓ savings.

8. The cost of things you must have to live is called
   Ⓕ resources.
   Ⓖ expenses.
   Ⓗ budget.
   Ⓙ savings.

Name Date

Social Studies: Economics

Directions: Answer the following questions about economic terms. Choose the best answer.

9. The study of how people use resources is called
- Ⓐ business.
- Ⓑ economics.
- Ⓒ division of labor.
- Ⓓ social studies.

10. Natural resources include all of the following <u>except</u>
- Ⓕ water.
- Ⓖ trees.
- Ⓗ oil.
- Ⓙ stores.

11. A fireman is a _____ resource.
- Ⓐ natural
- Ⓑ free
- Ⓒ consumer
- Ⓓ human

12. The price of an item is
- Ⓕ how much it costs.
- Ⓖ how it is used.
- Ⓗ where it is sold.
- Ⓙ what it is made of.

13. People work to earn a(n)
- Ⓐ expense.
- Ⓑ income.
- Ⓒ dividend.
- Ⓓ opportunity.

14. The price of an item may be higher if it is
- Ⓕ plentiful.
- Ⓖ damaged.
- Ⓗ scarce.
- Ⓙ pretty.

15. The price of a item is determined by _____ and demand.
- Ⓐ income
- Ⓑ supply
- Ⓒ business
- Ⓓ scarcity

16. Giving all workers a different job to do is
- Ⓕ division of labor.
- Ⓖ earning a living.
- Ⓗ saving money.
- Ⓙ human resources.

17. Of the following, which one is not a factory job?
- Ⓐ building cars
- Ⓑ sewing clothes
- Ⓒ making toys
- Ⓓ being a dentist

STOP

Name Date

Social Studies: Economics

Directions: Read the paragraph about resources. Use the information in the paragraph and the map to answer the questions that follow. Choose the best answer.

Natural resources are found in nature and used by people. They are also used to make other products. Natural resources include air, water, plants, soil, and minerals. The resource map of Texas shows where oil, cattle, cotton, dairy farms, and sheep are most plentiful.

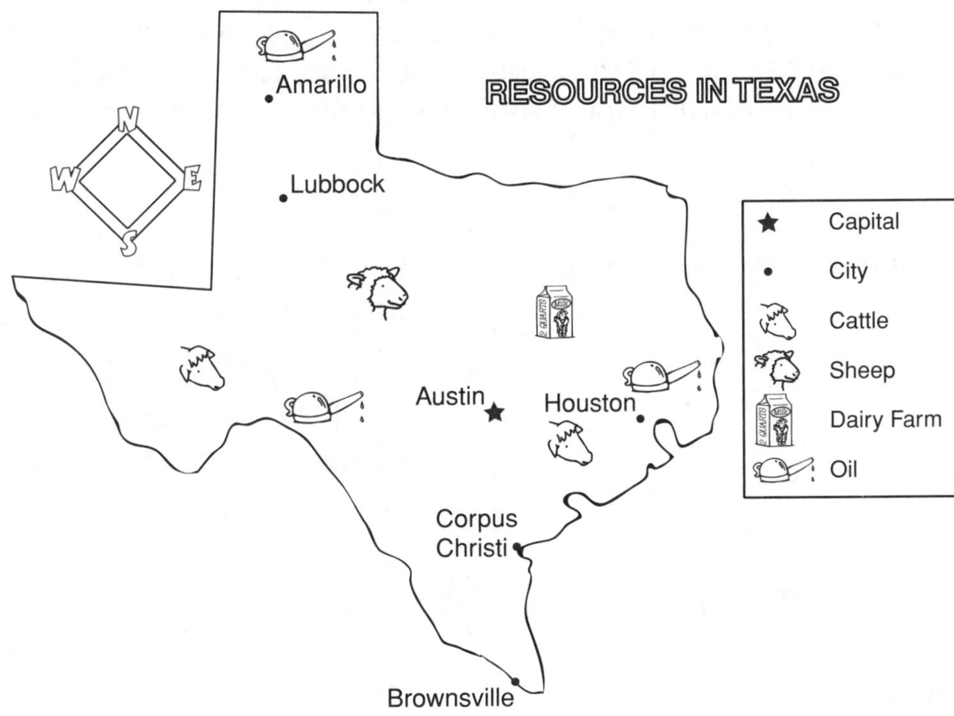

1. Which resource shown on the map cannot be replaced once it has all been used?
   Ⓐ cattle
   Ⓑ cotton
   Ⓒ oil
   Ⓓ sheep

2. Which one is not a resource found on this map of Texas?
   Ⓕ sheep
   Ⓖ oil
   Ⓗ fish
   Ⓙ dairy farms

3. How many cattle are produced in Texas?
   Ⓐ 2,000
   Ⓑ 3,000
   Ⓒ 30,000
   Ⓓ Not given

4. On the resource map what is represented by [oil symbol]?
   Ⓕ cattle
   Ⓖ oil
   Ⓗ sheep
   Ⓙ cotton

STOP

Name Date

Social Studies: Economics

Directions: Read the paragraph about resources and recycling. Use the information in the paragraph to answer the following questions. Choose the best answer.

Part of economics is studying the use of natural resources. Land, rocks, oil, iron, coal, water, plants, and animals are natural resources. Natural resources cannot be made by humans, but we use them to make many goods. Natural resources are also called raw materials. Some natural resources cannot be replaced if they are used up, so they should not be wasted. Fewer natural resources mean that fewer products can be made, and prices will go up. To try to prevent using all our natural resources, we recycle paper, glass, aluminum, and other materials from which more products can be made.

1. All of the following are natural resources except

Ⓐ land.
Ⓑ coal.
Ⓒ paper.
Ⓓ water.

2. Natural resources are materials that

Ⓕ are man-made.
Ⓖ occur in nature.
Ⓗ can be wasted.
Ⓙ will grow back.

3. We prevent natural resources from being used up by

Ⓐ wasting them.
Ⓑ making more raw materials.
Ⓒ recycling.
Ⓓ not using them.

4. One reason it is important to conserve natural resources is so that

Ⓕ prices will not go up.
Ⓖ we will not need to recycle.
Ⓗ we cannot make more products.
Ⓙ Not given

5. When we use natural resources to make goods, the resources are called

Ⓐ aluminum.
Ⓑ human resources.
Ⓒ raw materials.
Ⓓ factories.

STOP

Name Date

Social Studies: Economics

Directions: Use the pictograph to answer the following questions. Choose the best answer.

1. What type of book was the most popular?
   Ⓐ cookbooks
   Ⓑ fiction
   Ⓒ paperback
   Ⓓ children's

2. Which two types of books sold the same?
   Ⓕ cookbooks and nonfiction
   Ⓖ fiction and nonfiction
   Ⓗ paperback and children's
   Ⓙ None

3. How many children's books were sold?
   Ⓐ 70
   Ⓑ 80
   Ⓒ 90
   Ⓓ 100

4. Which type of book was the least popular?
   Ⓕ cookbooks
   Ⓖ biography
   Ⓗ fiction
   Ⓙ nonfiction

5. Which type of book sold half as many as cookbooks?
   Ⓐ nonfiction
   Ⓑ biography
   Ⓒ children's
   Ⓓ paperback

6. Which two categories combined sold as many books as the children's?
   Ⓕ paperback and biography
   Ⓖ nonfiction and cookbooks
   Ⓗ biography and fiction
   Ⓙ Not given

Name Date

Social Studies: Economics

Directions: Use Brandon's School Store to answer the following questions. Choose the best answer.

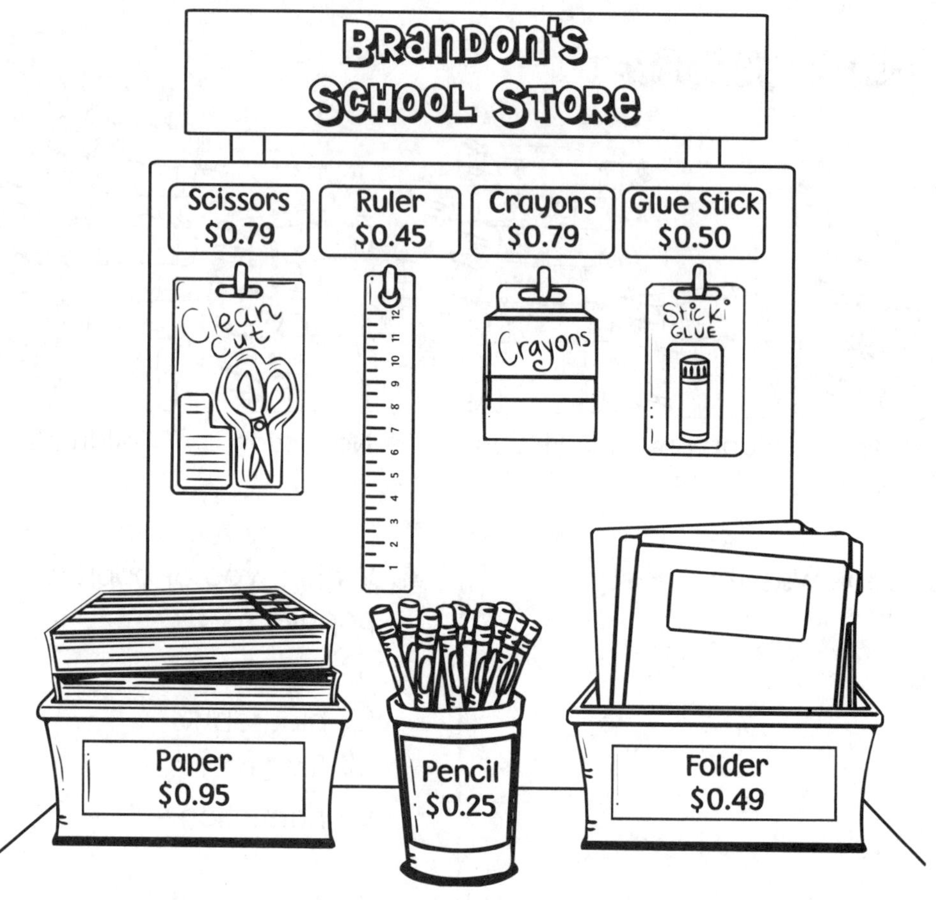

1. How many items are available in Brandon's School Store?
   - Ⓐ three
   - Ⓑ four
   - Ⓒ six
   - Ⓓ seven

2. What is the most expensive item in the school store?
   - Ⓕ crayons
   - Ⓖ scissors
   - Ⓗ folder
   - Ⓙ paper

3. Which two items are the same price?
   - Ⓐ crayons and scissors
   - Ⓑ glue stick and folder
   - Ⓒ folder and ruler
   - Ⓓ ruler and paper

4. If Leland bought paper, a pencil, and a ruler, how much change would he receive from $2.00?
   - Ⓕ $0.65
   - Ⓖ $0.45
   - Ⓗ $0.35
   - Ⓙ $0.25

STOP

Name Date

Social Studies: Sample Test

Directions: Read the question carefully. Then choose the best answer.

1. The imaginary line around the center of the earth is called the
   Ⓐ equator.
   Ⓑ hemisphere.
   Ⓒ zone.
   Ⓓ pole.

2. An area of lower land between hills or mountains is a(n)
   Ⓕ valley.
   Ⓖ island.
   Ⓗ river.
   Ⓙ bay.

3. Which of these names a model of the earth?
   Ⓐ compass rose
   Ⓑ world map
   Ⓒ globe
   Ⓓ pictograph

4. Which of the following are <u>not</u> physical features?
   Ⓕ mountains and valleys
   Ⓖ islands and rivers
   Ⓗ boundaries and state lines
   Ⓙ plains and hills

5. A body of land completely surrounded by water is
   Ⓐ a river.
   Ⓑ a valley.
   Ⓒ an ocean.
   Ⓓ an island.

6. A high, flat landform that rises steeply above surrounding land is called a(n)
   Ⓕ island.
   Ⓖ mountain.
   Ⓗ desert.
   Ⓙ plateau.

7. A large body of salt water is a(n)
   Ⓐ volcano.
   Ⓑ river.
   Ⓒ ocean.
   Ⓓ equator.

8. Which country is a neighbor of the United States to the south?
   Ⓕ Canada
   Ⓖ Mexico
   Ⓗ China
   Ⓙ Greenland

GO ON

Name Date

Social Studies: Sample Test

Directions: Read the question carefully. Then choose the best answer.

9. The first people to live in the United States were the

Ⓐ Europeans.
Ⓑ American Indians.
Ⓒ immigrants.
Ⓓ colonists.

10. When was the Constitution written?

Ⓕ after the Revolutionary War
Ⓖ during the Civil War
Ⓗ before the Revolutionary War
Ⓙ during World War I

11. What was the first permanent English settlement in America?

Ⓐ Boston
Ⓑ Philadelphia
Ⓒ Jamestown
Ⓓ Plymouth

12. Which branch of government sees that the laws are interpreted fairly?

Ⓕ executive
Ⓖ federal
Ⓗ judicial
Ⓙ legislative

13. The U.S. Congress's main role is to

Ⓐ conduct elections.
Ⓑ keep the peace.
Ⓒ make laws.
Ⓓ oversee transportation.

14. Money paid to support the government is called

Ⓕ interest.
Ⓖ fees.
Ⓗ fines.
Ⓙ taxes.

15. People who buy goods and services are called

Ⓐ actors.
Ⓑ consumers.
Ⓒ producers.
Ⓓ workers.

16. A plan for spending money you earn is called a(n)

Ⓕ budget.
Ⓖ expense.
Ⓗ income.
Ⓙ account.

17. The study of how people use resources is called

Ⓐ business.
Ⓑ division of labor.
Ⓒ economics.
Ⓓ social studies.

18. The price of an item may be higher if it is

Ⓕ damaged.
Ⓖ scarce.
Ⓗ plentiful
Ⓙ pretty.

Name Date

Social Studies: Sample Test

Directions: Use the map of Minnesota below to choose the best answer.

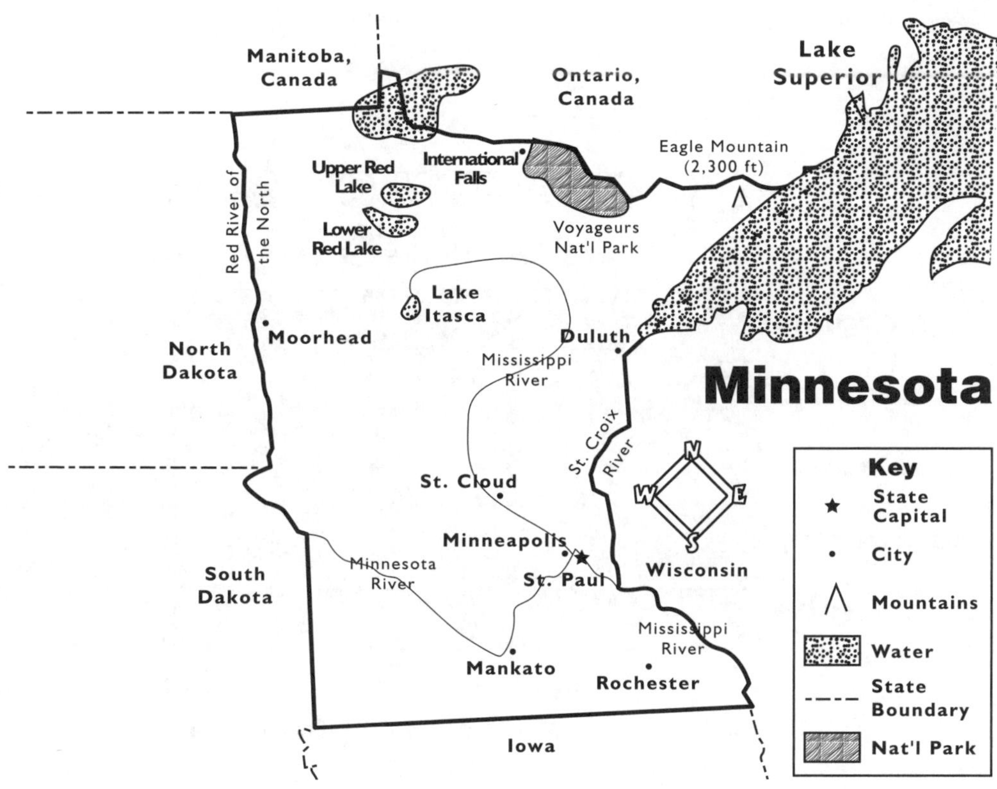

1. The capital of Minnesota is
   - Ⓐ Duluth.
   - Ⓑ Mankato.
   - Ⓒ St. Paul.
   - Ⓓ Rochester.

2. What state borders Minnesota on the east?
   - Ⓕ Iowa
   - Ⓖ Wisconsin
   - Ⓗ North Dakota
   - Ⓙ South Dakota

3. Which country borders Minnesota to the north?
   - Ⓐ Canada
   - Ⓑ North Dakota
   - Ⓒ South Dakota
   - Ⓓ Iowa

4. The large city near the southwestern end of Lake Superior is
   - Ⓕ International Falls.
   - Ⓖ Duluth.
   - Ⓗ Moorhead.
   - Ⓙ St. Cloud.

5. What river forms the northwestern border of Minnesota?
   - Ⓐ St. Croix
   - Ⓑ Red River
   - Ⓒ Mississippi
   - Ⓓ Superior

6. Which state borders Minnesota to the south?
   - Ⓕ Wisconsin
   - Ⓖ North Dakota
   - Ⓗ South Dakota
   - Ⓙ Iowa

STOP

Name Date

Social Studies: Sample Test

Directions: Use the "Population of American Colonies in 1700" graph below to choose the best answer.

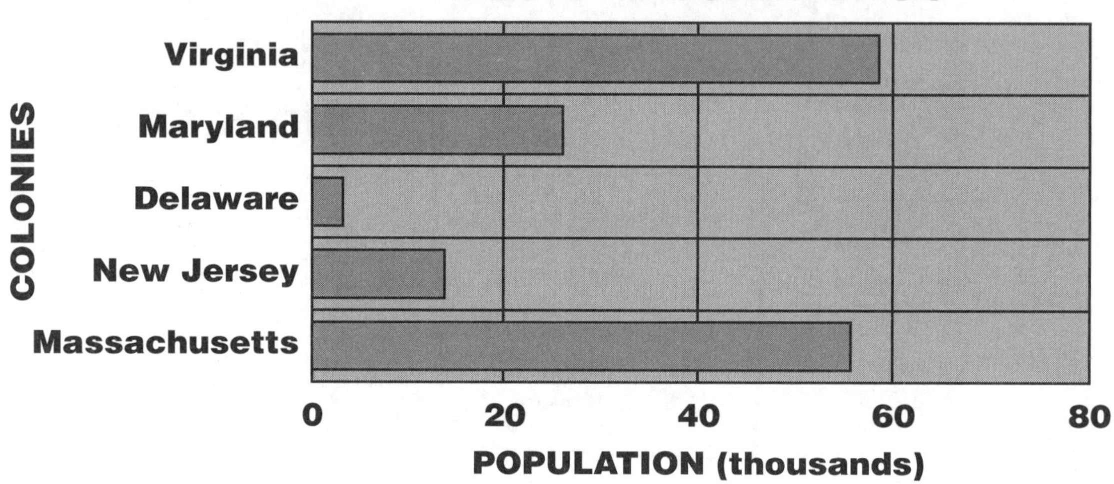

1. On the graph, how many colonies are represented?
   Ⓐ three
   Ⓑ four
   Ⓒ five
   Ⓓ six

2. According to this graph, which colony had the largest population in 1700?
   Ⓕ Massachusetts
   Ⓖ New Jersey
   Ⓗ Maryland
   Ⓙ Virginia

3. In 1700, Maryland's population was
   Ⓐ 25,000.
   Ⓑ 55,000.
   Ⓒ 18,000.
   Ⓓ 59,000.

4. The colony with the smallest population was
   Ⓕ Maryland.
   Ⓖ Delaware.
   Ⓗ New Jersey.
   Ⓙ Not given

STOP

Sample Answer Sheet

A B C D E
F G H J K
A B C D E
F G H J K
A B C D E
F G H J K
A B C D E
F G H J K
A B C D E
A B C D E
F G H J K
A B C D E
F G H J K
A B C D E
F G H J K
A B C D E
F G H J K
A B C D E
F G H J K
A B C D E
F G H J K
A B C D E
F G H J K
A B C D E
F G H J K
A B C D E
F G H J K
A B C D E
F G H J K
A B C D E
F G H J K
A B C D E
F G H J K
A B C D E
F G H J K
A B C D E
F G H J K
A B C D E
F G H J K
A B C D E

A B C D E
F G H J K
A B C D E
F G H J K
A B C D E
F G H J K
A B C D E
F G H J K
A B C D E
A B C D E
F G H J K
A B C D E
F G H J K
A B C D E
F G H J K
A B C D E
F G H J K
A B C D E
F G H J K
A B C D E
F G H J K
A B C D E
F G H J K
A B C D E
F G H J K
A B C D E
F G H J K
A B C D E
F G H J K
A B C D E
F G H J K
A B C D E
F G H J K
A B C D E
F G H J K
A B C D E
F G H J K
A B C D E
F G H J K
A B C D E

A B C D E
F G H J K
A B C D E
F G H J K
A B C D E
F G H J K
A B C D E
F G H J K
A B C D E
A B C D E
F G H J K
A B C D E
F G H J K
A B C D E
F G H J K
A B C D E
F G H J K
A B C D E
F G H J K
A B C D E
F G H J K
A B C D E
F G H J K
A B C D E
F G H J K
A B C D E
F G H J K
A B C D E
F G H J K
A B C D E
F G H J K
A B C D E
F G H J K
A B C D E
F G H J K
A B C D E
F G H J K
A B C D E
F G H J K
A B C D E

A B C D E
F G H J K
A B C D E
F G H J K
A B C D E
F G H J K
A B C D E
F G H J K
A B C D E
A B C D E
F G H J K
A B C D E
F G H J K
A B C D E
F G H J K
A B C D E
F G H J K
A B C D E
F G H J K
A B C D E
F G H J K
A B C D E
F G H J K
A B C D E
F G H J K
A B C D E
F G H J K
A B C D E
F G H J K
A B C D E
F G H J K
A B C D E
F G H J K
A B C D E
F G H J K
A B C D E
F G H J K
A B C D E
F G H J K
A B C D E

Answer Pages

Page 7

1. Ⓐ ● Ⓒ Ⓓ
2. Ⓕ Ⓖ ● Ⓙ
3. ● Ⓑ Ⓒ Ⓓ
4. Ⓕ Ⓖ Ⓗ ●
5. ● Ⓑ Ⓒ Ⓓ
6. Ⓕ ● Ⓗ Ⓙ

Page 8

1. Ⓐ ● Ⓒ Ⓓ
2. ● Ⓖ Ⓗ Ⓙ
3. Ⓐ ● Ⓒ Ⓓ
4. Ⓕ ● Ⓗ Ⓙ
5. ● Ⓑ Ⓒ Ⓓ
6. Ⓕ Ⓖ ● Ⓙ

Page 9

1. ● Ⓑ Ⓒ Ⓓ
2. Ⓕ ● Ⓗ Ⓙ
3. ● Ⓑ Ⓒ Ⓓ
4. Ⓕ ● Ⓗ Ⓙ
5. Ⓐ Ⓑ ● Ⓓ
6. Ⓕ Ⓖ ● Ⓙ

Page 10

1. Ⓐ Ⓑ Ⓒ ●
2. ● Ⓖ Ⓗ Ⓙ
3. Ⓐ ● Ⓒ Ⓓ
4. Ⓕ Ⓖ ● Ⓙ
5. ● Ⓑ Ⓒ Ⓓ
6. Ⓕ ● Ⓗ Ⓙ

Page 11

1. Ⓐ Ⓑ ● Ⓓ
2. ● Ⓖ Ⓗ Ⓙ
3. Ⓐ Ⓑ Ⓒ ●
4. Ⓕ Ⓖ ● Ⓙ
5. ● Ⓑ Ⓒ Ⓓ
6. Ⓕ Ⓖ ● Ⓙ

Page 12

1. Ⓐ Ⓑ ● Ⓓ
2. ● Ⓖ Ⓗ Ⓙ
3. Ⓐ ● Ⓒ Ⓓ
4. Ⓕ ● Ⓗ Ⓙ
5. ● Ⓑ Ⓒ Ⓓ
6. ● Ⓖ Ⓗ Ⓙ
7. Ⓐ Ⓑ Ⓒ ●
8. ● Ⓖ Ⓗ Ⓙ

Page 13

9. Ⓐ Ⓑ ● Ⓓ
10. ● Ⓖ Ⓗ Ⓙ
11. Ⓐ Ⓑ ● Ⓓ
12. Ⓕ ● Ⓗ Ⓙ
13. Ⓐ Ⓑ ● Ⓓ
14. Ⓕ Ⓖ Ⓗ ●
15. Ⓐ ● Ⓒ Ⓓ
16. Ⓕ Ⓖ ● Ⓙ
17. ● Ⓑ Ⓒ Ⓓ
18. Ⓕ Ⓖ Ⓗ ●

Page 14

1. ● Ⓑ Ⓒ Ⓓ
2. Ⓕ Ⓖ ● Ⓙ
3. Ⓐ ● Ⓒ Ⓓ

Page 15

4. ● Ⓖ Ⓗ Ⓙ
5. Ⓐ Ⓑ Ⓒ ●
6. Ⓕ Ⓖ ● Ⓙ

Page 16

1. ● Ⓑ Ⓒ Ⓓ
2. Ⓕ Ⓖ ● Ⓙ

Page 17

3. Ⓐ ● Ⓒ Ⓓ
4. Ⓕ ● Ⓗ Ⓙ
5. Ⓐ Ⓑ Ⓒ ●

Page 19

1. Ⓐ ● Ⓒ Ⓓ
2. Ⓕ Ⓖ ● Ⓙ
3. Ⓐ Ⓑ Ⓒ ●
4. Ⓕ Ⓖ Ⓗ ●
5. ● Ⓑ Ⓒ Ⓓ
6. Ⓕ Ⓖ ● Ⓙ
7. Ⓐ ● Ⓒ Ⓓ
8. Ⓕ ● Ⓗ Ⓙ

Page 20

1. Ⓐ Ⓑ ● Ⓓ
2. Ⓕ Ⓖ ● Ⓙ

Page 21

3. Ⓐ ● Ⓒ Ⓓ
4. Ⓕ Ⓖ Ⓗ ●
5. ● Ⓑ Ⓒ Ⓓ
6. Ⓕ Ⓖ ● Ⓙ

Page 22

1. Ⓐ ● Ⓒ Ⓓ
2. Ⓕ Ⓖ ● Ⓙ

Page 23

3. Ⓐ Ⓑ ● Ⓓ
4. ● Ⓖ Ⓗ Ⓙ
5. Ⓐ Ⓑ Ⓒ ●

Page 24

1. Ⓐ Ⓑ ● Ⓓ
2. Ⓕ Ⓖ Ⓗ ●

Page 25

3. ● Ⓑ Ⓒ Ⓓ
4. Ⓕ Ⓖ Ⓗ ●
5. ● Ⓑ Ⓒ Ⓓ
6. Ⓕ Ⓖ ● Ⓙ
7. Ⓐ ● Ⓒ Ⓓ
8. Ⓕ Ⓖ ● Ⓙ
9. Ⓐ Ⓑ ● Ⓓ
10. Ⓕ ● Ⓗ Ⓙ

Page 26

1. ● Ⓑ Ⓒ Ⓓ
2. Ⓕ Ⓖ ● Ⓙ
3. Ⓐ Ⓑ Ⓒ ●

Page 27

4. Ⓕ ● Ⓗ Ⓙ
5. Ⓐ Ⓑ Ⓒ ●
6. ● Ⓖ Ⓗ Ⓙ
7. Ⓐ Ⓑ Ⓒ ●
8. Ⓕ Ⓖ ● Ⓙ
9. Ⓐ ● Ⓒ Ⓓ

Page 28

1. Ⓐ Ⓑ Ⓒ ●
2. Ⓕ Ⓖ ● Ⓙ

Page 29

3. ● Ⓑ Ⓒ Ⓓ
4. Ⓕ Ⓖ Ⓗ ●
5. Ⓐ ● Ⓒ Ⓓ
6. Ⓕ ● Ⓗ Ⓙ
7. ● Ⓑ Ⓒ Ⓓ

Page 30

8. Ⓕ Ⓖ Ⓗ ●
9. Ⓐ Ⓑ ● Ⓓ
10. Ⓕ ● Ⓗ Ⓙ
11. Ⓐ Ⓑ ● Ⓓ
12. ● Ⓖ Ⓗ Ⓙ
13. Ⓐ ● Ⓒ Ⓓ

Page 31

14. Ⓕ Ⓖ Ⓗ ●
15. Ⓐ ● Ⓒ Ⓓ
16. ● Ⓖ Ⓗ Ⓙ
17. Ⓐ Ⓑ ● Ⓓ
18. ● Ⓖ Ⓗ Ⓙ
19. Ⓐ Ⓑ ● Ⓓ
20. Ⓕ Ⓖ Ⓗ ●
21. ● Ⓑ Ⓒ Ⓓ

Page 32

1. ● Ⓑ Ⓒ Ⓓ
2. Ⓕ ● Ⓗ Ⓙ
3. Ⓐ Ⓑ ● Ⓓ
4. Ⓕ Ⓖ ● Ⓙ
5. Ⓐ Ⓑ ● Ⓓ

Page 33

6. Ⓕ Ⓖ Ⓗ ●
7. Ⓐ Ⓑ ● Ⓓ
8. ● Ⓖ Ⓗ Ⓙ
9. Ⓐ ● Ⓒ Ⓓ
10. Ⓕ Ⓖ ● Ⓙ
11. ● Ⓑ Ⓒ Ⓓ
12. Ⓕ ● Ⓗ Ⓙ

Answer Pages

Page 34

1. ● Ⓑ Ⓒ Ⓓ
2. Ⓕ Ⓖ ● Ⓙ
3. Ⓐ ● Ⓒ Ⓓ
4. ● Ⓖ Ⓗ Ⓙ
5. Ⓐ Ⓑ Ⓒ ●
6. Ⓕ ● Ⓗ Ⓙ

Page 35

7. Ⓐ ● Ⓒ Ⓓ
8. ● Ⓖ Ⓗ Ⓙ
9. Ⓐ Ⓑ ● Ⓓ
10. ● Ⓖ Ⓗ Ⓙ
11. ● Ⓑ Ⓒ Ⓓ
12. Ⓕ ● Ⓗ Ⓙ
13. Ⓐ Ⓑ Ⓒ ●
14. Ⓕ ● Ⓗ Ⓙ

Page 36

1. Ⓐ ● Ⓒ Ⓓ
2. Ⓕ Ⓖ ● Ⓙ
3. Ⓐ ● Ⓒ Ⓓ
4. ● Ⓖ Ⓗ Ⓙ

Page 37

5. Ⓐ Ⓑ ● Ⓓ
6. ● Ⓖ Ⓗ Ⓙ
7. Ⓐ ● Ⓒ Ⓓ
8. Ⓕ Ⓖ ● Ⓙ
9. ● Ⓑ Ⓒ Ⓓ
10. Ⓕ Ⓖ Ⓗ ●
11. Ⓐ Ⓑ Ⓒ ●
12. Ⓕ ● Ⓗ Ⓙ
13. Ⓐ ● Ⓒ Ⓓ

Page 38

1. Ⓐ Ⓑ ● Ⓓ
2. ● Ⓖ Ⓗ Ⓙ
3. Ⓐ Ⓑ Ⓒ ●
4. Ⓕ ● Ⓗ Ⓙ
5. Ⓐ ● Ⓒ Ⓓ
6. Ⓕ Ⓖ Ⓗ ●
7. Ⓐ Ⓑ ● Ⓓ Ⓔ
8. Ⓕ ● Ⓗ Ⓙ Ⓚ
9. ● Ⓑ Ⓒ Ⓓ Ⓔ

Page 39

10. Ⓕ Ⓖ Ⓗ Ⓙ ●
11. Ⓐ ● Ⓒ Ⓓ Ⓔ
12. ● Ⓖ Ⓗ Ⓙ Ⓚ
13. ● Ⓑ Ⓒ Ⓓ Ⓔ
14. Ⓕ Ⓖ ● Ⓙ Ⓚ
15. Ⓐ ● Ⓒ Ⓓ Ⓔ
16. Ⓕ ● Ⓗ Ⓙ Ⓚ
17. Ⓐ Ⓑ Ⓒ Ⓓ ●
18. Ⓕ Ⓖ Ⓗ ● Ⓚ
19. Ⓐ Ⓑ Ⓒ ●
20. Ⓕ Ⓖ ● Ⓙ
21. Ⓐ ● Ⓒ Ⓓ
22. Ⓕ Ⓖ ● Ⓙ

Page 40

23. Ⓐ Ⓑ ● Ⓓ
24. Ⓕ Ⓖ ● Ⓙ
25. Ⓐ Ⓑ Ⓒ ●
26. Ⓕ ● Ⓗ Ⓙ
27. ● Ⓑ Ⓒ Ⓓ
28. Ⓕ Ⓖ ● Ⓙ
29. Ⓐ Ⓑ Ⓒ ●
30. Ⓕ ● Ⓗ Ⓙ
31. Ⓐ Ⓑ ● Ⓓ

Page 41

32. Ⓕ Ⓖ ● Ⓙ
33. Ⓐ ● Ⓒ Ⓓ
34. Ⓕ Ⓖ ● Ⓙ
35. Ⓐ ● Ⓒ Ⓓ
36. Ⓕ Ⓖ ● Ⓙ
37. ● Ⓑ Ⓒ Ⓓ
38. ● Ⓖ Ⓗ Ⓙ

Page 42

1. ● Ⓑ Ⓒ Ⓓ
2. Ⓕ Ⓖ ● Ⓙ
3. Ⓐ Ⓑ Ⓒ ●
4. Ⓕ Ⓖ Ⓗ ●
5. Ⓐ ● Ⓒ Ⓓ
6. Ⓕ Ⓖ Ⓗ ●

Page 43

7. ● Ⓑ Ⓒ Ⓓ
8. Ⓕ Ⓖ ● Ⓙ
9. Ⓐ Ⓑ Ⓒ ●
10. ● Ⓖ Ⓗ Ⓙ
11. Ⓐ ● Ⓒ Ⓓ

Page 44

12. Ⓕ ● Ⓗ Ⓙ Ⓚ
13. Ⓐ Ⓑ Ⓒ ● Ⓔ
14. Ⓕ Ⓖ Ⓗ Ⓙ ●
15. Ⓐ ● Ⓒ Ⓓ Ⓔ
16. Ⓕ Ⓖ ● Ⓙ Ⓚ
17. Ⓐ Ⓑ Ⓒ ● Ⓔ
18. ● Ⓖ Ⓗ Ⓙ Ⓚ
19. Ⓐ Ⓑ Ⓒ Ⓓ ●
20. Ⓕ Ⓖ Ⓗ ● Ⓚ
21. Ⓐ Ⓑ Ⓒ ●
22. Ⓕ ● Ⓗ Ⓙ
23. Ⓐ Ⓑ ● Ⓓ
24. ● Ⓖ Ⓗ Ⓙ
25. Ⓐ ● Ⓒ Ⓓ

Page 45

1. ● Ⓑ Ⓒ Ⓓ
2. Ⓕ Ⓖ Ⓗ ●
3. Ⓐ ● Ⓒ Ⓓ
4. Ⓕ Ⓖ ● Ⓙ
5. Ⓐ ● Ⓒ Ⓓ
6. Ⓕ Ⓖ ● Ⓙ
7. Ⓐ Ⓑ Ⓒ ●
8. ● Ⓖ Ⓗ Ⓙ

Page 46

1. Ⓐ Ⓑ ● Ⓓ
2. ● Ⓖ Ⓗ Ⓙ
3. Ⓐ Ⓑ Ⓒ ●
4. ● Ⓖ Ⓗ Ⓙ
5. Ⓐ ● Ⓒ Ⓓ
6. Ⓕ Ⓖ ● Ⓙ
7. Ⓐ ● Ⓒ Ⓓ
8. Ⓕ Ⓖ Ⓗ ●

Page 47

1. Ⓐ Ⓑ Ⓒ ●
2. ● Ⓖ Ⓗ Ⓙ
3. Ⓐ ● Ⓒ Ⓓ
4. Ⓕ Ⓖ Ⓗ ●
5. Ⓐ Ⓑ ● Ⓓ
6. ● Ⓖ Ⓗ Ⓙ
7. Ⓐ Ⓑ ● Ⓓ
8. Ⓕ ● Ⓗ Ⓙ

Page 48

1. Ⓐ ● Ⓒ Ⓓ
2. ● Ⓖ Ⓗ Ⓙ
3. Ⓐ Ⓑ ● Ⓓ
4. Ⓕ Ⓖ Ⓗ ●
5. Ⓐ Ⓑ Ⓒ ●
6. Ⓕ ● Ⓗ Ⓙ
7. ● Ⓑ Ⓒ Ⓓ
8. Ⓕ ● Ⓗ Ⓙ

Page 49

1. ● Ⓑ Ⓒ Ⓓ
2. Ⓕ Ⓖ Ⓗ ●
3. Ⓐ ● Ⓒ Ⓓ
4. Ⓕ Ⓖ Ⓗ ●
5. Ⓐ ● Ⓒ Ⓓ
6. ● Ⓖ Ⓗ Ⓙ
7. Ⓐ Ⓑ Ⓒ ●
8. Ⓕ ● Ⓗ Ⓙ

Page 50

1. ● Ⓑ Ⓒ Ⓓ
2. Ⓕ Ⓖ ● Ⓙ
3. Ⓐ Ⓑ Ⓒ ●
4. Ⓕ ● Ⓗ Ⓙ
5. Ⓐ Ⓑ Ⓒ ●
6. Ⓕ Ⓖ ● Ⓙ
7. Ⓐ Ⓑ Ⓒ ●
8. ● Ⓖ Ⓗ Ⓙ

Answer Pages

Page 51

1. ● Ⓑ Ⓒ Ⓓ
2. Ⓕ Ⓖ Ⓗ ●
3. Ⓐ Ⓑ ● Ⓓ
4. Ⓕ ● Ⓗ Ⓙ
5. ● Ⓑ Ⓒ Ⓓ
6. Ⓕ Ⓖ ● Ⓙ
7. Ⓐ ● Ⓒ Ⓓ
8. Ⓕ Ⓖ ● Ⓙ

Page 52

1. Ⓐ Ⓑ ● Ⓓ
2. Ⓕ ● Ⓗ Ⓙ

Page 53

1. Ⓐ ● Ⓒ Ⓓ
2. Ⓕ Ⓖ Ⓗ ●

Page 54

3. Ⓐ ● Ⓒ Ⓓ
4. Ⓕ Ⓖ ● Ⓙ
5. Ⓐ Ⓑ Ⓒ ●

Page 55

6. ● Ⓖ Ⓗ Ⓙ
7. Ⓐ Ⓑ Ⓒ ●
8. Ⓕ ● Ⓗ Ⓙ
9. Ⓐ ● Ⓒ Ⓓ

Page 56

1. Ⓐ ● Ⓒ Ⓓ
2. Ⓕ Ⓖ Ⓗ ●
3. Ⓐ ● Ⓒ Ⓓ
4. ● Ⓖ Ⓗ Ⓙ
5. Ⓐ Ⓑ Ⓒ ●
6. ● Ⓖ Ⓗ Ⓙ
7. Ⓐ Ⓑ ● Ⓓ
8. Ⓕ ● Ⓗ Ⓙ
9. Ⓐ Ⓑ Ⓒ ●

Page 57

10. Ⓕ Ⓖ Ⓗ ●
11. Ⓐ ● Ⓒ Ⓓ
12. Ⓕ ● Ⓗ Ⓙ
13. ● Ⓑ Ⓒ Ⓓ
14. Ⓕ Ⓖ Ⓗ ●
15. Ⓐ ● Ⓒ Ⓓ
16. ● Ⓖ Ⓗ Ⓙ
17. Ⓐ Ⓑ Ⓒ ●
18. Ⓕ Ⓖ ● Ⓙ
19. Ⓐ ● Ⓒ Ⓓ

Page 58

20. Ⓕ Ⓖ ● Ⓙ
21. Ⓐ ● Ⓒ Ⓓ
22. Ⓕ Ⓖ Ⓗ ●
23. ● Ⓑ Ⓒ Ⓓ

Page 59

1. Ⓐ Ⓑ ● Ⓓ
2. Ⓕ Ⓖ ● Ⓙ
3. Ⓐ Ⓑ Ⓒ ●
4. Ⓕ Ⓖ ● Ⓙ
5. ● Ⓑ Ⓒ Ⓓ
6. Ⓕ ● Ⓗ Ⓙ
7. Ⓐ ● Ⓒ Ⓓ
8. Ⓕ Ⓖ Ⓗ ●
9. Ⓐ Ⓑ ● Ⓓ
10. Ⓕ Ⓖ Ⓗ ●

Page 60

11. Ⓐ ● Ⓒ Ⓓ
12. ● Ⓖ Ⓗ Ⓙ
13. Ⓐ ● Ⓒ Ⓓ
14. Ⓕ Ⓖ ● Ⓙ
15. Ⓐ Ⓑ Ⓒ ●
16. Ⓕ Ⓖ ● Ⓙ
17. Ⓐ ● Ⓒ Ⓓ
18. Ⓕ Ⓖ ● Ⓙ
19. Ⓐ ● Ⓒ Ⓓ
20. Ⓕ Ⓖ ● Ⓙ
21. Ⓐ ● Ⓒ Ⓓ
22. Ⓕ Ⓖ ● Ⓙ

Page 61

23. Ⓐ Ⓑ ● Ⓓ
24. Ⓕ ● Ⓗ Ⓙ
25. ● Ⓑ Ⓒ Ⓓ
26. Ⓕ Ⓖ Ⓗ ●
27. Ⓐ Ⓑ ● Ⓓ
28. ● Ⓖ Ⓗ Ⓙ
29. Ⓐ Ⓑ ● Ⓓ

Page 62

1. Ⓐ ● Ⓒ Ⓓ
2. Ⓕ Ⓖ ● Ⓙ
3. Ⓐ Ⓑ Ⓒ ●
4. Ⓕ ● Ⓗ Ⓙ
5. Ⓐ Ⓑ ● Ⓓ
6. ● Ⓖ Ⓗ Ⓙ

Page 63

7. Ⓐ Ⓑ ● Ⓓ
8. Ⓕ ● Ⓗ Ⓙ
9. Ⓐ Ⓑ ● Ⓓ
10. Ⓕ Ⓖ Ⓗ ●
11. ● Ⓑ Ⓒ Ⓓ
12. Ⓕ Ⓖ Ⓗ ●
13. ● Ⓑ Ⓒ Ⓓ
14. Ⓕ Ⓖ ● Ⓙ

Page 64

15. Ⓐ Ⓑ Ⓒ ●
16. Ⓕ ● Ⓗ Ⓙ
17. Ⓐ Ⓑ Ⓒ ●
18. ● Ⓖ Ⓗ Ⓙ
19. Ⓐ Ⓑ ● Ⓓ
20. Ⓕ Ⓖ ● Ⓙ
21. Ⓐ Ⓑ ● Ⓓ

Page 65

1. Ⓐ Ⓑ Ⓒ ●
2. Ⓕ Ⓖ Ⓗ ●
3. Ⓐ ● Ⓒ Ⓓ
4. Ⓕ ● Ⓗ Ⓙ
5. ● Ⓑ Ⓒ Ⓓ
6. Ⓕ Ⓖ ● Ⓙ

Page 66

7. Ⓐ Ⓑ Ⓒ ●
8. Ⓕ ● Ⓗ Ⓙ
9. Ⓐ ● Ⓒ Ⓓ
10. ● Ⓖ Ⓗ Ⓙ
11. Ⓐ Ⓑ ● Ⓓ
12. Ⓕ Ⓖ ● Ⓙ
13. Ⓐ Ⓑ Ⓒ ●
14. ● Ⓖ Ⓗ Ⓙ
15. Ⓐ ● Ⓒ Ⓓ

Page 67

16. Ⓕ Ⓖ ● Ⓙ
17. ● Ⓑ Ⓒ Ⓓ
18. Ⓕ ● Ⓗ Ⓙ
19. Ⓐ ● Ⓒ Ⓓ
20. Ⓕ Ⓖ ● Ⓙ

Page 68

21. Ⓐ Ⓑ ● Ⓓ
22. ● Ⓖ Ⓗ Ⓙ
23. Ⓐ Ⓑ Ⓒ ●
24. Ⓕ ● Ⓗ Ⓙ
25. ● Ⓑ Ⓒ Ⓓ
26. Ⓕ Ⓖ Ⓗ ●
27. Ⓐ ● Ⓒ Ⓓ
28. Ⓕ Ⓖ ● Ⓙ

Page 69

1. Ⓐ Ⓑ ● Ⓓ
2. ● Ⓖ Ⓗ Ⓙ
3. Ⓐ Ⓑ ● Ⓓ
4. Ⓕ ● Ⓗ Ⓙ
5. Ⓐ Ⓑ Ⓒ ●
6. Ⓕ ● Ⓗ Ⓙ

Page 70

7. ● Ⓑ Ⓒ Ⓓ
8. Ⓕ ● Ⓗ Ⓙ
9. Ⓐ Ⓑ Ⓒ ●
10. ● Ⓖ Ⓗ Ⓙ
11. Ⓐ ● Ⓒ Ⓓ
12. Ⓕ Ⓖ ● Ⓙ
13. Ⓐ Ⓑ Ⓒ ●

Page 71

1. Ⓐ Ⓑ ● Ⓓ
2. Ⓕ Ⓖ ● Ⓙ
3. Ⓐ ● Ⓒ Ⓓ
4. Ⓕ ● Ⓗ Ⓙ
5. Ⓐ Ⓑ Ⓒ ●
6. Ⓕ Ⓖ ● Ⓙ

Answer Pages

Page 72

7. Ⓐ Ⓑ ● Ⓓ
8. ● Ⓖ Ⓗ Ⓙ
9. Ⓐ Ⓑ Ⓒ ●
10. Ⓕ ● Ⓗ Ⓙ
11. Ⓐ Ⓑ ● Ⓓ
12. Ⓕ Ⓖ Ⓗ ●
13. Ⓐ Ⓑ ● Ⓓ
14. Ⓕ Ⓖ Ⓗ ●
15. Ⓐ ● Ⓒ Ⓓ
16. ● Ⓖ Ⓗ Ⓙ

Page 73

17. Ⓐ Ⓑ Ⓒ ●
18. ● Ⓖ Ⓗ Ⓙ
19. Ⓐ Ⓑ ● Ⓓ
20. Ⓕ ● Ⓗ Ⓙ
21. Ⓐ Ⓑ Ⓒ ●
22. Ⓕ Ⓖ Ⓗ ●
23. Ⓐ Ⓑ ● Ⓓ
24. Ⓕ ● Ⓗ Ⓙ

Page 74

1. ● Ⓑ Ⓒ Ⓓ Ⓔ
2. Ⓕ ● Ⓗ Ⓙ Ⓚ
3. Ⓐ Ⓑ ● Ⓓ Ⓔ
4. Ⓕ Ⓖ Ⓗ ● Ⓚ
5. Ⓐ Ⓑ ● Ⓓ Ⓔ
6. Ⓕ Ⓖ Ⓗ ● Ⓚ

Page 75

7. Ⓐ ● Ⓒ Ⓓ Ⓔ
8. Ⓕ Ⓖ ● Ⓙ Ⓚ
9. ● Ⓑ Ⓒ Ⓓ Ⓔ
10. Ⓕ Ⓖ Ⓗ Ⓙ ●
11. Ⓐ Ⓑ ● Ⓓ Ⓔ
12. Ⓕ Ⓖ ● Ⓙ Ⓚ
13. ● Ⓑ Ⓒ Ⓓ Ⓔ
14. Ⓕ Ⓖ ● Ⓙ Ⓚ
15. Ⓐ Ⓑ Ⓒ ● Ⓔ
16. Ⓕ Ⓖ ● Ⓙ Ⓚ
17. Ⓐ ● Ⓒ Ⓓ Ⓔ
18. Ⓕ Ⓖ Ⓗ Ⓙ ●

Page 76

1. Ⓐ Ⓑ Ⓒ Ⓓ ●
2. ● Ⓖ Ⓗ Ⓙ Ⓚ
3. Ⓐ Ⓑ Ⓒ ● Ⓔ
4. Ⓕ ● Ⓗ Ⓙ Ⓚ
5. Ⓐ Ⓑ Ⓒ ● Ⓔ
6. Ⓕ Ⓖ Ⓗ Ⓙ ●

Page 77

7. Ⓐ ● Ⓒ Ⓓ Ⓔ
8. Ⓕ Ⓖ Ⓗ Ⓙ ●
9. Ⓐ Ⓑ Ⓒ ● Ⓔ
10. Ⓕ Ⓖ Ⓗ Ⓙ ●
11. ● Ⓑ Ⓒ Ⓓ Ⓔ
12. Ⓕ Ⓖ Ⓗ ● Ⓚ
13. Ⓐ Ⓑ ● Ⓓ Ⓔ
14. Ⓕ Ⓖ Ⓗ ● Ⓚ
15. Ⓐ ● Ⓒ Ⓓ Ⓔ
16. Ⓕ Ⓖ Ⓗ Ⓙ ●
17. Ⓐ ● Ⓒ Ⓓ Ⓔ
18. Ⓕ ● Ⓗ Ⓙ Ⓚ

Page 78

1. Ⓐ ● Ⓒ Ⓓ Ⓔ
2. Ⓕ ● Ⓗ Ⓙ Ⓚ
3. Ⓐ Ⓑ ● Ⓓ Ⓔ
4. Ⓕ Ⓖ ● Ⓙ Ⓚ
5. Ⓐ ● Ⓒ Ⓓ Ⓔ
6. ● Ⓖ Ⓗ Ⓙ Ⓚ
7. Ⓐ Ⓑ Ⓒ Ⓓ ●
8. Ⓕ Ⓖ Ⓗ ● Ⓚ

Page 79

9. Ⓐ Ⓑ Ⓒ ● Ⓔ
10. Ⓕ Ⓖ ● Ⓙ Ⓚ
11. ● Ⓑ Ⓒ Ⓓ Ⓔ
12. Ⓕ ● Ⓗ Ⓙ Ⓚ
13. Ⓐ Ⓑ ● Ⓓ Ⓔ
14. Ⓕ ● Ⓗ Ⓙ Ⓚ
15. Ⓐ Ⓑ ● Ⓓ Ⓔ
16. Ⓕ Ⓖ Ⓗ ● Ⓚ
17. Ⓐ Ⓑ Ⓒ Ⓓ ●
18. Ⓕ ● Ⓗ Ⓙ Ⓚ
19. Ⓐ Ⓑ Ⓒ ● Ⓔ
20. Ⓕ Ⓖ ● Ⓙ Ⓚ

Page 80

21. Ⓐ ● Ⓒ Ⓓ Ⓔ
22. Ⓕ ● Ⓗ Ⓙ Ⓚ
23. Ⓐ Ⓑ Ⓒ ● Ⓔ
24. Ⓕ ● Ⓗ Ⓙ Ⓚ
25. Ⓐ Ⓑ ● Ⓓ Ⓔ
26. ● Ⓖ Ⓗ Ⓙ Ⓚ
27. Ⓐ ● Ⓒ Ⓓ Ⓔ
28. Ⓕ Ⓖ Ⓗ ● Ⓚ
29. Ⓐ Ⓑ ● Ⓓ Ⓔ
30. Ⓕ ● Ⓗ Ⓙ Ⓚ
31. Ⓐ ● Ⓒ Ⓓ Ⓔ
32. Ⓕ Ⓖ Ⓗ Ⓙ ●

Page 81

33. Ⓐ Ⓑ Ⓒ ● Ⓔ
34. ● Ⓖ Ⓗ Ⓙ Ⓚ
35. ● Ⓑ Ⓒ Ⓓ Ⓔ
36. Ⓕ Ⓖ ● Ⓙ Ⓚ
37. Ⓐ Ⓑ ● Ⓓ Ⓔ
38. Ⓕ Ⓖ Ⓗ Ⓙ ●
39. ● Ⓑ Ⓒ Ⓓ Ⓔ
40. Ⓕ Ⓖ ● Ⓙ Ⓚ
41. Ⓐ ● Ⓒ Ⓓ Ⓔ
42. Ⓕ Ⓖ ● Ⓙ Ⓚ
43. Ⓐ ● Ⓒ Ⓓ Ⓔ
44. ● Ⓖ Ⓗ Ⓙ Ⓚ

Page 82

1. Ⓐ ● Ⓒ Ⓓ Ⓔ
2. Ⓕ Ⓖ Ⓗ ● Ⓚ
3. Ⓐ ● Ⓒ Ⓓ Ⓔ
4. Ⓕ Ⓖ Ⓗ ● Ⓚ
5. ● Ⓑ Ⓒ Ⓓ Ⓔ
6. Ⓕ ● Ⓗ Ⓙ Ⓚ
7. Ⓐ Ⓑ ● Ⓓ Ⓔ
8. Ⓕ Ⓖ Ⓗ ● Ⓚ
9. Ⓐ Ⓑ Ⓒ Ⓓ ●
10. Ⓕ ● Ⓗ Ⓙ Ⓚ

Page 83

11. Ⓐ Ⓑ ● Ⓓ Ⓔ
12. Ⓕ ● Ⓗ Ⓙ Ⓚ
13. Ⓐ ● Ⓒ Ⓓ Ⓔ
14. ● Ⓖ Ⓗ Ⓙ Ⓚ
15. Ⓐ Ⓑ ● Ⓓ Ⓔ
16. Ⓕ Ⓖ Ⓗ ● Ⓚ
17. Ⓐ Ⓑ ● Ⓓ Ⓔ
18. Ⓕ ● Ⓗ Ⓙ Ⓚ
19. Ⓐ Ⓑ Ⓒ ● Ⓔ
20. Ⓕ Ⓖ ● Ⓙ Ⓚ
21. ● Ⓑ Ⓒ Ⓓ Ⓔ
22. Ⓕ ● Ⓗ Ⓙ Ⓚ

Page 84

23. Ⓐ Ⓑ Ⓒ ● Ⓔ
24. Ⓕ ● Ⓗ Ⓙ Ⓚ
25. ● Ⓑ Ⓒ Ⓓ Ⓔ
26. Ⓕ Ⓖ ● Ⓙ Ⓚ
27. Ⓐ Ⓑ Ⓒ Ⓓ ●
28. Ⓕ Ⓖ Ⓗ ● Ⓚ
29. ● Ⓑ Ⓒ Ⓓ Ⓔ
30. Ⓕ Ⓖ ● Ⓙ Ⓚ
31. Ⓐ Ⓑ Ⓒ Ⓓ ●
32. Ⓕ ● Ⓗ Ⓙ Ⓚ
33. Ⓐ Ⓑ ● Ⓓ Ⓔ
34. Ⓕ ● Ⓗ Ⓙ Ⓚ

Page 85

1. Ⓐ Ⓑ ● Ⓓ
2. Ⓕ Ⓖ Ⓗ ●
3. Ⓐ Ⓑ Ⓒ ●
4. Ⓕ Ⓖ Ⓗ ●
5. Ⓐ ● Ⓒ Ⓓ

Page 86

6. ● Ⓖ Ⓗ Ⓙ
7. ● Ⓑ Ⓒ Ⓓ
8. Ⓕ Ⓖ Ⓗ ●
9. Ⓐ Ⓑ Ⓒ ●
10. ● Ⓖ Ⓗ Ⓙ
11. Ⓐ ● Ⓒ Ⓓ

Answer Pages

Page 87
1. Ⓐ ● Ⓒ Ⓓ
2. Ⓕ Ⓖ Ⓗ ●
3. Ⓐ Ⓑ ● Ⓓ
4. Ⓕ ● Ⓗ Ⓙ

Page 88
5. Ⓐ ● Ⓒ Ⓓ
6. Ⓕ Ⓖ Ⓗ ●
7. Ⓐ Ⓑ ● Ⓓ
8. ● Ⓖ Ⓗ Ⓙ
9. Ⓐ ● Ⓒ Ⓓ
10. Ⓕ Ⓖ Ⓗ ●
11. ● Ⓑ Ⓒ Ⓓ
12. Ⓕ Ⓖ ● Ⓙ

Page 89
13. Ⓐ ● Ⓒ Ⓓ
14. ● Ⓖ Ⓗ Ⓙ
15. Ⓐ Ⓑ Ⓒ ●
16. Ⓕ Ⓖ ● Ⓙ
17. Ⓐ ● Ⓒ Ⓓ
18. Ⓕ Ⓖ Ⓗ ●
19. Ⓐ Ⓑ ● Ⓓ
20. ● Ⓖ Ⓗ Ⓙ
21. ● Ⓑ Ⓒ Ⓓ
22. Ⓕ ● Ⓗ Ⓙ

Page 90
23. Ⓐ Ⓑ ● Ⓓ
24. Ⓕ ● Ⓗ Ⓙ
25. Ⓐ Ⓑ ● Ⓓ
26. Ⓕ ● Ⓗ Ⓙ
27. ● Ⓑ Ⓒ Ⓓ
28. Ⓕ Ⓖ Ⓗ ●
29. Ⓐ Ⓑ ● Ⓓ
30. ● Ⓖ Ⓗ Ⓙ

Page 91
1. Ⓐ Ⓑ Ⓒ ●
2. Ⓕ Ⓖ Ⓗ ●
3. ● Ⓑ Ⓒ Ⓓ
4. Ⓕ ● Ⓗ Ⓙ

Page 92
5. Ⓐ Ⓑ Ⓒ ●
6. ● Ⓖ Ⓗ Ⓙ
7. Ⓐ ● Ⓒ Ⓓ
8. Ⓕ Ⓖ ● Ⓙ
9. Ⓐ Ⓑ Ⓒ ●
10. Ⓕ Ⓖ Ⓗ ●
11. ● Ⓑ Ⓒ Ⓓ
12. ● Ⓖ Ⓗ Ⓙ

Page 93
13. Ⓐ ● Ⓒ Ⓓ
14. Ⓕ Ⓖ Ⓗ ●
15. Ⓐ ● Ⓒ Ⓓ
16. Ⓕ Ⓖ ● Ⓙ
17. Ⓐ ● Ⓒ Ⓓ
18. ● Ⓖ Ⓗ Ⓙ
19. Ⓐ Ⓑ ● Ⓓ

Page 94
20. Ⓕ ● Ⓗ Ⓙ
21. Ⓐ Ⓑ Ⓒ ●
22. Ⓕ Ⓖ ● Ⓙ
23. ● Ⓑ Ⓒ Ⓓ
24. ● Ⓖ Ⓗ Ⓙ
25. Ⓐ Ⓑ Ⓒ ●
26. Ⓕ Ⓖ ● Ⓙ

Page 95
1. Ⓐ Ⓑ Ⓒ ●
2. ● Ⓖ Ⓗ Ⓙ
3. Ⓐ ● Ⓒ Ⓓ
4. Ⓕ Ⓖ ● Ⓙ
5. Ⓐ Ⓑ Ⓒ ●

Page 96
6. ● Ⓖ Ⓗ Ⓙ
7. Ⓐ Ⓑ ● Ⓓ
8. Ⓕ ● Ⓗ Ⓙ
9. ● Ⓑ Ⓒ Ⓓ
10. Ⓕ ● Ⓗ Ⓙ
11. Ⓐ Ⓑ ● Ⓓ
12. Ⓕ Ⓖ ● Ⓙ
13. Ⓐ Ⓑ ● Ⓓ

Page 97
14. Ⓕ Ⓖ ● Ⓙ
15. Ⓐ Ⓑ Ⓒ ●
16. ● Ⓖ Ⓗ Ⓙ
17. Ⓐ Ⓑ Ⓒ ●
18. Ⓕ ● Ⓗ Ⓙ
19. Ⓐ ● Ⓒ Ⓓ
20. ● Ⓖ Ⓗ Ⓙ

Page 98
1. ● Ⓑ Ⓒ Ⓓ
2. Ⓕ Ⓖ Ⓗ ●
3. Ⓐ ● Ⓒ Ⓓ
4. ● Ⓖ Ⓗ Ⓙ

Page 99
5. Ⓐ Ⓑ Ⓒ ●
6. ● Ⓖ Ⓗ Ⓙ
7. ● Ⓑ Ⓒ Ⓓ
8. Ⓕ Ⓖ ● Ⓙ
9. ● Ⓑ Ⓒ Ⓓ
10. Ⓕ Ⓖ ● Ⓙ
11. Ⓐ ● Ⓒ Ⓓ
12. Ⓕ ● Ⓗ Ⓙ

Page 100
13. Ⓐ Ⓑ Ⓒ ●
14. ● Ⓖ Ⓗ Ⓙ
15. Ⓐ ● Ⓒ Ⓓ
16. Ⓕ ● Ⓗ Ⓙ
17. Ⓐ Ⓑ ● Ⓓ
18. Ⓕ Ⓖ Ⓗ ●
19. Ⓐ ● Ⓒ Ⓓ
20. Ⓕ Ⓖ Ⓗ ●

Page 101
21. Ⓐ Ⓑ Ⓒ ●
22. Ⓕ Ⓖ ● Ⓙ
23. ● Ⓑ Ⓒ Ⓓ
24. Ⓕ Ⓖ Ⓗ ●
25. Ⓐ Ⓑ ● Ⓓ
26. Ⓕ Ⓖ Ⓗ ●
27. Ⓐ ● Ⓒ Ⓓ

Page 102
28. ● Ⓖ Ⓗ Ⓙ
29. Ⓐ Ⓑ ● Ⓓ
30. Ⓕ Ⓖ Ⓗ ●
31. Ⓐ ● Ⓒ Ⓓ
32. ● Ⓖ Ⓗ Ⓙ
33. Ⓐ Ⓑ ● Ⓓ
34. Ⓕ ● Ⓗ Ⓙ

Page 103
35. Ⓐ ● Ⓒ Ⓓ
36. Ⓕ Ⓖ Ⓗ ●
37. Ⓐ Ⓑ Ⓒ ●
38. Ⓕ Ⓖ ● Ⓙ
39. Ⓐ Ⓑ Ⓒ ●
40. Ⓕ ● Ⓗ Ⓙ
41. Ⓐ ● Ⓒ Ⓓ
42. Ⓕ Ⓖ ● Ⓙ

Page 104
1. ● Ⓑ Ⓒ Ⓓ
2. Ⓕ Ⓖ ● Ⓙ
3. Ⓐ Ⓑ Ⓒ ●
4. Ⓕ ● Ⓗ Ⓙ
5. Ⓐ ● Ⓒ Ⓓ
6. Ⓕ Ⓖ ● Ⓙ
7. ● Ⓑ Ⓒ Ⓓ

Page 105
8. ● Ⓖ Ⓗ Ⓙ
9. Ⓐ Ⓑ Ⓒ ●
10. Ⓕ ● Ⓗ Ⓙ
11. Ⓐ Ⓑ Ⓒ ●
12. Ⓕ Ⓖ Ⓗ ●
13. Ⓐ Ⓑ ● Ⓓ
14. Ⓕ Ⓖ ● Ⓙ

Page 106
15. Ⓐ Ⓑ Ⓒ ●
16. Ⓕ Ⓖ ● Ⓙ
17. Ⓐ Ⓑ Ⓒ ●
18. Ⓕ ● Ⓗ Ⓙ
19. Ⓐ Ⓑ ● Ⓓ
20. ● Ⓖ Ⓗ Ⓙ
21. Ⓐ Ⓑ ● Ⓓ

Answer Pages

Page 107
22. Ⓕ Ⓖ ● Ⓙ
23. Ⓐ Ⓑ Ⓒ ●
24. Ⓕ ● Ⓗ Ⓙ
25. Ⓐ Ⓑ Ⓒ ●
26. Ⓕ Ⓖ Ⓗ ●
27. Ⓐ ● Ⓒ Ⓓ

Page 108
1. Ⓐ Ⓑ Ⓒ ●
2. ● Ⓖ Ⓗ Ⓙ
3. Ⓐ Ⓑ ● Ⓓ
4. Ⓕ ● Ⓗ Ⓙ
5. Ⓐ Ⓑ ● Ⓓ

Page 109
1. Ⓐ ● Ⓒ Ⓓ
2. Ⓕ Ⓖ Ⓗ ●
3. ● Ⓑ Ⓒ Ⓓ
4. Ⓕ Ⓖ ● Ⓙ

Page 110
1. Ⓐ Ⓑ ● Ⓓ
2. Ⓕ Ⓖ Ⓗ ●
3. ● Ⓑ Ⓒ Ⓓ
4. Ⓕ ● Ⓗ Ⓙ

Page 111
1. Ⓐ ● Ⓒ Ⓓ
2. Ⓕ Ⓖ ● Ⓙ
3. Ⓐ Ⓑ ● Ⓓ
4. ● Ⓖ Ⓗ Ⓙ

Page 112
1. Ⓐ ● Ⓒ Ⓓ
2. Ⓕ Ⓖ ● Ⓙ
3. Ⓐ Ⓑ Ⓒ ●
4. ● Ⓖ Ⓗ Ⓙ
5. Ⓐ Ⓑ ● Ⓓ
6. Ⓕ ● Ⓗ Ⓙ
7. Ⓐ Ⓑ Ⓒ ●
8. Ⓕ Ⓖ ● Ⓙ

Page 113
1. Ⓐ ● Ⓒ Ⓓ
2. Ⓕ Ⓖ Ⓗ ●
3. Ⓐ Ⓑ ● Ⓓ
4. ● Ⓖ Ⓗ Ⓙ

Page 114
1. Ⓐ Ⓑ ● Ⓓ
2. Ⓕ ● Ⓗ Ⓙ
3. ● Ⓑ Ⓒ Ⓓ
4. Ⓕ Ⓖ ● Ⓙ
5. Ⓐ Ⓑ Ⓒ ●
6. Ⓕ Ⓖ Ⓗ ●

Page 115
1. ● Ⓑ Ⓒ Ⓓ
2. Ⓕ ● Ⓗ Ⓙ
3. Ⓐ Ⓑ Ⓒ ●
4. Ⓕ Ⓖ ● Ⓙ
5. Ⓐ Ⓑ ● Ⓓ

Page 116
1. Ⓐ ● Ⓒ Ⓓ
2. ● Ⓖ Ⓗ Ⓙ
3. Ⓐ ● Ⓒ Ⓓ
4. Ⓕ Ⓖ ● Ⓙ

Page 117
1. ● Ⓑ Ⓒ Ⓓ
2. ● Ⓖ Ⓗ Ⓙ
3. Ⓐ Ⓑ Ⓒ ●
4. Ⓕ Ⓖ ● Ⓙ

Page 118
1. Ⓐ Ⓑ ● Ⓓ
2. Ⓕ ● Ⓗ Ⓙ
3. Ⓐ Ⓑ Ⓒ ●
4. ● Ⓖ Ⓗ Ⓙ

Page 119
1. Ⓐ Ⓑ ● Ⓓ
2. Ⓕ ● Ⓗ Ⓙ
3. Ⓐ Ⓑ ● Ⓓ
4. Ⓕ Ⓖ Ⓗ ●
5. ● Ⓑ Ⓒ Ⓓ
6. Ⓕ Ⓖ ● Ⓙ

Page 120
1. ● Ⓑ Ⓒ Ⓓ
2. Ⓕ Ⓖ ● Ⓙ
3. Ⓐ Ⓑ Ⓒ ●
4. Ⓕ ● Ⓗ Ⓙ
5. Ⓐ Ⓑ Ⓒ ●
6. ● Ⓖ Ⓗ Ⓙ
7. Ⓐ Ⓑ Ⓒ ●
8. ● Ⓖ Ⓗ Ⓙ
9. Ⓐ ● Ⓒ Ⓓ

Page 121
10. Ⓕ Ⓖ ● Ⓙ
11. ● Ⓑ Ⓒ Ⓓ
12. Ⓕ Ⓖ Ⓗ ●
13. Ⓐ ● Ⓒ Ⓓ
14. Ⓕ Ⓖ Ⓗ ●
15. Ⓐ ● Ⓒ Ⓓ
16. Ⓕ Ⓖ Ⓗ ●
17. ● Ⓑ Ⓒ Ⓓ
18. Ⓕ Ⓖ Ⓗ ●

Page 122
19. Ⓐ ● Ⓒ Ⓓ
20. Ⓕ Ⓖ Ⓗ ●
21. Ⓐ Ⓑ Ⓒ ●
22. Ⓕ Ⓖ Ⓗ ●
23. ● Ⓑ Ⓒ Ⓓ
24. Ⓕ Ⓖ ● Ⓙ
25. Ⓐ Ⓑ Ⓒ ●
26. ● Ⓖ Ⓗ Ⓙ
27. Ⓐ Ⓑ ● Ⓓ

Page 123
1. ● Ⓑ Ⓒ Ⓓ
2. Ⓕ Ⓖ ● Ⓙ
3. Ⓐ Ⓑ ● Ⓓ
4. Ⓕ Ⓖ Ⓗ ●
5. Ⓐ Ⓑ ● Ⓓ
6. Ⓕ Ⓖ Ⓗ ●

Page 124
7. Ⓐ ● Ⓒ Ⓓ
8. Ⓕ Ⓖ Ⓗ ●
9. Ⓐ Ⓑ Ⓒ ●
10. ● Ⓖ Ⓗ Ⓙ
11. Ⓐ Ⓑ ● Ⓓ
12. Ⓕ ● Ⓗ Ⓙ
13. Ⓐ Ⓑ Ⓒ ●
14. ● Ⓖ Ⓗ Ⓙ

Page 125
1. Ⓐ Ⓑ ● Ⓓ
2. Ⓕ ● Ⓗ Ⓙ
3. Ⓐ Ⓑ ● Ⓓ
4. Ⓕ ● Ⓗ Ⓙ
5. Ⓐ Ⓑ Ⓒ ●
6. Ⓕ ● Ⓗ Ⓙ

Page 126
1. Ⓐ Ⓑ ● Ⓓ
2. ● Ⓖ Ⓗ Ⓙ
3. Ⓐ Ⓑ ● Ⓓ
4. Ⓕ ● Ⓗ Ⓙ
5. Ⓐ ● Ⓒ Ⓓ
6. ● Ⓖ Ⓗ Ⓙ

Page 127
1. Ⓐ Ⓑ ● Ⓓ
2. ● Ⓖ Ⓗ Ⓙ
3. Ⓐ Ⓑ Ⓒ ●
4. Ⓕ ● Ⓗ Ⓙ
5. ● Ⓑ Ⓒ Ⓓ
6. Ⓕ ● Ⓗ Ⓙ

Page 128
1. Ⓐ Ⓑ Ⓒ ●
2. Ⓕ Ⓖ ● Ⓙ
3. Ⓐ ● Ⓒ Ⓓ
4. ● Ⓖ Ⓗ Ⓙ
5. Ⓐ ● Ⓒ Ⓓ
6. Ⓕ Ⓖ ● Ⓙ

Answer Pages

Page 129

1. Ⓐ ● Ⓒ Ⓓ
2. Ⓕ Ⓖ Ⓗ ●
3. Ⓐ Ⓑ ● Ⓓ
4. Ⓕ ● Ⓗ Ⓙ

Page 130

1. Ⓐ Ⓑ ● Ⓓ
2. Ⓕ ● Ⓗ Ⓙ
3. Ⓐ Ⓑ Ⓒ ●
4. ● Ⓖ Ⓗ Ⓙ

Page 131

1. Ⓐ Ⓑ ● Ⓓ
2. Ⓕ ● Ⓗ Ⓙ
3. Ⓐ Ⓑ Ⓒ ●
4. Ⓕ Ⓖ ● Ⓙ
5. Ⓐ ● Ⓒ Ⓓ
6. Ⓕ Ⓖ ● Ⓙ
7. Ⓐ Ⓑ ● Ⓓ
8. ● Ⓖ Ⓗ Ⓙ

Page 132

9. Ⓐ Ⓑ Ⓒ ●
10. Ⓕ Ⓖ ● Ⓙ
11. Ⓐ ● Ⓒ Ⓓ
12. Ⓕ Ⓖ Ⓗ ●
13. Ⓐ Ⓑ ● Ⓓ
14. ● Ⓖ Ⓗ Ⓙ
15. Ⓐ Ⓑ ● Ⓓ
16. Ⓕ Ⓖ Ⓗ ●

Page 134

1. Ⓐ ● Ⓒ Ⓓ
2. ● Ⓖ Ⓗ Ⓙ
3. Ⓐ ● Ⓒ Ⓓ
4. ● Ⓖ Ⓗ Ⓙ
5. Ⓐ Ⓑ ● Ⓓ
6. Ⓕ Ⓖ ● Ⓙ
7. Ⓐ Ⓑ Ⓒ ●

Page 136

1. Ⓐ Ⓑ Ⓒ ●
2. Ⓕ ● Ⓗ Ⓙ
3. ● Ⓑ Ⓒ Ⓓ
4. Ⓕ Ⓖ Ⓗ ●
5. Ⓐ ● Ⓒ Ⓓ
6. Ⓕ Ⓖ ● Ⓙ
7. Ⓐ ● Ⓒ Ⓓ
8. ● Ⓖ Ⓗ Ⓙ

Page 137

1. Ⓐ ● Ⓒ Ⓓ
2. Ⓕ Ⓖ ● Ⓙ
3. Ⓐ Ⓑ ● Ⓓ
4. Ⓕ ● Ⓗ Ⓙ

Page 138

1. Ⓐ ● Ⓒ Ⓓ
2. Ⓕ Ⓖ ● Ⓙ
3. ● Ⓑ Ⓒ Ⓓ
4. Ⓕ Ⓖ ● Ⓙ

Page 139

1. Ⓐ Ⓑ ● Ⓓ
2. ● Ⓖ Ⓗ Ⓙ
3. Ⓐ Ⓑ ● Ⓓ
4. ● Ⓖ Ⓗ Ⓙ
5. Ⓐ Ⓑ ● Ⓓ
6. ● Ⓖ Ⓗ Ⓙ
7. Ⓐ Ⓑ ● Ⓓ
8. Ⓕ Ⓖ ● Ⓙ

Page 140

9. ● Ⓑ Ⓒ Ⓓ
10. Ⓕ Ⓖ ● Ⓙ
11. Ⓐ Ⓑ ● Ⓓ
12. Ⓕ Ⓖ ● Ⓙ
13. ● Ⓑ Ⓒ Ⓓ
14. ● Ⓖ Ⓗ Ⓙ
15. Ⓐ ● Ⓒ Ⓓ
16. Ⓕ Ⓖ Ⓗ ●

Page 141

1. ● Ⓑ Ⓒ Ⓓ
2. Ⓕ ● Ⓗ Ⓙ
3. Ⓐ Ⓑ Ⓒ ●
4. Ⓕ Ⓖ ● Ⓙ

Page 142

1. Ⓐ ● Ⓒ Ⓓ
2. Ⓕ Ⓖ ● Ⓙ
3. Ⓐ Ⓑ ● Ⓓ
4. Ⓕ Ⓖ Ⓗ ●
5. Ⓐ ● Ⓒ Ⓓ
6. Ⓕ ● Ⓗ Ⓙ

Page 143

1. ● Ⓑ Ⓒ Ⓓ
2. Ⓕ Ⓖ ● Ⓙ
3. Ⓐ Ⓑ Ⓒ ●
4. Ⓕ ● Ⓗ Ⓙ
5. ● Ⓑ Ⓒ Ⓓ
6. Ⓕ Ⓖ ● Ⓙ
7. Ⓐ Ⓑ Ⓒ ●
8. Ⓕ ● Ⓗ Ⓙ

Page 144

9. Ⓐ ● Ⓒ Ⓓ
10. Ⓕ Ⓖ Ⓗ ●
11. Ⓐ Ⓑ Ⓒ ●
12. ● Ⓖ Ⓗ Ⓙ
13. Ⓐ ● Ⓒ Ⓓ
14. Ⓕ Ⓖ ● Ⓙ
15. Ⓐ ● Ⓒ Ⓓ
16. ● Ⓖ Ⓗ Ⓙ
17. Ⓐ Ⓑ Ⓒ ●

Page 145

1. Ⓐ Ⓑ ● Ⓓ
2. Ⓕ Ⓖ ● Ⓙ
3. Ⓐ Ⓑ Ⓒ ●
4. Ⓕ ● Ⓗ Ⓙ

Page 146

1. Ⓐ Ⓑ ● Ⓓ
2. Ⓕ ● Ⓗ Ⓙ
3. Ⓐ Ⓑ ● Ⓓ
4. ● Ⓖ Ⓗ Ⓙ
5. Ⓐ Ⓑ ● Ⓓ

Page 147

1. Ⓐ Ⓑ Ⓒ ●
2. Ⓕ Ⓖ Ⓗ ●
3. Ⓐ Ⓑ Ⓒ ●
4. Ⓕ ● Ⓗ Ⓙ
5. Ⓐ ● Ⓒ Ⓓ
6. Ⓕ Ⓖ ● Ⓙ

Page 148

1. Ⓐ Ⓑ Ⓒ ●
2. Ⓕ Ⓖ Ⓗ ●
3. ● Ⓑ Ⓒ Ⓓ
4. Ⓕ Ⓖ ● Ⓙ

Page 149

1. ● Ⓑ Ⓒ Ⓓ
2. ● Ⓖ Ⓗ Ⓙ
3. Ⓐ Ⓑ ● Ⓓ
4. Ⓕ Ⓖ ● Ⓙ
5. Ⓐ Ⓑ Ⓒ ●
6. Ⓕ Ⓖ Ⓗ ●
7. Ⓐ Ⓑ ● Ⓓ
8. Ⓕ ● Ⓗ Ⓙ

Page 150

9. Ⓐ ● Ⓒ Ⓓ
10. ● Ⓖ Ⓗ Ⓙ
11. Ⓐ Ⓑ ● Ⓓ
12. Ⓕ Ⓖ ● Ⓙ
13. Ⓐ Ⓑ ● Ⓓ
14. Ⓕ Ⓖ Ⓗ ●
15. Ⓐ ● Ⓒ Ⓓ
16. ● Ⓖ Ⓗ Ⓙ
17. Ⓐ Ⓑ ● Ⓓ
18. Ⓕ ● Ⓗ Ⓙ

Page 151

1. Ⓐ Ⓑ ● Ⓓ
2. Ⓕ ● Ⓗ Ⓙ
3. ● Ⓑ Ⓒ Ⓓ
4. Ⓕ ● Ⓗ Ⓙ
5. Ⓐ ● Ⓒ Ⓓ
6. Ⓕ Ⓖ Ⓗ ●

Page 152

1. Ⓐ Ⓑ ● Ⓓ
2. Ⓕ Ⓖ Ⓗ ●
3. ● Ⓑ Ⓒ Ⓓ
4. Ⓕ ● Ⓗ Ⓙ